WHEN THE KNEAD RISES

CREATIVE BREADS AND MORE

by

JACKIE E. GUICE

ILLUSTRATIONS AND COVER DESIGN

by

MITCH HOWELL

GINGERBREAD PRESS, INC.

1992

FIRST EDITION

Library of Congress Catalog Number 92-097009

ISBN 0-9634026-0-9

Printed in the USA by
WIMMER BROTHERS
A Wimmer Company
Memphis • Dallas

This book is dedicated to my Dad, G. C. Edwards, on celebrating many enjoyable years of baking, eating, sharing with others and being an inspiration to us all. I appreciate the support and encouragement given by my children, John, Annette, and Edward. I also want to thank my cousin Ruth, researcher of family traditions, and my friends who generously shared recipes and time.

Baker's Award of Appreciation

Illustrator: Mitch Howell, cover designer and illustrator from Hartselle, Alabama, is primarily a water color portraitist, but she has done a number of book covers and illustrations. Mitch, a fine arts graduate, is listed in Who's Who in American Art, International Who's Who in Art and Antiques and is a member of the Water Color Society of Alabama.

Technical: Mary Jo Belt, Charles Belt, Joe Long and Gayla Bailey. Kenneth Shelton, Judy Sibrans, Gail Hurst and Lee Coon.

Writing: Regina Wright, Pat DePoyster, Joyce Wingard, Betty Jo Atkinson, Jo Shelton, Anne Sidwell, Barbara Ann Straker, Ann Ozier and Joy Gabriel.

Foods: Bette Haney, Betty Sims, Dr. Rae Hansberry, Joanne Mounger, Julie Dutton, Cathy Gottler, Dr. Benji Mikel, Auburn University and U.S. Department of Agriculture.

Publications:

Diggs, Mitchell, *BIRMINGHAM POST HERALD*, June, 1991

Graham, Sylvester, *TREATISE ON BREAD AND BREAD-MAKING*, Boston and Stearns, 1 Cornhill, 1837

McKay, Dr. Clieve, *THE CORNELL BREAD BOOK*, Dover Publications, 1980, New York

McKay, Jeanette, by Special Permission

Michner, James A., *ALASKA*, First Edition, 1988, Random House, New York

Silver, Joel, Public Services, The Lilly Library, Indiana University, Bloomington, Indiana

THE DECATUR DAILY, Decatur, Alabama

THE KNOXVILLE NEWS-SENTINEL, Knoxville, Tennessee

Wheeler Basin Regional Library Reference, Library Staff, Margarete Lange and Jennifer Humiston

Ideas and Recipes Shared

Isabel Armbrister

Ann Anderson

Andrea Aitken

Charlotte Atchley

Joyce Atchley

Kathryn Barthold

Mara Becker

Linda Belew

Sylvia Brazelton

Billee Brooks

Sue Burns

Peggy Campbell

Janet Cannon

Alfred Caro

Elizabeth Carter

Owen Chapman

Ann Cochran

Emma Copeland

Wilma Curtis

Grace Dalton

Evelyn Darden

Ann Davenport

Billie Davis

Ann and Morley Denbo

MeMe Dupes

Carrie Edwards

Dawn Edwards

Dottie Evans

Ann Eyster

Boots Finney

Imogene Ford

Sandy Freeman

Jim Gabriel

Ann Gebhart

Laurie Gilbert

Charlotte Gill

Melody Guice

Marguerite Hamilton

Irene Henderson

Florence Hilsenbeck

Yvonne Hogland

Charlie Holland

Sally Holmes

Jo Hosey

Jan Howell

Glenda Jenkins

Helen Johnson

Billie Kantola

Diane Killian

Carolyn King

Virginia King

Kitty Knight

Marjorie Kurz

Nancy Large

Dyann Lentz

Loyetta Lenser

Carroll Lewis

Mary Marlow

John Melonas

Attie Ming

Ellen Montgomery

Jim Montgomery

Milade Mounsoor

Peggy Murphree

Jennie Nance

Bay Naylor

Lowella Needham

Sandy Nix

Louise Oden

June Odom

Blythe Orr

Betty Parker

Doris Peltier

Laurie Pennington

Mary Quattlebaum

Patsy Riggins

Mary Salter

Maria Delia Ugalde de Sandoval

Phyllis Schmidbauer

Diane Shirley

Janis Shirley

Ruth Shirley

Walt Sidwell

Virginia Simpson

Sally Smart

Carolyn Sparks

Rose Stutts

Sara and Stanley Szczepanski

Pat Taylor

Sherry Tunstill

Lu Underwood

Margaret Vann

Jean and Mannie Villar

Gay Voss

Cheri Warren

Evelyn Welch

Margaret Wenzler

Jo and Jim Wilhite

Esther Wilkening

Katherine Wilks

June Wilson

Charlotte White

Ann Word

Mary Wright

Peepie Yarbrough

Helpful Measurements, Substitutions and Equivalents of Ingredients

Ingredients	Amount	Substitution or Equivalent
Allspice	1 teaspoon	½ teaspoon Cinnamon and ½ teaspoon Cloves
Bread	1 slice dry	⅓ cup dry breadcrumbs
Bread	1 slice soft	¾ cup soft breadcrumbs
Chocolate, unsweetened	1-ounce or square	3 tablespoons cocoa and 1 tablespoon shortening
Cornmeal, self-rising	1 cup	1½ teaspoons baking powder and ½ teaspoon salt in 1 cup cornmeal
Flour	1 pound	4 cups sifted flour or 3¾ cups whole wheat flour
Flour, self-rising	1 cup	Add 1½ teaspoons baking powder and ½ teaspoon salt to 1 cup all-purpose flour
Herbs, fresh	1 tablespoon chopped	½ teaspoon dried, crushed herbs
Lemon	1 medium	1 to 3 tablespoons juice and 1 to 3 teaspoons grated peel
Milk, skim	1 cup	5 tablespoons nonfat dry milk powder to 1 cup water
Orange	1 medium	⅓ to ½ cup juice and 2-3 tablespoons grated peel
Sour milk or buttermilk	1 cup	1 cup plain yogurt or 1 cup milk plus 1 tablespoon lemon juice or white vinegar
Sugar, brown	1 cup firmly packed	1 cup granulated sugar
Sugar, powdered	1 pound	2¾ cups powdered sugar
Yeast, active dry	2½ teaspoons	1 package active dry yeast

BEFORE YOU START...

USE STANDARD MEASURING CUPS AND SPOONS, EVEN THOUGH GRANDMOTHER USED A "HEAPING TEA CUP" OF FLOUR AND LARD THE "SIZE OF A HEN EGG".

1. Loosen flour in a container with a spoon or pour into a bowl before measuring. **Flour does not have to be sifted if lightly spooned into a cup for dry measurements and leveled with a knife.** Baking mixes are lightly spooned into measuring cups, leveling off excess.

2. Granulated sugar, baking powder and baking soda are measured with a set of standard spoons or cups and leveled with a knife. **Dry ingredients do not have to be sifted together if they are thoroughly combined.**

3. **Margarine can be substituted for all butter in the recipes.** Pack shortening in cups or spoons, leveling with a knife; oil must be scraped off sides of the cup. Vegetable cooking sprays can be used on doughs, bowls and pans instead of shortening.

4. Liquids are most accurate when measured with a glass or clear plastic measurer at eye level. Large eggs were used in recipes.

5. Unless otherwise directed, ovens are preheated to the specified temperature. All temperatures are in degrees Fahrenheit.

6. Encourage all ages to "help" you bake. Do not include the animals! Reinforce clean kitchen rules: clean hands, clean containers and fresh, good quality ingredients.

TABLE OF CONTENTS

Dear Baker...

Few things are as well remembered from my childhood as the warm, comforting aroma of yeasty, feathery hot rolls. As my mother loved to cook and bake, through the years, we sampled an array of crunchy golden cornbread, pungent sweet sourdough loaves, tender flaky biscuits and shiny crusty French bread. Then there were soft rounded muffins, flaky pastry, fragrant rich sweet breads and hearty, healthful whole grain loaves. Her recipes are here, as well as those of friends and family, unfolding for the beginning cook or an experienced chef as creativity abounds. Substitutions and variations throughout the book are for all ages and degrees of experience.

For the last twelve years my friends and I have pounded and floured in my kitchen, baking simple and exotic breads. We always chose mornings in January or February, for even in the sunny South, those months can sometimes be dismal. A dark, cold winter day loses some of its chill when delectable aromas float on clouds of flour through the kitchen. The chill of the air is forgotten with a taste of hot bread with butter melting down the side. Recalled with nostalgia are the treasured moments of special friendship and warmth enriched by these breadbaking sessions.

I hope you, your friends and family enjoy this book as much as I enjoyed creating it for you.

Happy Baking!

Jackie Guice

YEAST BREADS

REFRIGERATOR ROLLS

AUNT MARY'S POTATO ROLLS AND LOAVES (REFRIGERATOR)

My First Rolls; Flavorful and Yeasty

Years ago The Knoxville News-Sentinel, in their "Cook's Corner," featured Aunt Mary's Rolls — still a winner today with new mixing and baking options. Only one rising is required.

2 packages dry yeast	½ cup sugar
½ cup warm water	1½ teaspoons salt
1 cup mashed potatoes (can use instant)	2 eggs
	1 cup warm milk
⅔ cup shortening	6-7 cups bread flour, divided

Sprinkle yeast over warm water in a large bowl; stir until dissolved. Using a spoon or a heavy duty mixer with beaters or dough hooks, beat in potatoes, shortening, sugar, salt and eggs until smooth. Do not exceed warm temperature, 105-115°, with any ingredient. Beat in milk; mix in 3 cups flour, beating for 3 minutes on high speed. Slowly add more flour until too difficult for mixer, scraping bowl as necessary. Finish mixing by hand, adding only enough flour to form a soft, manageable dough. Knead dough on a lightly floured surface, adding more flour if necessary until smooth and elastic.

NEW BAKER: For helpful hints and more information, see *Kneads of Yeast Breads* (page 241).

REFRIGERATOR DOUGH: Cover in a bowl, up to 5 days, use as needed. As necessary, punch down dough (flatten with hand to release air bubbles as dough slowly rises in refrigerator).

SHAPED DOUGH: Shape dough as desired or use the following directions for rolls or loaves. Cover formed rolls to rise in a warm place until double in size and light to touch, about 1-1 ½ hours. Bake at 400° for 15-20 minutes. Remove from pans to cool on wire rack.

SHAPE AND BAKE VARIATIONS:

POCKETBOOK FOLD-OVER ROLLS: Divide dough into 4 balls; roll each ball into a 12-inch circle. Brush with butter; cut with a 2 ¾-inch floured biscuit cutter. Make a light crease with a knife to one side of the center of each cut roll; fold wider side over and press edges together as a pocketbook closing. Place rolls touching in greased baking pans. If desired, brush rolls with melted butter. Let rise; bake at 400° for 15-20 minutes. Yields 60 rolls.

FAST FOLD-OVER OR PAN ROLLS: Divide dough in 4 parts; roll each part into an 8-inch square. Cut each square into 16 (2-inch) squares. Fold each square over, lightly pressing edges together as a pocketbook.

For pan rolls, gather edges together underneath roll to form a smooth round ball. Place rolls, touching, on a greased pan. If desired brush with melted butter. Let rise; bake at 400° for 15-20 minutes. Yields 64 rolls.

LOAVES: Divide dough in half; gently roll each half, with a rolling pin, into a 9x15-inch rectangle. Starting with the short side, completely roll up dough, pressing outside edges to seal. Turn ends under; place loaves seam side down in 2 greased 9x5x3-inch loaf pans. Let rise until double and light, about 1 hour. Bake at 375° for 25-30 minutes.

REFRIGERATOR RISING FOR ROLLS AND LOAVES: Refrigerate shaped rolls and loaves, loosely covered, in their baking pans. When convenient, after a few hours or up to 24 hours, remove from refrigerator to continue rising in a warm place until double the original size and light to touch, about 20-25 minutes. Rising time depends on the refrigerator and "warm place" temperatures. Bake as usual.

BROWN TO SERVE ROLLS AND LOAVES: Bake risen rolls 20-25 minutes at 275°; do not brown. Bake risen loaves 250° for 30-35 minutes. Cool; refrigerate in pan covered with plastic for up to a week. To serve hot bread, bake 10 minutes for rolls and 20 minutes for loaves at 400° until brown.

BAKER'S ADVENTURE: Aunt Mary's Potato Rolls is "User Friendly" — a good recipe for your first roll-making adventure. Share your fun and enjoyment with the children. Since long ago, mothers, grandmothers and cooks pacified children by pulling off pieces of dough for the children's play. Children still love to play with dough "scraps" or extra dough as well as adding ingredients or kneading the real dough.

AUNT MARY'S HURRY-UP POTATO ROLLS (REFRIGERATOR)

Yields 30 Rolls

¹/₃ cup instant potato flakes	3-3½ cups bread flour, divided
¼ cup sugar	¾ cup water (120-130°)
1 teaspoon salt	½ cup milk
1 package dry yeast, rapid or regular	¹/₃ cup shortening
	1 egg

With a mixer, thoroughly combine the potato flakes, sugar, salt, undissolved yeast and 1½ cups flour in a large bowl. Heat water, milk and shortening to 120-130°; test temperature with a thermometer, as liquid must be the correct temperature. Slowly add to dry ingredients, beating 2 minutes on medium. Scrape bowl if necessary. Add 1 cup flour and 1 egg; beat on high speed for 3 minutes. Add enough flour by hand to form a manageable dough. Knead dough until smooth on a floured surface, adding more flour if necessary. Form into rolls. Let rise covered in a warm place until light and double in size. Bake at 400° for 15-20 minutes.

Variations:

FOOD PROCESSOR: Place 3 cups flour and all dry ingredients in a food processor (strong enough for kneading) using the steel blade. Thoroughly combine all dry ingredients by processing about 10 seconds. Add liquid (105-115°), shortening and egg; process about 15 seconds. Add flour, 1 tablespoon at a time, if dough is too wet. When dough forms around blade, process for 60 seconds to knead or until a moist, soft dough forms. Refrigerate dough (covered) or lightly knead with more flour, if necessary, to form rolls or loaves immediately.

RAPID HAND MIXING: Place ½ cup flour to the side for reserve when kneading dough. In large bowl, mix remaining flour, sugar, potato flakes, salt and rapid yeast. Stir water, milk and shortening (120-130°) into dry mixture. Beat in egg and enough flour to form a soft dough. Knead, form into rolls and let rise covered in a warm place until light and double in size, about 50 minutes. Bake at 400° for 15-20 minutes.

MICROWAVE SPEED-UP RISING: Follow manufacturers directions; yeast rising is recommended only on high wattage ovens which put out small amounts of power (10%) on the low setting. Time depends on how many rolls or loaves in the oven and the temperature of the dough.

Experiment with your oven by placing an oven-proof container with 2 cups hot water in the corner of the oven. Place microwave-safe containers of rolls or loaves in the microwave oven covered with a towel. Microwave on the lowest power for 1 minute. Feel the dough in the corners, sides and bottom of the container. Rising temperature too high will cook the dough and kill the yeast. The best rising temperature is 85 to 90°. When first working with microwave rising, check dough temperature each minute, turning container a quarter turn. Unless dough is becoming too warm, repeat the process for about 5 minutes or until dough is nearly double. Allow dough to continue rising in microwave (power off) until double in size and light to touch. Better to be a little cautious with those yummy rolls and loaves!

FAVORITE REFRIGERATOR ROLLS
(NO KNEADING)

Easy on inexperienced bakers, waistline and budget!

¼ cup shortening	1 package dry yeast
1 cup water	1 cup warm water (105-115°)
½ cup sugar	1 egg, slightly beaten
1 teaspoon salt	5-6 cups all-purpose flour

Heat shortening until dissolved with water, sugar and salt; cool to a warm 105-115°. In a large bowl, sprinkle yeast over warm water; stir to dissolve. Mix in shortening mixture, egg and 3 cups flour. Beat until smooth, adding only enough more flour to form a soft dough. Place dough in large, floured, sealable, plastic food storage bags with air pressed out or in a greased bowl, turning dough over to grease top of dough. Cover bowl; refrigerate overnight, dough can be used the next morning. Punch refrigerated dough down (flatten with hand to release air bubbles) as necessary. Dough can be refrigerated up to 5 days.

Variations:

CRESCENT ROLLS: Divide dough into 4 balls; roll each ball in a 12-inch circle on a lightly floured surface; brush with melted butter. Cut into 12 wedges. Roll up, starting with wide end; place point down on a greased baking pan with rolls touching. Let rise, covered, in a warm place until double and light, about 1 ½ hours. Bake at 400° for 15-20 minutes or until lightly browned. Makes 4 dozen crescent rolls.

PIZZA CRUSTS: Roll out ¼ of dough to fit a 12-inch greased pizza pan. Form a rim around the outside edge. Bake at 400° for 10 minutes. Spread with an Italian sauce, toppings and cheese. Bake 450° for 10-12 minutes more or until cheese has melted.

WHOLE WHEAT: Substitute ½ whole wheat flour for ½ all-purpose flour.

HURRIED BAKER: Add 1 package dry yeast for a total of 2 packages dry yeast.

ANN'S BUTTERMILK ROLLS

No egg - Refrigerator

Very similar ingredients to Betty's Yeast Biscuits, but Ann Anderson's rolls are more yeasty and lower in calories.

2 cups buttermilk	¼ cup warm water (105-115°)
¼ cup sugar	5 cups all-purpose flour
¼ cup shortening	½ teaspoon baking soda
1 teaspoon salt	1 teaspoon baking powder
2 packages dry yeast	

Warm buttermilk and mix with sugar, shortening and salt until blended. Dissolve yeast in water in a large bowl; add to milk mixture, cooled to 105-115°. Mix in flour, combined with soda and baking powder, to form a soft dough. Knead lightly, adding more flour as necessary, on a floured board. Cover and store in refrigerator until ready for use. About two hours before baking time, form into rolls; let rise until double. Bake at 400° for about 15 minutes.

BAKER'S APPLAUSE: Would you like rave notices at the dinner party? Dip your rolls in butter; roll in fine graham cracker crumbs, before rolls rise. Bake as usual.

EMMA'S "FOOL-PROOF" ROLLS

1 cup warm water (105-115° Fahrenheit)	1 cup boiling water
2 packages dry yeast	¾ cup sugar
½ cup margarine	2 eggs, beaten
¾ cup shortening	7 cups self-rising flour

In a large bowl, dissolve yeast in warm water. Combine margarine, shortening and sugar in boiling water; let cool to 105-115° Fahrenheit. Add to yeast; beat with eggs and 2 cups flour until smooth. Slowly add flour until a soft manageable dough is formed. Refrigerate a few hours or overnight.

CLOVER LEAF ROLLS: Form dough into 4 long rolls; cut in 3-inch pieces; divide pieces into 3 balls. Place 3 balls in each greased (2½x1½-inch) muffin pan section. Brush with melted butter.

FAST CLOVER LEAF ROLLS: Place large balls, not divided, in greased muffin pans. Cut dough in half with scissors; cut in half again, forming quarters. Brush with melted butter. Let rise for 1 hour or until double. Bake at 400° for 10-15 minutes until light brown. Yields about 3 dozen clover leaf rolls.

This dough makes a quick base for your sweet dough coffee cakes. The self-rising flour provides extra assurance for rising.

COMPANY WHOLE WHEAT REFRIGERATOR ROLLS
Can Refrigerate For 5 Days

1 cup hot water	1 cup lukewarm water
1 cup shortening or margarine	2 eggs
½ cup sugar	3 cups whole wheat flour
1 tablespoon salt	3 cups all-purpose flour
2 packages dry yeast	

Pour hot water over shortening, sugar and salt in a large mixing bowl. Dissolve yeast in warm water. When hot water mixture is lukewarm, add yeast mixture; beat in the eggs and flour. Oil bowl and top of dough; cover and refrigerate overnight.

FINGER OR PARTY ROLLS: Roll dough on lightly floured board, adding flour if necessary. Cut dough the length and size of a small finger, smoothing top. Can also form by pressing dough into a tablespoon; remove and smooth into an oblong size. Place in greased pan, brushing with melted butter. Let rise until double. Bake about 400° for 20 minutes or until lightly browned. Split these small rolls to spread with meat fillings for a buffet.

PULL AWAY WHOLE WHEAT ROLLS: Roll dough ½-inch thick; cut with serrated knife in 2-inch squares or use a 2-inch biscuit cutter. Dip each roll in butter; arrange in greased 10-inch Bundt pan, filling about half full. Let rise until double in size. Bake at 375° for 40-45 minutes or until light brown. Invert rolls on serving plate; guests serve themselves.

CORNMEAL BUNS OR ROLLS

Light, Mild Flavored Barbecue, Fish, Hamburger or Hot Dog Holders

1¼ cups water (120 to 130°)
¼ cup butter
⅓ cup instant nonfat dry milk
2 packages dry yeast
¼ cup sugar

1½ teaspoons salt
½ cup cornmeal
3 ½-4 cups all-purpose flour
1 egg

Mix very warm water with butter. With mixer, in a large bowl, combine dry milk, yeast, sugar, salt, cornmeal and 1½ cups flour. Beat in butter mixture. Add ½ cup more flour and egg; mix at high speed for 3 minutes. Add more flour until a soft dough is formed; knead only until smooth. Place in a greased bowl to rise until double or refrigerate dough to form rolls the next day. Divide dough in half. Roll dough ½-inch thick, cut with a 2 ½-inch cutter or form into desired shapes. Let rise until double on a greased pan. Bake at 400° for 15-20 minutes until golden brown. Brush tops with butter. Yields approximately 1 ½ dozen buns.

FESTIVE DILL ROLLS

3 packages dry yeast
⅔ cup warm water
¼ cup sugar
2½ cups small curd cottage
    cheese
1 teaspoon salt
1 package dried onion soup mix
3 tablespoons butter

1 tablespoon fresh parsley or
    dried parsley minced
3 teaspoons dill seeds
3 eggs
½ teaspoon baking soda
7 cups all-purpose flour
melted butter, optional

Dissolve yeast in warm water. Combine sugar, cottage cheese, salt, soup mix, butter, parsley and dill in a sauce pan. Heat just until warm; beat in dissolved yeast, eggs, soda and enough flour to be manageable. Knead dough on a floured surface until smooth. Place in a greased bowl; let rise until double. Punch down; form into rolls or buns.

SANDWICH ROLLS: Form into sandwich rolls which easily hold meats and fillings. Use lightly floured biscuit cutter, 2-inch, or any size desired, to cut ½-inch thick rolled dough. Place each cut out roll on greased baking sheet, brush with butter and top with another cut out roll. Makes a natural indention for a sandwich. Brush rolls with melted butter; let rise until double. Bake at 400° for 15-20 minutes. Brush with melted butter when removed from oven. Yields about 5 dozen rolls.

MARGUERITE'S ONION-CHEESE ROLLS: Mix a small green pepper (½ cup chopped), a bunch of spring onions (½ cup chopped), 2 cups grated cheddar cheese and 1 cup mayonnaise together. Fill rolls with small amount of mixture. Heat until rolls are hot.

Can spread mixture on small bread slices. Heat in oven until bubbly.

BAKER'S MAIN-DISH IDEA: All meats from pork roast to corned beef are delicious matched with appropriate dressings and topped with cheese in these already baked rolls. Place the filled rolls in oven-safe rectangular casseroles. Cover with foil and refrigerate until serving time. Heat, covered, in a 325° oven until rolls are heated throughout. Serve hot from casserole.

BAKER'S CHEESY IDEA: Sprinkle tops of unbaked rolls with Parmesan cheese; when baked fill with a favorite meat salad.

ONE-RISE PUDDIN' ROLLS

Fun to Make!

2 packages dry yeast	¼ cup oil
1 cup warm water	½ teaspoon salt
1 (3½-ounce) package instant vanilla pudding mix	2-3 cups all-purpose flour

Soften yeast in warm water in large bowl. Add pudding mix, oil and salt. Combine until dissolved. Add flour until a manageable dough is formed or use less flour for a sticky, drop dough for muffin pans. Beat or knead until smooth and elastic.

Pat into rolls or roll dough ½-inch thick; cut into 2-inch rounds. Place in greased pan, let rise about 1 hour or until light. Bake at 400° for 10 minutes. Makes approximately 18 rolls.

BAKER'S IDEA: Children would enjoy helping make this slightly sweet, novelty dough. Let them add ½ cup raisins and ½ teaspoon cinnamon for a variation. Sprinkle tops with sugar. Drop the dough in greased muffin pans, filling half full.

QUICKER ROLLS

The so called quick "one-hour rolls" are like playing the Minute Waltz with the piano judges watching you. I do things like falling over my feet, dropping the flour and tripping over the cat trying to make the deadline, but...I have found some short cuts.

QUICK BATTER ROLLS
Good Luncheon Addition

2 cups self-rising flour
3 tablespoons instant nonfat dry
  milk
1 package rapid dry yeast

2 tablespoons sugar
¹/₃ cup cooking oil
¾ cup hot water (125-130°)
1 egg

Mix flour, dry milk, yeast and sugar, in a large bowl, with electric mixer. Beat in oil and water; beat in egg. Fill 24 small greased muffin pans ½ full. Bake after 10 minutes or let rise until batter reaches top of muffin tins. Bake at 400° for 10-12 minutes or until light brown. Yields 24 small rolls. Serve hot with dinner. Can refrigerate dough a few days.

Variations:

MOCK ORANGE ROLLS: Add 1 tablespoon grated orange rind to dough. When baked, ice while hot with any orange roll toppings.

PECAN-NUTMEG QUICK BATTER ROLLS: Add ¼ teaspoon ground nutmeg and ¼ teaspoon ground mace with the flour and ½ cup chopped toasted pecans.

YEASTY BAKING MIX GEMS

1 package dry yeast
½ cup warm water
½ cup milk

1 egg
2 cups baking mix (page 121)

Dissolve yeast in a medium bowl with water; whisk or beat in milk and egg. Add baking mix, stirring until moistened. Drop by rounded teaspoons into greased small muffin pans; bake immediately or, for a lighter muffin, allow to rise in a warm place 10-15 minutes. Bake at 400° for 12-18 minutes or until light brown. Serve piping hot with herbed butter. Yields 2 dozen small muffins.

HERBED BUTTER: Blend the following dried herbs: ¼ teaspoon thyme, ⅛ teaspoon cinnamon, ⅛ teaspoon ginger, 1 teaspoon parsley, 1 teaspoon Parmesan cheese, ¼ teaspoon marjoram with 1 stick butter in the blender until smooth.

MA MA'S ONE-RISE BUTTERMILK ROLLS

No Eggs

1 cup lukewarm buttermilk (105-115°)
¼ teaspoon baking soda
2 teaspoons sugar
½ teaspoon salt

1 package dry yeast
4 tablespoons melted margarine
3 cups all-purpose flour

Combine buttermilk and soda; thoroughly mix in sugar, salt and yeast. Add melted margarine and enough flour to form a soft dough. Turn out on a lightly floured surface; knead until smooth. Divide dough and roll into 2 circles. Cut each circle into 12 wedges. Begin at wide end rolling up to form a crescent roll. Place end of point down on greased pan; brush with melted margarine. Let rise until double in size. Bake at 400° for 12 to 15 minutes. Makes 2 dozen light, delicious rolls.

Jennie Nance still carries on her Ma Ma's bread baking art. She encourages and inspires others to bake for family and friends. While traveling with her minister husband she brought new recipes and opportunities to share foods with others.

Variations:

MA MA'S QUICK MIXER METHOD: Combine sugar, salt, yeast and 2 cups flour in the large mixer bowl. Beat in buttermilk (120-130°) mixed with soda and margarine, beating for 3 minutes on high speed. Slowly add rest of flour by hand until a soft dough forms. Liberally grease an 11x8x2-inch baking pan. Press dough into pan with fingers; cut rolls into 24 squares with a sharp serrated knife. Let rise until double in a warm place. Bake at 400° for 20-25 minutes. Brush tops with melted margarine. Yields 24 squares.

BETTE'S BUSY DAY ROLL MIX
Similar to Commercial Roll Mix

$3^1/_3$-$3^2/_3$ cups bread flour
¾ teaspoon salt
2 tablespoons sugar
1 package rapid dry yeast
2 tablespoons cooking oil

1 cup water (120-130°)
1 egg
1 teaspoon vanilla, optional for
   sweet breads

Place ⅔ cup flour to the side for a reserve. Mix rest of flour, salt, sugar and yeast in a large bowl; stir in oil and hot water. Add egg and vanilla; mix in enough reserved flour to form a manageable dough. Knead dough until smooth and elastic on a lightly floured surface. Cover dough to rest for 10 minutes. Elongate dough into a 16-inch roll; cut into 16 large rolls or 32 smaller rolls. Let rise until double, covered, in a warm place. Bake at 400° for 15-20 minutes.

Yields 2 (7½x3 ½x2-inch) loaves. Bake in 400° oven for 25-30 minutes.

Variations:

BETTE'S FAST AND LUSCIOUS CINNAMON ROLLS: Roll dough to a 13x6-inch rectangle. Cut 8 tablespoons cold butter, ½ cup, into 20 slices; cut slices into small pieces. Place butter pieces evenly on rectangles, leaving a ⅛-inch border. Sprinkle evenly with sugar and cinnamon; roll as a jelly roll. Cut the roll into 10 pieces; place cut side down in 2 greased 9-inch square pans about ½-inch apart. Let rise until double. Bake at 375° for 25-30 minutes. Carefully turn rolls onto a serving plate. Watch - syrup is hot! Drizzle on powdered sugar glaze.

Bette takes this mix to the beach, as a special breakfast surprise, or as an antidote for that rainy, gloomy beach afternoon. No rolling pin? Try a bottle or a glass.

MIX-IN-A-BAG: Form a sponge by combining 1 cup flour, salt, sugar and yeast (use regular yeast) with 1 cup warm water (105-115°) in a gallon heavy-duty freezer bag. Press bag to remove air; close bag. Mix by moving and working ingredients by hand. Add oil, egg and enough flour to form a soft dough. Combine until dough pulls away from the sides of bag as kneading. Can add more flour as necessary. Form dough as desired. Great project for children.

LOAVES, STICKS AND PRETZELS

MICROWAVE ENGLISH MUFFIN BREAD

Morning Fitness Bread: Low Sugar, No Shortening and a Complete Protein

1 cup bread flour	1 teaspoon salt
1 cup whole wheat	$^1/_8$ teaspoon baking soda
¼ cup wheat germ	1 teaspoon cinnamon
¼ cup soy flour	½ cup plumped raisins
1 package dry yeast	1 cup milk
1 tablespoon sugar	¼ cup water

Using the food processor, combine all dry ingredients (except raisins), flours, yeast, sugar, salt, soda and cinnamon, for about 10 seconds. Add warm milk and water; process for 15 seconds. When dough gathers around the blade, pulling away from the sides of the bowl, process for about 1 minute. Add raisins, processing just until combined. Spoon thick batter into a greased and coated with cornmeal 8½x4½x2½-inch glass loaf container.

Refrigerate loosely covered loaf overnight (try a plastic food storage bag). Uncover in the morning, let stand in a warm place, 10-20 minutes. Sprinkle loaf top with cornmeal. Microwave on high (100%) power for 6 ½-7 minutes. Bread top will be firm to touch, flat and light in color. Let rest for 5 minutes; remove to slice and toast.

Variation:

OAT-BRAN ENGLISH MUFFIN BREAD: Substitute ¼ cup uncooked, old-fashioned oats for the wheat germ. Substitute ¼ cup shredded bran cereal (crushed in blender) instead of the soy flour and substitute ½ cup dried, plumped apricots (chopped) for the raisins. Add ½ cup lightly toasted chopped nuts.

BRAN 'N GRAHAM ROLLS, LOAVES AND BUNS

Makes 5 dozen rolls, 2 loaves and 28 buns

2¼ cups water
½ cup margarine
½ cup shortening
1½ teaspoons salt
1 cup shreds of 100 % wheat bran
  cereal (not bran flakes)

½ cup graham cracker crumbs
3 packages dry yeast
⅔ cup sugar
2 eggs
6 cups all-purpose flour

Heat water, margarine and shortening until mixture reaches 120-130°. With a mixer, combine salt, cereal, cracker crumbs, yeast, sugar, and 2 cups flour in a large bowl. Gradually add liquid ingredients, beating on high for 3 minutes. Add eggs and 1 cup flour; beat well. Add enough flour to form a soft dough; knead only until smooth and elastic. Place in a greased bowl, turning to grease top; let rise until double, about 1½-2 hours. When dough is double in size, punch down.

Rolls and Buns: Form by hand, into desired shapes; smooth tops and tuck any excess under the roll. Can roll dough ½-inch thick to cut buns with a 3-inch cutter or use a 2-inch cutter for rolls.

Loaves: Form by dividing dough in half. Lightly knead dough to remove air. Smooth loaf top by gently tucking dough towards the underside of loaf. Press together any excess dough under loaf; turn under ends, pressing to seal. Place loaves seam side down in 2 greased 8½x4½x2½-inch loaf pans. Let rise until double. The bread loaves will take approximately 30-40 minutes at 375° or until a light golden brown color. Bake rolls at 400° for 15-20 minutes.

HOLIDAY BAKER: Use these light, flavorful buns for Thanksgiving or special celebration leftovers. Add spicy mustard, horseradish sauce or mayonnaise with leftover turkey, beef, barbecue or ham for a continued feast.

HURRIED BAKER: After mixing dough, can refrigerate for a few days.

AUSTRALIAN ROSEMARY-PEPPER BREAD STICKS

**Outback folks cooked their large bread sticks
on thick bark over the campfire coals.**

4 cups bread flour, divided
1 package dry yeast
1 teaspoon salt
1 tablespoon sugar
1 teaspoon crushed dried rosemary
¼ cup grated Parmesan cheese

½ teaspoon ground black pepper
1¼ cups water (120-130°)
2 tablespoons margarine
Egg White Glaze
crushed rosemary
garlic salt

Mix 2 cups flour, yeast, salt, sugar, rosemary, Parmesan cheese and black pepper in a large bowl. Beat in the water and margarine with mixer or dough hooks for 3-4 minutes. Stir in enough flour to form a manageable dough. Knead on a floured surface until smooth and elastic, adding flour as necessary. Place in a greased bowl turning to grease top. Let rise until double, about 1 hour.

Punch down dough; divide in half, cutting each half into 12 pieces. Roll each piece about 6 inches long. Place on a greased baking sheet 1-inch apart. Brush bread sticks with 1 egg white beaten with 1 tablespoon water. Sprinkle with rosemary and garlic salt. Let rise until double. Bake at 375° for 20 minutes until light brown. Remove carefully from pan to cool on wire rack. Yields 24 bread sticks. For crispy, light bread sticks, roll dough thinner.

Variation:

FOOD PROCESSOR: Use rapid dry yeast; change water temperature to 105-115°. Set aside 1 cup flour. Process all dry ingredients until mixed; add water and margarine through feed tube. Process ingredients until combined. When dough gathers in a ball around blades, process for 1 minute or until smooth and elastic. Add more flour if too wet. Let dough rest 10 minutes. form into bread sticks; let rise until double, about 20 minutes.

LINDA'S SOFT PRETZELS

Children love forming these good-for-you shapes.

1 package dry yeast	2 cups all-purpose flour
2/3 cup warm water	Egg Glaze
1/2 teaspoon salt	Coarse Kosher or table salt

In a medium bowl dissolve yeast in warm water; mix slowly with salt and enough flour to form a manageable dough. Knead dough on a lightly floured surface until smooth and elastic, about 10 minutes. Cover and let rise in a warm place for 1 hour or until doubled in size. Divide dough into 10 parts; roll each part with floured hands into a rope 16-inches long. Form rope into a circle, twist loose ends of rope at end of circle, bringing rope ends across middle of circle, sealing loose ends under the circle on either side. Rising is not necessary, as dough will rise some while being shaped.

Lower pretzels, with a spatula, into simmering water. Linda uses an electric skillet or wok half full of simmering water. Cook about 3 minutes, turning once. Pretzels should hold their shape. Remove to a wire rack to dry for 8-10 minutes. Brush each pretzel with egg yolk beaten with 2 tablespoons water; sprinkle with salt. Place pretzels on a greased wire rack, baking at 400° for 30 minutes or until golden. Best served warm. Yields 10 large pretzels.

Variations:

CRISP PRETZELS: After dough rises, divide into 20 parts; roll each part into a rope. Shape as desired; place on greased baking sheet. Brush with glaze; sprinkle top with salt or herbs. Bake at 400° for 10-15 minutes or until golden brown.

WHOLE WHEAT PRETZELS: Substitute 1 cup whole wheat flour for 1 cup all-purpose flour.

DIANE'S SOFT EGG PRETZELS: Add 2 tablespoons margarine, 2 tablespoons sugar and 1 egg white to the dough. Mix into the dough; add more flour as necessary. After forming desired shapes, let rise until double. Do **not** place in boiling water. Glaze and bake as usual. Added ingredients help these stay fresher.

BRAIDS AND LOAVES

PEGGY'S YEAST BRAIDS
Beautiful and Delicate Texture

¾ cup vegetable shortening
1½ cups milk
¾ cup sugar
1 tablespoon salt
3 packages dry yeast

¾ cup warm water (105-115°)
3 slightly beaten eggs
9-11 cups all-purpose flour
Egg White glaze
Sesame seeds or poppy seeds

Melt shortening; add milk, sugar and salt in a large bowl. Dissolve yeast in water; combine with eggs and warm milk mixture. Slowly add approximately 8 cups flour, mixing with a spoon until dough can be kneaded; add extra flour if necessary for kneading until smooth. Place in greased bowl to rise until double in bulk (about 1½ hours). Punch down; divide dough in 6 parts. Divide 6 loaf parts into 3 parts each. Roll each part into a rope-like coil. Place the 3 coils parallel, pinch the 3 ends together, braid the 3 coils, pinch the ends together and tuck ends under. Does not require a second rising.

Brush tops with an egg white beaten with 1 tablespoon water; sprinkle tops with seeds. Bake on greased baking sheets at 350° for 25-30 minutes. Cool loaves on wire racks. Yields 6 loaves.

VIRGINIA'S HIWASSEE BREAD
Flavor and Texture Reminiscent of Sourdough

2 packages active dry yeast
½ cup warm water
½ cup shortening
¾ cup hot water

½ cup sugar
¾ cup cold water
6-6½ cups self-rising flour

Dissolve yeast in warm water in a large bowl. Melt shortening in hot water adding sugar; mix in cold water, cooling to lukewarm (105-115°). Mix in all water and ½ of the flour with the yeast. Using the mixer, beat for 3 minutes on high. Mix in only enough flour, by hand, to be a manageable thick dough. Knead until dough is elastic and smooth. Place in floured bowl, turn dough over to flour top, and cover or place in large, floured plastic food storage bag. Refrigerate for at least an hour. Divide dough; roll each half with a rolling pin, or by hand, into a rectangle. Fold dough in half, pressing edges and ends to seal. Fold ends under; place in greased pans. In a warm place, let rise until double or dough rounds over top of pans. Bake at 350° for 35 minutes or until light brown. Cool on racks. Yields 2 loaves.

Handle with care, as the soft bread mashes easily. Cool, seal in foil to refrigerate or freeze. To serve: slice and let thaw; heat at 350°, in foil, until thoroughly hot for serving. Also makes scrumptious toast!

Hiwassee College, founded in 1849, is tucked away in picturesque hills between Chattanooga and Knoxville, Tennessee. The great granddaughter of the second president of Hiwassee College, Virginia Brunner Simpson, has just retired as Hiwassee's cafeteria kitchen manager.

Her advice to new bread enthusiasts is, "Even an experienced baker turns out a lemon now and then." She uses that for "kitchen bread". She still loves to bake after helping to bake about 100 loaves a week.

ELIZABETH'S CHALLAH BREAD
A Jewish Sabbath Loaf

Elizabeth Bohling's family began baking this bread in Illinois in the early 1800's—long before her birth. She continued this baking tradition throughout her long life.

1 package dry yeast	4 cups all-purpose flour, divided
1 cup warm water	2 eggs
1 teaspoon salt	Egg Glaze
2 teaspoons sugar	Poppy or sesame seeds
1 tablespoon salad oil	

Dissolve yeast in warm water in a large bowl; add to salt, sugar, oil and 1½ cups flour. Beat until smooth; add 2 eggs and beat again. Mix in enough remaining flour to form a manageable dough. Knead for 8-10 minutes or until smooth and elastic. Place in a greased bowl, cover and let rise for 1 hour. Punch down dough; roll out into three parts. Divide each dough part into three pieces to braid. Place on a greased baking sheet; brush with 1 egg beaten with 1 tablespoon water. Sprinkle with poppy or sesame seeds; let rise until double. Bake at 350° for 25-30 minutes. Cool loaves on a wire rack. Makes three individual braided loaves or 1 large braided loaf.

SALLY LUNN YEAST BREAD

1½ cups hot water (120-130°)	1 package dry yeast
⅓ cup margarine or butter	1 teaspoon salt
⅓ cup instant nonfat dry milk	2 eggs
3 tablespoons sugar	3 cups all-purpose flour

Combine water and margarine. In a large bowl mix dry milk, sugar, yeast and salt with a mixer or by hand; stir in margarine mixture with eggs and flour. Beat for 3 minutes. Let rise, covered, in a warm place until double. Stir down batter by beating until close to original size. Pour batter into a well greased 9-inch bundt pan, tube pan or fluted mold. Place in refrigerator to rise overnight or let rise in a warm place until doubled or almost 1-inch from top of pan. Bake for 35-45 minutes at 375°.

This sponge-like, porous bread, reminiscent of an 1800's English breakfast, is good cold or hot. Hope for leftovers as it makes delicious toast!

BAKER'S IDEA: Let rise in the refrigerator overnight; allow to stand at room temperature for 20 minutes before baking for breakfast.

WORK-AROUND-YOUR-SCHEDULE-FRENCH BRIOCHE

Braid or Individual Buns

1 package dry yeast	¼ cup sugar
3 tablespoons warm water	⅓ cup soft butter
⅓ cup warm milk	3 eggs
3 cups all-purpose flour, divided	Egg Glaze
½ teaspoon salt	

Dissolve yeast in water using a large bowl. With an electric mixer, beat in milk, 1 cup flour, salt and sugar; beat in butter and eggs alternately with 1 cup flour, beating on high until dough is smooth and comes away from bowl sides, (about 3 minutes). Add more flour; finish beating by hand. Refrigerate dough in a greased, covered bowl overnight or for a few days. Can let dough rise immediately by covering at room temperature for 2-3 hours until double.

Braid: Form dough in a 14-inch long roll. Flatten dough; cut lengthwise in 3 even strips almost to the end. Braid; tuck dough ends under braid. Brush top with 1 egg beaten with 1 tablespoon water. Let rise until double on a greased baking sheet. Bake at 375° for 25-30 minutes or until a golden brown. Yields 1 braided loaf.

Brioche a Tête Buns: Small individual buns with a topknot are elegant favorites! Grease a 12 cup muffin pan. Divide dough into 16 balls; place a ball in each muffin cup. Divide leftover balls into 12 smaller balls; elongate one end of each ball (top knot) as a teardrop. Cut a 1-inch deep hole in center of dough in muffin pans to hold pointed end of topknot. Press dough around topknot. Brush with egg glaze, following above directions for Brioche braid, baking only 15-20 minutes or until golden brown. Remove from pan; cool on wire rack. Yields 12 individual brioches.

Cut top off Brioche a Tête scooping out some of inside; serve as an elegant, edible container for scrambled eggs, chicken or seafood salad. Replace top; pass a bowl of hot cheese sauce as a topping. Serve this pièce de résistance with fruit and a mixed green salad.

CHEESE, FRUIT AND VEGETABLE LOAVES

RUTH'S CHEESE BREAD
Subtle Way to add Extra Calcium

2 packages dry yeast
2 cups warm water (105-115°)
2 tablespoons sugar
½ teaspoon salt
2 tablespoons vegetable oil

½ cup instant nonfat dry milk
5¼ cups all-purpose flour, divided
1 cup sharp, grated cheddar cheese

Use a large bowl to dissolve yeast in warm water; add sugar, salt and oil. Beat in dry milk with 2 cups of flour; stir in cheese and remaining flour. Beat until well blended. Let rise, covered, in a warm place 45 minutes or until doubled in bulk. Stir dough down, (removing air bubbles); beat vigorously about 5 strokes.

Spoon into well greased 8 cup fluted mold, baking dish or bundt cake pan. Let rise for about 30 minutes or until doubled. Bake at 350° for 1 hour and 10 minutes or until golden brown. Cool completely on a wire rack. Yields 1 loaf. Cut slices for dinner; freeze rest for sandwiches.

Variations:

CHEESE CARAWAY BREAD: Add 1 tablespoon, whole or crushed, caraway seeds with the cheese.

DELICATESSEN SANDWICH: Cut across 1 round loaf twice, forming 3 layers.

Mustard
Mayonnaise
½ pound thinly sliced turkey

½ pound thinly sliced ham
¼ pound Swiss cheese, sliced

Place bottom bread layer on heavy foil on baking sheet. Use enough foil to cover the entire loaf and fasten together on the top. Spread mustard and mayonnaise on the cut side of the bottom layer; add layers of thinly sliced turkey. Place middle bread layer on top; spread with mayonnaise, layers of thinly sliced ham and slices of Swiss cheese. Add top of bread; cut with a serrated knife into 6 individual wedge servings. Do not cut through the foil; cover and seal the foil. Heat for 20 minutes at 350° or until completely hot. Serves 6.

Add a spinach salad with a cup of canned cream of tomato soup made with milk, simmered with fresh chopped tomatoes and a handful of chopped celery for a scrumptious, beautiful meal.

NUTTY-ORANGE BREAD

A Honey of a Loaf

1 package dry yeast	1 egg
¼ cup warm water	¼ cup butter, melted
1 seedless orange	½ cup honey
3½ cups all-purpose flour	½ cup raisins
1 teaspoon salt	½ cup chopped nuts

Dissolve yeast in warm water. In a blender or food processor grind orange, cut in sections, until fine. Using mixer, food processor or by hand combine dissolved yeast, orange mixture, flour, salt, egg, butter and honey. Mix well; stir in the raisins and nuts. Add more flour to form a soft manageable dough; knead until smooth. Let rise until doubled; punch down. Place in a greased, 9x5x3-inch loaf pan. Let rise about 50-60 minutes or until doubled. Bake at 350° for 50 minutes until light brown. Yields 1 loaf.

Optional: Mix ¾ cup powdered sugar and enough orange juice to glaze loaf top.

RUTH'S PUMPKIN SPICE BREAD

Colorful and Delicately Spiced

½ cup pumpkin (use 16-ounce can)	3½ to 4 cups all-purpose flour
1 teaspoon salt	1 teaspoon cinnamon
¼ cup sugar	¼ teaspoon nutmeg
3 tablespoons margarine	¼ teaspoon mace or pumpkin pie spice
2 packages dry yeast	2 eggs, slightly beaten
½ cup warm water	

Microwave pumpkin, salt, sugar and margarine until warm; beat until smooth; let cool to 105-115°. Dissolve yeast in warm water in a large bowl. Mix in 3 cups flour and spices; stir in pumpkin mixture, yeast and eggs. Add enough flour to knead until smooth. Cover, in a greased bowl, to rise until double; punch down. Shape into a loaf for a 9x5x3-inch greased loaf pan. Let rise until double; bake at 375° for 35-40 minutes. Cover with foil if bread becomes too brown. Remove from pan to a rack; brush with melted butter. Yields 1 loaf. Slice; serve with Pumpkin Butter.

PUMPKIN BUTTER
Welcome Gift at Thanksgiving or Christmas

1½ cups pumpkin, remaining
   pumpkin
¾ cup brown or white sugar
1 teaspoon cinnamon

⅛ teaspoon cloves
⅛ teaspoon nutmeg
¼ cup orange juice

Cook until thick and spreadable. Makes 2 small jars of pumpkin butter.

YUM-YUM TOMATO BREAD
Ultimate in B.L.T's and Cheese Toast

2 cups tomato juice, warmed
2 tablespoons honey
3 tablespoons cooking oil
1 tablespoon worcestershire
  sauce
1 teaspoon lemon juice
1 tablespoon dried parsley or 3
  tablespoons minced fresh
  parsley
1 tablespoon dehydrated onion
  flakes or 3 tablespoons minced
  or blended fresh onion

1 teaspoon celery salt
1 teaspoon garlic salt
½ teaspoon black pepper
5 drops hot sauce, or for a hot
  zippy flavor, add 1 small
  seeded jalapeno pepper
  blended with tomato juice,
  optional
¼ cup warm water
1 package dry yeast
3-3½ cups bread flour
2½ cups all-purpose flour

Whisk juice, honey, oil, worcestershire, lemon juice, parsley, onion, salts, pepper and hot sauce in a large bowl; add yeast dissolved in warm water. Beat in enough flour to form a manageable dough. Knead on floured board 5 to 8 minutes or until dough is smooth and elastic. Flip dough over in greased bowl; cover to rise in warm area until double, about 1½ hours.

Punch dough down; divide in 2 loaves, placing in greased 9x5x3-inch loaf pans. Bake 30-35 minutes at 350°. Watch, will not appear brown. Brush loaves with oil when nearly done if brown tops are desired. Remove loaves from pans; cool on racks. Yields 2 loaves.

Serve warm bread slices, cut in strips, with homemade pimento cheese for a sensational appetizer.

CHERI'S SHEEPHERDER'S BREAD

Southern California Low-Fat Bread

3½ cups warm water, divided
3 tablespoons sugar
3 packages dry yeast

8-9½ cups bread flour, divided
1 tablespoon salt

Mix ½ cup water (105-115°), sugar and yeast in a large bowl; let stand until bubbly. Mix in 3 cups flour, salt, yeast mixture and remaining water. Mix in only enough flour, a few cups at a time, for a manageable dough. Knead for about 10 minutes until smooth and elastic using extra flour, if needed. Let rise in a greased, covered bowl until doubled.

Line, with foil, the bottom of a 10x3-inch Dutch oven, using a tight fitting lid. Grease the foil, pan surface and lid thoroughly. Punch down risen dough, kneading a few turns; form into a round ball, placing in the Dutch oven. Cover with lid; let rise until dough begins to lift lid, 20-25 minutes. Bake at 350° for 1 hour and 5 minutes. After 25-30 minutes, lift lid to check on dough; place lid back on bread. Remove lid for the last 10 minutes to brown the top. Test with a cake tester in the center for doneness. Turn out of Dutch oven to cool on wire rack. Makes a very large loaf.

This unique, beautiful hunk of bread reminds Cheri of small town California baking and eating.

If you don't have any hungry sheepherders to call, family, neighbors and friends will do just fine!

BAKER'S IDEA: For a low-calorie spread for the warm bread, blend a pinch of crushed herbs, such as thyme, marjoram and basil, into farmers cheese.

FRENCH AND ITALIAN BREADS

Slash risen, round or long loaves with a very sharp knife. If dough has risen too long, don't slash loaf; bake immediately. If shaped loaf falls, gently faltten dough; reshape dough for another rising.

Enjoy eating the warm loaves; keep extra loaves fresh by freezing. Being low in fat, sugar, and eggs, these breads do not remain fresh long.

CLASSIC FRENCH BREAD

No fat added

2 packages dry yeast	6 cups bread flour, divided
2 cups warm water	cornmeal
1 tablespoon sugar	Egg White Glaze
1½ teaspoons salt	sesame seeds, optional

Dissolve yeast in warm water; mix in sugar, salt and 3 cups of bread flour. Allow to rise for 30 minutes. Add rest of flour until manageable; knead on floured surface until smooth and elastic, about 8-10 minutes, adding flour as needed. Cover bowl and let rise in warm place until double in bulk. Punch down; cover dough for 10 minute rest. Divide dough in 2 parts; roll each part into 15x9-inch rectangles. Start with long side to roll tightly as a jelly roll. Roll to taper ends. Place loaf, seam down, diagonally across a greased, cornmeal sprinkled baking sheet, or place in greased cylinder pans. Let rise in warm oven with a cup of hot water until double in size. Brush bread with 1 egg white beaten with 1 tablespoon water; sprinkle on seeds. Slash tops diagonally, ½-inch deep and 1½-inches apart. Place a pan of hot water in a preheated 425° oven. Bake loaves for 10 minutes. Reduce heat to 400° for 20-25 minutes longer. Adjust time with loaf size. Bread will be a light golden brown and have a hollow sound when tapped. Cool on wire racks. Yields 2 large loaves or 4 long batons.

Variations:

OATMEAL FRENCH BREAD: Add ½ cup quick raw oats mixed with ½ cup boiling water, 2 tablespoons sugar (total of 3) and ½ cup cooking oil to French Bread batter before adding rest of flour. Increase flour as necessary.

FEATHER-LIGHT FRENCH BREAD: After 30 minute rising, add 1 egg white, stiffly beaten; continue with recipe. Increase flour as necessary.

WHOLE WHEAT FRENCH BREAD: Can substitute whole wheat flour for ½ of bread flour.

MARY PANZICA'S ITALIAN BREAD

Weekend Chef's Special "User-Friendly" Dough

10 cups bread flour	2¾ cups water, (120-130°)
2 packages dry yeast	¼ cup pure, virgin olive oil or
1 teaspoon salt	cooking oil

Combine with an electric mixer in a large bowl, 3 cups flour, yeast and salt. Add water and olive oil; beat for 3 minutes. Add more flour until a manageable soft dough forms. Knead until smooth and elastic, about 5 to 8 minutes. Flip dough over in a very large greased bowl to grease top; let rise, covered, in a warm place until doubled. While dough rests, grease 2 baking sheets. Divide dough into 4 parts. Lightly knead, pushing and rolling dough into a rectangle wider than the pan and 2 inches shorter than pan length. Roll dough jelly roll fashion, placing seam side under dough, tapering ends. Let rise in warm, draft free area until double. Slash tops of loaves; brush with water. Place pan of hot water in the 400° oven. Bake loaves for 20-25 minutes or until bread sounds hollow when tapped. Cool on cake rack. Yields 4 loaves.

Mary would mix the dough with her hands, kneading until lively and resilient. Long thin loaves, tapered rolls and round loaves, rolled between her hands and the table surface, were all her specialities. Rose Stutts and the rest of Mary's children wistfully remember this bread hot out of the oven, pieces broken from the loaf, dipped in olive oil and eaten with gusto, yet savoring the aroma and flavor. Rose has her mother's European flare for baking and for generous sharing of epicurean foods.

RICOTTA CHEESE-WICH: For a snack, Mary's family would spread sliced warm bread with crumbled ricotta cheese, sprinkled with salt.

Variations: The following variations of Mary Panzica's Italian Bread use kneaded and risen dough:

ITALIAN PESTO SWIRL LOAF: Roll ¼ of dough into a 9x15-inch rectangle, brush with melted butter and spread with Pesto leaving a ⅛-inch border around the edges. Roll tightly as a jelly roll, pressing all edges to seal with each turn. Place seam side down on a greased baking sheet; let rise until double in a warm place. Brush or spray with water; bake, with a pan of hot water, at 400° about 25 minutes or until golden brown.

PESTO: Combine in a food processor or blender until smooth:

1 cup fresh basil leaves, lightly packed	1 clove garlic
	2 tablespoons English
⅓ cup grated Parmesan and Romano cheese	Walnuts or pine nuts
	1 tablespoon fresh parsley
2 tablespoons olive oil	

GARLIC LOVERS ONLY:

ITALIAN GARLIC BOW KNOT ROLLS: Into ½ of Italian dough, knead 4 cloves of garlic, mashed in a garlic press, into dough. Form dough in a long roll, cut into 18 pieces and roll each piece into a 6-inch rope. To form small bow knot rolls, cross rope over as tying a knot, leaving top of one end in the middle of the roll. Tuck loose end under roll. Brush all rolls with olive oil and sprinkle tops with garlic salt, crushed oregano and thyme.

ITALIAN GARLIC SNAIL ROLLS: To form snails, press center of rope to greased pan; circle rest of dough around center as a snail. Call the children to make these.

ITALIAN FRIED GARLIC NUGGETS: Form into small balls, using rounded teaspoon of dough. When light and doubled in size, cook in 375° oil until pale golden brown and done. Sprinkle with garlic salt, crushed oregano and thyme.

ITALIAN SPIRAL GARLIC LOAF OR ROLLS: Roll ½ of Italian dough into a ½-inch thick rectangle. Spread garlic butter over dough. Roll dough as a jelly roll starting with long side. Press seam to seal, placing seam side down on a greased baking sheet or cut ¼ to ½-inch rolls, depending on the size desired. Place small rolls, cut side down, on a greased pan, close together. Brush dough with garlic glaze and sprinkle with oregano. After rising until double, bake for 15-20 minutes at 400° for small rolls or 25-30 minutes for whole loaf.

GARLIC BUTTER: Cream all ingredients.

½ cup butter	2 teaspoons dried parsley flakes
1 teaspoon garlic powder	

GARLIC GLAZE: Combine all ingredients except oregano.

¼ cup melted butter	1 tablespoon beaten egg
½ teaspoon garlic powder	oregano flakes

JIM'S GARLIC TOAST: Cut garlic clove in half, rub on sliced, slightly toasted Italian or French bread. Brush with melted butter. Toast in oven until lightly brown. Top with a layer of ricotta cheese. Umm good!

VIRGINIA'S ROASTED GARLIC TOAST: Roast large garlic cloves in a 300° oven until soft. Spread on Italian bread slices. Low-calorie, good-for-you spread!

More Italian Bread Variations:

ITALIAN CRISPY OR SOFT BREAD STICKS: Roll ¼ of Italian dough ½-inch thick; cut in strips, roll pencil thin or desired thickness. Let rise, brush with egg white glaze and coarse salt. Bake at 400° for 10-15 minutes or until brown. Use for appetizers with dips, salads or Italian meals.

SERVE NOW OR LATER ITALIAN PIZZA CRUST: Roll ¼ of Italian dough into 2 (12-inch) pizza crusts with a ridge on outer edge. Bake pizza crusts in lightly greased pans for 8 minutes at 400°. Cool, plastic wrap and refrigerate for several days. Use desired fillings.

BAKER'S FAVORITE — VEGGIE PIZZA: Place crust in pan, spread with pizza sauce, add a layer of thinly sliced onions, squash, zucchini and green pepper and top with low-fat mozzarella cheese. Bake for 15-20 minutes at 425°.

CUBAN BREAD: Use ½ of Italian dough after kneading, first rising and resting. Roll into a 15-inch rectangle. Roll up, press edges together, place seam side down on greased baking sheet and cut a lengthwise slash down the center top of the bread. Brush or spray loaves with water. Let rise until almost double. Start baking in cold oven with a pan of hot water on the lower shelf. Turn oven to 400° for 35 to 40 minutes, or until loaves sound hollow when tapped. Cool on wire racks. The bread is sliced lengthwise adding your favorite cold, thinly sliced meats, swiss cheese, sharp cheddar, mustard, mayonnaise and thinly sliced dill pickles.

CROWD PLEASING ITALIAN SAUSAGE ROLL

Jean and Mannie Villar serve this do ahead "meal-in-one" for ball game gatherings or very special Florida occasions.

½ of Mary Panzica's Italian Bread
  Dough
1 large bell pepper, chopped
8 ounces fresh sliced mushrooms
1 large onion, chopped

2 tablespoons olive oil
1 pound mild Italian or Kielbasa
  sausage
1 pound grated mozzarella
  cheese

Saute pepper, mushrooms and onion in olive oil. Add sausage cooked in water, drained, removed from casing and chopped. Place dough rolled to a 12x18-inch rectangle on a greased, foil lined baking sheet. Spread filling down the center of the rectangle and sprinkle cheese on top. Fold sides and ends of dough to the middle to enclose filling. Pinch edges together to seal. Brush with an egg white or cornstarch glaze. Pierce top dough in 3 places.

Cut only through top layer, to allow steam to escape. Bake at 375° for 20-25 minutes or until golden brown. Cool a few minutes, slice and serve hot.

Individual calzone servings can be made by filling half of a small dough rectangle, folding over and pinching edges to seal. Pierce top with a fork. Form extra dough into ropes to make symbols for schools or initials for top of roll.

The aroma from baking will whet the appetites of the most avid ball fans.

RAPID YEAST PIZZA DOUGH
Dough for 2 (12-inch) Crusts

1½ cups whole wheat flour	1 package dry yeast
1½ cups all-purpose flour	1 cup hot water, (125-130°)
1 teaspoon salt	2 tablespoons cooking oil

Combine flours in mixing bowl. Take out 1 cup of flour for reserve. Mix salt and yeast with flour; add water and oil. Beat with mixer until smooth, about 3 minutes. Add enough reserved flour to form a manageable dough. Knead on a lightly floured board until smooth and elastic. Cover dough with bowl to rest for 10 minutes. Divide dough in half; roll 1-inch larger than pizza pans. Can use 2 pizza pans or 2 baking sheets; grease pans and sprinkle with cornmeal, which acts as a baking stone to brown crust. Fit dough in pans, form a rim around edge of pizza and pinch up edges. Prick with a fork several times over the surface. Bake at 400° for 10-12 minutes or until light brown.

Now ready for filling!

BAKER'S MOST FAVORITE - SLICED TOMATO PIZZA: Spread on pizza sauce; add drained, cooked sausage, sprinkle with shredded mozzarella cheese and cover with thin sliced ripe tomatoes. Add a covering of grated Parmesan and cover with more mozzarella. Bake for 10-12 minutes at 450°. *Enjoy!*

BAKER'S PIZZA PARTY: Form and bake pizza dough in greased, small pizza pans. Spread on pizza sauce. Allow guests to build their own individual pizzas from thinly sliced, crumbled or chopped vegetables, meats and cheeses. Bake in oven while guests help themselves to salad.

BASIC MAXI-BREAD DOUGH

Bake and Freeze Weeks Ahead

Choose from these varieties: 10 French breads, 2 Novelty breads and 8 different Whole Grain breads

1 cup warm water (105-115°)	1 tablespoon salt
²/₃ cup instant nonfat dry milk	2 packages active dry yeast
¹/₃ cup shortening	3 cups warm water (105-115°)
¹/₃ cup sugar	12 cups bread flour, divided

Combine water, dry milk, shortening, sugar and salt. In a large bowl, dissolve yeast in water; stir in milk mixture. Mix in 3 cups flour, beat until smooth. Stir in 3 more cups flour, adding more flour until difficult to stir or dough is manageable. Turn out onto lightly floured surface. Knead until smooth and elastic, about 8 minutes, adding flour as necessary. Let dough rise, covered, in a warm place, until double.

Now for the creativity! Whatever your mood or need for bread the rest of the week, you can do now. Divide dough into sections or divide by weight. Refrigerate dough in a large plastic bag for a few days or freeze if your schedule becomes hectic.

GLAZES:

EGG GLAZE: Whisk 1 whole egg and 1 tablespoon water.

EGG WHITE GLAZE: Whisk 1 egg white and 1 tablespoon water.

Brush egg or egg white glaze on bread before last rising, when bread is changing color in the oven and when it is removed from the oven. Seeds or toppings hold onto the bread crust easily with these glazes.

CORNSTARCH GLAZE:

1 teaspoon cornstarch	¼ teaspoon salt, optional
¼ cup cold water	

Continuously mix cornstarch, salt and water together bringing only to a complete boil over medium heat. Brush slightly cooled glaze over tops and sides of bread loaves before rising, middle of bread baking and after removing hot from oven for a shiny crust.

MOTTLED GLAZE: Mix ½ package dry yeast (1¼ teaspoons), 1 teaspoon sugar, 2 tablespoons cornstarch, 1 teaspoon oil and 2 tablespoons water. Allow to stand until bubbly, about 25 minutes. Brush on this thick glaze, for a crinkled hide effect for breads and creative novelty breads, before rising and baking.

Variations of Basic Maxi-Bread Dough:

Each of the following large French bread loaves requires ¼ of Maxi-Dough kneaded, risen and rolled to a 9x15-inch rectangle. Roll dough starting with the long side. Press edges and ends to seal. Place completely rolled loaf seam side down on greased, foil-lined baking sheet large enough to allow for rising. Can form two small long or round loaves.

Baking of Basic Maxi-Bread Dough Variations:

After formed loaves rise until double, carefully make ¼-inch deep slashes at an angle every 1½-inches across the bread tops with a sharp knife. Brush with an egg white glaze. Place in a 400° oven, with a pan of hot water, for 25-30 minutes until light brown and hollow sounding when tapped. Glaze bread again, sprinkle with sesame seeds if desired.

FRENCH ROLLS: Form ¼ of Maxi-Dough into 2 dozen egg shaped, oblong rolls. Place about 1-inch apart on greased pan. Smooth the top and tuck under edges. After rising, cut slash around top or down middle using a sharp knife. Glaze with egg white glaze. Bake at 400° for 15-20 minutes.

FRESH HERB FRENCH BREAD: Use a medium size skillet to lightly saute vegetables and herbs; add salts and pepper. When cool mix in egg yolk.

2 tablespoons butter
1 small onion, finely chopped
¾ cup fresh parsley, finely chopped
¼ cup total, fresh, mixed or matched finely chopped dill, sweet basil, thyme, summer savory, rosemary or marjarom

¼ teaspoon celery salt
¼ teaspoon garlic salt
¹/₈ teaspoon cayenne pepper
1 egg, separated and beaten

Spread filling on dough rectangle to within 1-inch of edges. Roll dough from the long side, pressing to seal roll and ends with each turn; place seam side down on a greased baking sheet. Brush the loaf with egg white mixed with 1 tablespoon of water. Let rise until double. Bake at 375° for 30-35 minutes until brown and has a hollow sound when tapped. Cool on rack. Yields 1 loaf.

LOW-FAT BAKER: Process the filling in the food processor, omitting egg and butter.

More Variations of Basic Maxi-Bread Dough:

For each of the following, flatten ¼ of the Maxi-Bread Dough (page 40) into a 9x15-inch rectangle. Add ingredients within ¼-inch of edges. Tightly roll, starting with the long side, pressing and pinching edges together. Place seam side down on a greased baking pan. Let rise until double; bake at 375° for 25-30 minutes

CREOLE FRENCH BREAD: Brush dough rectangle with butter; sprinkle 1 tablespoon creole seasoning on top of butter. Sprinkle with 1 cup shredded mozzarella cheese.

CHEESE AND CHILIES FRENCH BREAD: Brush rectangle with butter; sprinkle with about 3½ tablespoons chopped, drained, canned hot or mild green chilies. Sprinkle over the top 1¼ cups medium or sharp cheddar cheese.

ONION FRENCH BREAD: Spread dough rectangle with softened butter. Crush a 1.3 ounce envelope of onion soup mix before opening. Sprinkle crushed soup mix over dough; sprinkle with 1 cup shredded mozzarella or cheddar cheese.

DRIED HERB FRENCH BREAD: Brush dough rectangle with melted butter; sprinkle with the following ingredients:

1 tablespoon dried parsley	¼ teaspoon garlic salt
1 tablespoon total, mix or match dried basil, thyme, oregano, marjarom, rosemary or dill	¼ teaspoon onion salt
	$1/8$ teaspoon cayenne pepper
1 tablespoon, mix or match favorite seeds if desired, caraway, aniseed, fennel, cumin seeds	

CHEESE HERB FRENCH BREAD:

Variation of Dried Herb French Bread

Add ¼ cup Parmesan cheese and ⅔ cup cheddar cheese to the herb mixture on the Dried Herb French Bread dough rectangle.

More Variations of Basic Maxi-Bread Dough:

MUSTARD-HERB FRENCH BREAD: Spread creamed ingredients over dough rectangle.

2 tablespoons softened butter
1 teaspoon worcestershire sauce
1 teaspoon onion powder
2 teaspoons dried parsley flakes
½ teaspoon crushed, dried thyme
½ teaspoon crushed, dried rosemary

1 teaspoon dried, minced onion
2 teaspoons spicy brown mustard
2 teaspoons honey

MUSHROOM-SPINACH BRAID: Lightly saute mushrooms, onion and garlic; mix in spinach, cottage cheese and spices.

½ pound fresh mushrooms, sliced
½ cup chopped onion
2 cloves garlic, minced
1 package (10 ounce) frozen chopped spinach, thaw, drain and squeeze out juice
½ cup cottage cheese, drained

¼ teaspoon lemon-pepper or ¼ teaspoon grated lemon and $1/8$ teaspoon pepper
¼ teaspoon seasoned salt
¼ teaspoon nutmeg
¼ teaspoon thyme
1 beaten egg, divided
¾ cup shredded mozzarella cheese

Roll ¼ of the Maxi-Dough (page 40) in a 15x12-inch rectangle; place on a greased baking sheet. Brush dough surface with beaten egg. Spread filling in center of rectangle. Cut dough in 1-inch strips to the filling, on both long sides. Fold alternately at an angle across the filling to the center giving a braided effect. Brush outside with remaining egg and 1 teaspoon water. Let rise until double. Bake at 375° for 20 minutes. Makes 4 servings.

BAKER'S IDEA: Make this meal-in-a-loaf a special picnic bread. Add a salad and your favorite tea bread.

More Variations of Basic Maxi-Bread Dough:

NOVELTY BREADS

Use Maxi-Dough to form simple lines of turtles, fish, mice, rabbits, monsters or fun critters. Fruits and leaves, intricate coils, braids and initials can be added to the rising bread for decorations. Let children create with the dough, using their imagination — just for the fun of it!

JULIE DUTTON'S DINOSAUR BREAD: Divide ¼ of the Maxi-Dough in half. Shape one of the halves into an 8x4-inch half circle on a greased baking sheet. Gently pull and stretch right angled corner of dough to form a 3½-inch head, tapering end and shaping neck. With sharp knife, make 1-inch cut at end of head to form mouth; press raisin in head for eye. Gently pull and stretch left corner of dough to form 6-inch tail; taper end, flatten tail and curve.

Remove ¼ of remaining dough; divide into 2 equal pieces shaping into 2 (4-inch) rectangles for legs. Attach legs by pressing to body; turn up ends of legs to form feet, making 3 cuts on each foot to form toes.

Divide remaining dough into 3 equal pieces. Divide to form into squares, using three sizes, large, medium and small. Cut squares in half to form triangles. Arrange triangles in a row along back of dinosaur, gently pressing to hold, slightly overlapping, with large triangles at center and smaller triangles tapering down near head and tail. Brush with egg white, beaten with 1 tablespoon water. Let rise until double.

Carefully redefine shape if necessary. Form any extra dough into "rocks", rolled in cinnamon and sugar before baking, to place around dinosaur. Bake at 350° for 30 minutes or until light brown.

TEDDY BEAR BREAD: Divide ½ of Maxi-Dough into 3 balls. Divide first ball into 6 equal balls for ears, arms and legs. Pinch off small part of second ball for nose, reshaping remainder for head. Leave third ball intact for body. Fit pieces of the bear together on a greased baking sheet; add raisins for eyes and buttons. Glaze and bake as Julie's Dinosaur Bread.

More Variations of Basic Maxi-Bread Dough:

GOOD-FOR-YOU WHOLE-GRAINS
INTRODUCE YOUR FAMILY AND FRIENDS
TO EATING WHOLE-GRAINS

Added Bonus: Have the adventure of traveling through time and space to unravel the exciting past of whole grains.

Use ¼ of the Maxi-Dough (page 40) to form any of the varieties below. Knead in a small amount of different grains to form a healthful, flavorful, crunchy whole grain loaf. Flatten loaf to an oblong shape, folding and pressing dough to fit pan. Place dough in a greased 9x5x3-inch loaf pan, letting rise in a warm place, covered, until double. Dough will rise to the top, rounding above the rim. Bake at 375° for 30-35 minutes.

CRACKED WHEAT BREAD: Knead 2 tablespoons honey, ½ cup cracked wheat and 1 teaspoon orange rind into ½ of the Maxi-Dough until combined. Before rising spread honey over loaf and sprinkle with cracked wheat.

WHEAT GERM-BRAN BREAD: Knead 1 tablespoon honey, 2 tablespoons wheat germ and 2 tablespoons bran into ½ of the Maxi-Dough. Before rising spread honey over loaf and sprinkle with wheat germ.

MOLASSES-RYE BREAD: Knead 1 tablespoon orange marmalade, 1 tablespoon molasses, ½ teaspoon ginger and ½ cup rye flour into ½ of the Maxi-Dough. Add more rye flour for kneading if dough is sticky. Before rising spread orange marmalade over top of bread loaf and sprinkle caraway seeds over top.

MILLET-SOY-MOLASSES BREAD: Knead 2 tablespoons molasses, ½ cup millet flour and ½ cup soy flour into ½ of the Maxi-Dough. Before rising brush top of loaf with molasses, sprinkling on whole hulled millet.

OATMEAL-BARLEY BREAD: Knead 2 tablespoons maple syrup into ½ of the Maxi-Dough with ½ cup oatmeal, ½ cup barley, 1 teaspoon lemon rind and ½ teaspoon ginger. Before rising spread maple syrup over loaf and sprinkle with oats.

BREAKFAST CEREAL BREAD: Add ½ cup cooked cereal or cooked, drained rice to ¼ of the Maxi-Dough; add flour if necessary.

More Variations of Basic Maxi-Bread Dough:

SPROUTED GRAINS, SEEDS AND WHOLE WHEAT BREAD: Wheat, rye, barley, millet, oats, various beans, such as lentils and mung beans, and seeds such as alfalfa, not processed by heat or crushing, can be sprouted. Use a large mouth canning jar to soak grains, beans or seeds over night. Drain off the water. Allow grains, beans or seeds to stick to jar side. Cover top with cheese cloth or paper towel fastened with jar band or rubber band. Place on side in dark cabinet. Place a dated note on cupboard door to prevent forgetting or someone throwing them away.

Each day rinse and drain sprouts or sprinkle water on them. Do not leave too wet. If desired, after sprouting, place in light to form green leaves.

Saute leftover sprouts in butter. Add to your favorite rice or bean dish.

Knead ½ cup drained, chopped sprouts into ¼ of Maxi-Dough (page 40), adding enough whole wheat flour for a manageable dough.

EZEKIEL BREAD, the complete protein bread recipe God gave to the Israelites. *"Take wheat, barley, lentils, millet and spelt, put them in one vessel and make them into bread for yourself..."* Ezekiel 4:9

Substitute professionally milled Ezekiel flour (look in health food stores) for ¼ to ½ of the flour in loaf breads, using with bread flour.

Make your own Ezekiel flour by grinding dried lentils and beans. Add 1 tablespoon honey and a little liquid if necessary when adding 1 tablespoon each barley, millet, whole wheat, lentils and beans to form an Ezekiel Bread with ¼ of the Maxi-Dough (page 40).

Save leftover cooked, mashed and drained dried lentils, split peas and beans in the freezer to add to bread dough. Add ¼ to ½ cup cooked mixed or matched legumes with enough barley, millet and whole wheat flour to form a manageable dough with ¼ of the Maxi-Dough.

Form into a long loaf or make hamburger or hotdog buns shaped by hand. Place on greased pan sprinkled with corn meal for a crispy crust. Glaze with a cornstarch glaze or brush with melted butter, rolling in bran or sesame seeds.

This bread with its rough, golden crust will be a conversation topic. A tasty introduction to whole grains, legumes and eating high on the food chain. Dried legume flour contains 2 to 4 times as much protein as grain flours.

By encouraging children to help add and knead whole-grains in the dough, coaxing to eat "their" loaf won't be necessary.

WHOLE-GRAIN YEAST BREADS

Combine varieties of whole-grain flour with bread flour to yield a lighter product. Knead a 100% whole-grain dough well, to utilize the gluten available. Enjoy the compact, chewy texture and nut-like flavor.

The American public's view on the nutritional importance of whole-grains has come full circle since Sylvester Graham's 1800's "health" lectures. He was an advocate of baking with good quality whole-grain flour, such as his graham flour — coarsely ground and unsifted. He refers to natural whole-grain breads as "made of the whole substance of the grain," in his book, *Treatise on Bread and Bread-Making*, published in 1837.

ANN'S WHOLE WHEAT SHEEPHERDER'S BREAD

½ cup butter
1½ teaspoons salt
2½ cups hot water
2 packages dry yeast

½ cup warm water
4½ cups all-purpose flour
5 cups whole wheat flour

Add butter and salt to hot water. Dissolve yeast in ½ cup warm water. Add cooled, lukewarm butter mixture to yeast, gradually beating in the 4 ½ cups all-purpose flour. Beat in rest of whole wheat flour as necessary for kneading. Knead until smooth and elastic, about 10 minutes. Let rise in a greased, covered bowl until doubled.

Punch down risen dough, kneading a few times. Form and bake as Cheri's Sheepherder's bread (page 34) or use washed, new clay pots lined with foil and greased. Fill pots half full of dough. This will make about 9 (4¼x4-inch) flower pots of dough. Greased and floured cans or molds can also be used. Let rise until double. Bake at 350° for 25-30 minutes or until done, depending on size.

Cooking in a clay container or a closed Dutch oven gives a similar effect to baking in the round adobe ovens used by the Pueblos and other Southwest Indians.

JENNIE'S WHOLE WHEAT BREAD AND ROLLS

¾ cup hot milk
⅓ cup brown sugar
1 tablespoon salt
¼ cup margarine

2 packages dry yeast
1½ cups warm water
3 cups whole wheat flour
3½ cups bread flour

Mix milk, sugar, salt and margarine together; cool (105-115°). Dissolve yeast in warm water; beat in milk mixture and whole wheat flour. Add enough bread flour to be manageable; knead dough about 10 minutes or until smooth and elastic. Place in oiled bowl, cover and let rise in warm place until double in size. Punch down and divide dough in half. Pat dough to fit 2 greased 9x5x3-inch loaf pans or form into buns or rolls. Bake at 400° for 15 minutes. For loaves, change oven temperature to 375° to bake for 15 minutes more or until loaves are a golden brown and sound hollow when tapped. If bread is becoming too brown, cover with foil.

Jennie sometimes uses regular all-purpose flour instead of bread flour with good results (a little more compact).

Variations:

WHOLE WHEAT PITA BREAD — MIDDLE EASTERN POCKET BREAD: Use ½ of Jennie's recipe. After first rising, let dough rest 10 minutes. Divide dough into 7 parts. Shape into balls. Starting in the center, use a rolling pin to roll each ball evenly, to form a smooth 6-inch round. Place on a lightly greased baking sheet. Brush tops with milk or evaporated milk. Let rise, covered, in a warm place until **partially** risen and a little puffy, about 30 minutes. Place baking sheet on lowest rack in a 475° oven for 5-10 minutes or until puffed and light brown. To serve, cut part way along one side and stuff with sandwich filling or cut in half for two sandwiches.

BAKER'S HINT: Dough rising too much will result in large rolls instead of the desired pita bread. Without some rising, Arab bread will form.

WHOLE-WHEAT ARAB BREAD: Use ½ of Jennie's recipe. After rising and resting, divide dough into 7 balls. Roll each into an 8-inch circle. Place in a hot, greased 8-inch iron skillet, on the lowest oven rack, in a 450° oven. Bake for 5-8 minutes.

HONEY-BUTTER SPREAD: Cream ½ cup softened butter with 2 tablespoons honey; add ½ teaspoon cinnamon for an extra oomph!

Fresh whole-grain flour, such as Falls Mill's stone-ground flour, gives this bread more texture. John and Jane Lovett operate this restored 1873 water-powered mill in Belvidere, Tennessee, 35 miles northeast of Huntsville, Alabama.

REFRIGERATOR HONEY-WHEAT BREAD

Serve hot with honey spread

2½ to 3 cups whole wheat, divided
2 packages dry yeast
1 tablespoon salt
⅓ cup instant nonfat dry milk

2¾ cups water
¼ cup cooking oil
¼ cup honey
4 cups bread flour
1 cup chopped pecans, optional

Combine 2½ cups whole wheat flour, yeast, salt and dry milk in a large mixer bowl. Beat water, oil and honey, heated to 120-130°, into dry ingredients, beating for three minutes on high. Add pecans and whole wheat flour until too thick for mixer. Add white flour to form a manageable dough; knead until smooth and elastic, about 5-8 minutes.

Cover dough and let rise in a warm place. Punch down; place in two greased 9x5x3-inch loaf pans. Brush with oil; cover with plastic wrap, allowing for expansion, and refrigerate overnight. When ready to use, let stand at room temperature until light, about 15-20 minutes. If bubbles appear on surface, deflate with a toothpick. Bake in 400° oven 35-40 minutes. Cool on wire rack. Yields 2 loaves.

TRADITIONAL ANADAMA BREAD

The old story is told about the irate farmer, who tired of eating his wife Anna's cornmeal mush every night, threw in some yeast and more flour to bake the mixture. Ah...Anadama Bread was born! An unusual name for an equally unusual, low in fat, bread.

½ cup cornmeal
2 teaspoons salt
2 packages dry yeast
⅓ cup instant nonfat dry milk

5-6 cups all-purpose flour, divided
½ cup molasses
2 tablespoons shortening
2 cups water (120-130° F.)

Using mixer, combine cornmeal, salt, yeast, dry milk and 2 ½ cups flour in a large bowl; beat in shortening, molasses and water, beating for 3 minutes on high. Add flour to form a manageable dough. Knead on a floured surface until smooth and elastic. Let rise until double. Punch dough down; divide in half. Shape in 2 greased 9x5x3-inch pans. Cover to rise in warm, draft-free place for 45 minutes or until double in size. Bake at 375° for 35-45 minutes. Remove from pan; cool loaves on racks. Yields 2 loaves.

JOHN'S 100% WHOLE WHEAT BREAD
100 % Healthy

2 packages dry yeast	3 teaspoons salt
2¼ cups water (105-115°)	⅓ cup molasses or honey
⅔ cup instant nonfat dry milk	2 eggs
3 tablespoons cooking oil	6-6½ cups whole wheat flour

Dissolve yeast with 2¼ cups water in a large bowl; beat in dry milk, oil, salt, molasses and eggs. Add flour, a few cups at a time, beating after each addition, until a soft dough is formed. Knead on a floured board for about 10 minutes or until smooth and elastic; must knead well to utilize gluten. Let rise in a greased bowl, turning dough over to grease surface of dough, until double in size. Punch down the dough. Knead dough again for a few turns. Form one half of dough in a loaf shape; place in a greased 9x5x3-inch loaf pan. The other half of the bread can be formed into a fresh herb loaf as follows:

FRESH ONION-HERB BREAD: Knead in 1 finely chopped small onion and ½ cup finely chopped fresh green herbs to half of the 100% Whole Wheat Bread dough. Mix or match Italian basil, parsley, thyme, marjoram, dill and oregano. Form herb dough to fit greased 9x5x3-inch pan.

Place both loaves of bread, covered, in a warm place to rise until double. Bake at 400° for 10 minutes. Turn oven to 375° for 25 more minutes. The bread should sound hollow when tapped. If loaf bottom is not done enough, turn over in pan to bake a few more minutes. Cover top with foil if too brown. Brush tops with melted butter. Yields 2 loaves.

Chop and freeze leftover fresh parsley, chives, dill or other herbs to add to this bread. Measure before freezing. Frozen herbs, as well as dried herbs, are more concentrated.

MAMA GILLS' OATMEAL BREAD

1 cup old-fashioned oats	2 packages regular or rapid dry
2 cups boiling water	yeast
5-6 cups bread flour, can substi-	2 teaspoons salt
tute 1 cup whole wheat flour	½ cup honey or molasses
for 1 cup bread flour	3 tablespoons cooking oil

Combine oats and boiling water; let stand ½ hour. Using mixer, combine 3 cups flour, yeast and salt in large bowl. Add oat mixture with molasses and oil, cooled to 125-130°, to the dry ingredients; beat for 3 minutes. Add rest of flour as necessary to form a manageable dough. Knead on a floured surface for 5 minutes or until dough is smooth and elastic. Let rest for 10 minutes for rapid yeast, or let rise until double for regular yeast before punching down the dough. Divide dough; place in 2 greased 9x5x2-inch pans. Cover in warm place; let rise until double, about 45-50 minutes. Bake at 350° for 30 minutes. Yields 2 loaves.

MaMa, who lived with the Gills for many years, used the conventional method (sprinkling regular yeast over warm water to dissolve) to make her bread each week for the family. Her daughter-in-law Charlotte, continues the tradition in their North Carolina home. For variety she adds ½ cup orange marmalade or 1 cup raisins.

JOHN'S WHOLE-GRAIN BATTER BREAD

Packed with good nutrition and go power!

5½ cups whole wheat flour	⅔ cup instant nonfat dry milk
½ cup barley flour	⅓ cup brown sugar
½ cup soy flour	1 teaspoon salt
¼ cup cracked wheat	2 packages dry yeast
¼ cup wheat germ	3½ cups hot water

Combine 3 cups of the whole wheat, plus all the barley, soy, cracked wheat, wheat germ, dry milk, sugar, salt and yeast in a large bowl. Add hot water. Beat 3 minutes with a mixer and continue beating by hand. John only beats this 150 strokes, but he gives it a hefty hand mixing. Add the rest of the whole wheat flour to form a soft batter dough; beat until smooth, pulling away from bowl sides. Divide dough between 2 greased 9x5x2-inch bread pans. Let rise until double. Bake at 400° for 15 minutes. Reduce temperature to 375° for 25 minutes, or until bread sounds hollow. Yields 2 loaves.

LOW-CALORIE BAKER: Dieters, this is the bread for you! Help stop the sweet attacks and between meal cravings with this filling, satisfying bread. Makes sandwiches even better.

MARJORIE KURZ'S QUICK THREE WHEAT BATTER BREAD

Health Bonus!

1 package dry yeast
½ cup warm water
3 tablespoons honey
2 tablespoons cooking oil
12 ounces evaporated milk
2½ cups bread flour

1¼ cups whole wheat flour
1 teaspoon salt
½ cup wheat germ
¼ cup cracked wheat
⅛ teaspoon ginger

Dissolve yeast in warm water in a large mixer bowl; mix in honey, oil and milk. Slowly add flours combined with salt, wheat germ, cracked wheat and ginger to liquid ingredients; beat until smooth and dough pulls away from bowl sides. Fill 2 greased, pound coffee cans ½ full; place greased, plastic coffee can lid on top. Let rise in warm place. When lid pops off or bread has risen to the top of the can, bake bread at 400° for 25-30 minutes. Let bread cool 10 minutes; remove from can to cool on wire rack. Yields 2 loaves; freeze one and eat one.

BAKER'S IDEA: Substitute oat or wheat bran for cracked wheat.

MARJORIE'S HIGH FIBER PECAN BREAD

Tasty and Nutritious!

2 packages active dry yeast
¼ cup warm water
2 cups warm (115-120°) water
2 tablespoons honey
¼ cup softened margarine
1 cup quick cooking oats

2 teaspoons salt
½ cup instant nonfat dry milk
2 cup whole wheat flour
3-3½ cups unbleached flour
½ cup raisins
¾ cup chopped pecans

Dissolve yeast in water. Blend water with honey, margarine, oats, salt and dry milk in a large bowl; mix in yeast mixture and whole wheat flour. Add enough remaining flour to form a manageable dough. On a lightly floured surface knead until smooth and elastic, about 8-10 minutes, adding extra flour if necessary. Knead pecans and raisins into the dough. Shape in ball; place in greased bowl, turning to grease top. Let rise, covered, in warm place until double, 1-1½ hours. Punch dough down; divide in half. Flatten each half into a rectangle. Start with the short side, rolling dough into a roll. Turn ends under and seal edges. Place seam side down in greased

9x5x3-inch loaf pans. Let rise, covered, in a warm place until double. Bake at 350° for 35-40 minutes. Remove from pans; cool on rack. Makes 2 loaves.

Taught to bake by her father when she was 12 years old, Marjorie continues to love making bread. Her husband and family love her baking too!

MULTI-GRAIN BREAD

Rapid Yeast Method

Anna's husband would sing her praises with this multi-grain bread, especially today, living in our nutrition and health conscious society. The name would change from the Traditional Anadama Bread (page 49) to Analove!

2 packages rapid dry yeast	2 teaspoons salt
½ cup cornmeal	2 tablespoons cooking oil
¾ cup wheat germ	½ cup molasses
1½ cups whole wheat flour	1½ cups very hot water (125-130°)
1 cup cracked wheat	1½ cups bread flour

Using mixer, combine yeast, cornmeal, wheat germ, whole wheat flour, cracked wheat and salt in a large bowl. Combine oil, molasses and hot water; add to dry ingredients, beating with mixer for 3 minutes. Add enough bread flour to form a manageable dough. Knead on a floured surface for 5-8 minutes or until elastic and easy to handle. Let rest for 10 minutes. Divide dough and shape to fit 2 greased 9x5x3-inch loaf pans. Let rise until double. Bake in a 375° oven for 30-35 minutes or until bread is brown and sounds hollow when tapped. Lightly cover with foil to prevent over-browning the last 10 minutes of baking. Remove from pan to cool on a wire rack. Yields 2 loaves.

Even a bad day at the office will soon be forgotten after a hot slice of this hearty bread.

BAKER'S IDEA: Use ½ of this dough for the Mushroom-Spinach Braid (page 43) to make this meal-in-one especially healthy.

RYE AND COMPANY

Even though traditionally baked with caraway seeds, rye bread, with its own unique, rich flavor, does not require additional seeds or herbs. The caraway seed, anise seed (licorice flavor) and the cumin seed (alias a chili herb) are often combined with rye to give a different effect.

Fresh or frozen grated orange or lemon rind adds a special flavor and fragrance to rye and whole-grain breads. Add about 1 teaspoon grated rind to a dough containing approximately 5½-6 cups flour. A teaspoon of ground ginger and ¼ cup chopped onion adds another flavor dimension.

To accent initials or designs, cover the surface by pressing white flour or seeds against the free-form round or oval loaves. Cover with foil, if over browning. Remember that whole wheat, cornmeal, oat flour, cracked wheat, barley flour and rye flour produce a heavier product because of their low-or no-gluten content.

LIGHT PUMPERNICKEL BREAD

2 packages dry yeast
1 teaspoon sugar
½ cup warm water
1¼ cups boiling water
⅓ cup cornmeal
2 tablespoons cooking oil
3 tablespoons dark molasses
1 cup mashed potatoes, can use
   instant

1 tablespoon dark brown sugar
1 drop anise oil
2½ teaspoons salt
1½ cups rye flour
1½ cups whole wheat flour
2-2½ cups bread flour
1 tablespoon caraway seeds,
   whole or crushed

Dissolve yeast in sugar and water. Pour boiling water over cornmeal, oil, molasses, potatoes, brown sugar, anise and salt. Mix and allow to cool (105-115°). Combine with yeast mixture, rye, whole wheat and enough bread flour to form a manageable dough. Mix until smooth after each addition. Knead with seeds and extra bread flour about 10 minutes or until smooth and elastic. Let rise covered in greased bowl, in a warm area, until double in size. Punch down dough; knead dough 2 or 3 turns, flatten and shape to fit 2 greased 8½x4½x2½-inch loaf pans. Let rise until double. Spray tops with water; sprinkle with seeds. Bake at 375° for 20 minutes; spray with water again. Bake 15-20 minutes more or until bread sounds hollow when tapped. Cover top with foil if bread becomes too brown. Remove pan; let cool on wire rack. Yields 2 loaves.

SWEDISH RYE BREAD

Jewish rye bread often contains caraway seeds; Swedish rye bread often has caraway or fennel added. Good plain or with crushed or whole seeds.

2 packages dry yeast
2 cups warm water
3 tablespoons dried cultured
   buttermilk or substitute ½ cup
   fresh buttermilk for ½ cup
   water
½ tablespoon sugar
¼ cup molasses

¼ cup honey
¼ cup melted butter
1½ teaspoons salt
2½ cups rye flour
½ cup whole wheat flour
3 cups bread flour
1 tablespoon caraway, optional
1 teaspoon fennel, optional

Dissolve yeast in warm water in a large bowl; mix in powdered buttermilk and sugar allowing to stand until bubbly. Mix in molasses, honey, butter, salt, whole-grain flours and enough bread flour to be manageable. Rye dough tends to be sticky. Add seeds; knead until smooth and elastic, about 8 to 10 minutes. Let rise, covered, until double. Punch down dough, lightly kneading to shape 2 loaves for 9x5x3-inch loaf pans or shape into 2 round loaves, placing on greased baking sheets. Let rise until double. Bake at 375° for 35-40 minutes. Yields 2 loaves.

OATS AND COMPANY POWER BREAD

Oats, millet, rye and whole wheat = a bread for champions!

1½ cups warm water
1 package dry yeast
*¹⁄₃ cup dried cultured buttermilk
¼ cup molasses or honey
1 cup bread flour
1 teaspoon salt
2 tablespoons oil

½ cup millet flour
½ cup rye flour
1 cup whole wheat flour
1 cup old fashioned oats
1 teaspoon grated orange rind
Egg white glaze
oat flakes

* Substitute 1 cup fresh buttermilk for dried buttermilk; decrease water to ½ cup total.

Dissolve yeast in warm water; whisk in powdered buttermilk, molasses and bread flour. Let stand until bubbly. Add salt, oil, 3 flours, oats and orange rind, beating well after each addition. Beat with mixer until mixture comes away from the sides of bowl. Pour batter into 1 greased 9x5x3-inch bread pan; let rise. Brush top with egg white beaten with 1 tablespoon water; sprinkle with raw oats. Bake for 30-35 minutes at 375°. Cover with foil if top becomes too brown. Remove from pan; cool on wire rack. Yields 1 loaf.

BETTY'S QUICK RYE BREAD

2 cups bread flour
1 cup rye flour
1 package rapid dry yeast
1 teaspoon caraway seeds or
   cumin seeds

1 teaspoon salt
1 tablespoon molasses
3 tablespoons margarine
¾ cup plus two tablespoons
   water (105-115°)

In the food processor, mix flours, yeast, seeds and salt until combined; add molasses, margarine and water to the food processor through the feed tube with motor running. When a ball forms, process another minute or until smooth and elastic.

Place in a large, floured plastic food storage bag, squeeze out the air and seal the top. Let rise until double in a warm place, about 1 hour. Punch dough down. If desired refrigerate dough overnight.

Allow dough to rest, covered, for 10 minutes before shaping loaf. Press out air bubbles. Smooth top by tucking under dough; press edges to seal. Place in a greased 8½x4½x2½-inch loaf pan or in a greased round bowl, covered, to rise until double. Bake at 400° for 25-30 minutes or until brown and sounds hollow when tapped. Cool on wire rack. Yields 1 loaf.

Variation:

ONION RYE BREAD: Press (risen and punched down) dough in a 15x10x¾-inch jelly roll pan. Chop 2 cups onion in food processor. Microwave onion for 2 minutes with 1 tablespoon honey in a covered container. Drain; add 1 tablespoon parsley, ¼ tablespoon thyme and ½ teaspoon seasoned salt. Spread onion mixture over dough. Sprinkle more sasoned salt lightly over the top. Bake at 400° for 20 minutes. *A low-fat version of Italian focaccia.*

BETTY SIMS' REUBEN FOLD-OVER

1 recipe of Betty's Quick Rye
   Bread.
1 pound jar sauerkraut
3 tablespoons Thousand Island
   dressing
1 tablespoon spicy mustard,
   optional

½ pound Swiss cheese slices
½ pound corned beef, thinly
   sliced
1 egg, beaten

Make dough; let rise. Roll Quick Rye dough on a floured surface to a 16x8-inch rectangle; place on a greased baking sheet.

Rinse and drain sauerkraut; squeeze out juice. Mix dressing and mustard with sauerkraut. Cover right side of rectangle with half of corned beef; layer with sauerkraut mixture, cheese and remaining corned beef, leaving a ½-inch border around the end and sides. Brush remaining half of dough with beaten egg. Fold egg brushed dough side over filling; seal edges by pressing with fingers and tucking under dough edges. With a sharp knife, make 3 cuts, 4-inches long and 2-inches apart, starting in the center top of the foldover. Brush with egg. Cover; let rest 15 minutes. Bake at 375° for 25-30 minutes or until brown. Makes 8 regular servings; can be cut into narrow slices or smaller rectangles.

Betty, a renowned epicurean and creative baker since high school, shared these recipes in a cooking class at her Johnston Street Cafe in Decatur, Alabama. Her specialties are gourmet baked delicacies and elegant catered party fare.

JEANETTE McCAY'S ENRICHED LOAF

Jeanette's husband, Clieve M. McCay, a research nutritionist in the 1930's at Cornell University, pioneered a method of improving health through diet by adding extra protein, minerals and vitamins to man's staple food — bread.

Jeanette continues as an advocate of healthful diets as she bakes her own bread, always adding the "Cornell formula" — dry milk, wheat germ and soy flour. She often starts her bread as a sponge the night before, timing the loaf to be "table ready" for lunch. Her advice to the busy women of today, "Let dad and children bake...and enjoy bread baking."

3½ cups bread flour, divided	2 tablespoons wheat germ
1 package dry yeast	¼ cup soy flour
1 ½ cups warm water	½ cup raisins
2 tablespoons brown sugar	¼ cup chopped apricots or other
1 teaspoon salt	dried fruit
1 tablespoon cooking oil	¼ cup toasted sunflower seeds or
⅓ cup instant non-fat dry milk	chopped nuts

Mix a sponge with 2 cups of flour, yeast, water and sugar in a bowl; cover in a warm place overnight. In the morning, add the salt, oil, dry milk, wheat germ and soy flour to the bubbly sponge. Beat by hand or with the mixer for 1 minute until well blended. Add dried fruits and nuts or today's favorite combination. Continue to beat for 2 to 3 minutes or until batter leaves the sides of the bowl. Pour into a greased 9x5x3-inch baking pan. Let rise until double, 1-1 ½ hours. Bake at 375° for 45-50 minutes. Bread will sound hollow when done; cool on wire rack. Yields 1 loaf.

THE AUTOMATIC BREAD MACHINE

The home bakers with an automatic breadmaker can use many *When The Knead Rises* variations and ideas to adapt to their bakery-in-a-box. Even though the breadmaker doesn't take the place of enjoying the feel (hands on) of dough kneading and rising, it can save time.

Avid bread makers Jim and Ellen Montgomery have had fun creating new breads with their automatic bread machine. The following are some of Jim's bread machine tips.

1. **Precise**, careful measuring with accurate measuring cups and spoons is very important.

2. When experimenting, write down exact amounts of ingredients.

3. Can use the baker to mix, knead and let dough rise. Remove dough for forming rolls or desired shapes.

4. When adding moist ingredients (for example, plumped raisins or dates) or baking during very rainy weather, feel the dough when mixer is off. If the dough is sticky, add a sprinkling of flour, by the teaspoon. Dough should feel moist.

5. When mixing ½ or more whole grain flour, repeat the mixing cycle.

6. Take bread out of baker when finished, if possible.

The following recipes are adapted for a bread machine using approximately 2 cups of flour. Increase the ingredients by ⅓ for a machine which holds 3 cups of flour. When using a conventional oven, mix dough, knead, let rise and punch down. Form dough into a loaf for an 8½x4½x2½-inch greased loaf pan. Let rise until double. Bake at 375° for 30-35 minutes.

BREAD MACHINE'S LIGHT WHEAT BREAD
Good Freshly Baked or Toasted

1½ teaspoons dry yeast
1¼ cups bread flour
½ cup self-rising flour
⅓ cup + 1 tablespoon whole
   wheat flour
¾ teaspoon salt
1 tablespoon sugar

1 tablespoon instant nonfat dry
   milk
1 tablespoon butter
1 large egg (place in 1 cup measuring cup)
warm water
¼ teaspoon ginger, optional

Add yeast to inner baking container. Add rest of ingredients except for egg and water. Add egg to 1 cup standard measuring cup; add enough warm water with egg to fill measuring cup. Add egg and water to baking container. Set bread maker for automatic control. Remove bread when done. Yields 1 loaf.

BREAD MACHINE'S LIGHT HEALTH LOAF
Added Natural Nutrients

1½ teaspoons dry yeast
1¼ cups bread flour
¼ cup whole wheat
½ cup self-rising flour
2 tablespoons soy flour
2 tablespoons wheat germ
1 tablespoon sugar
1 teaspoon salt

2 tablespoons dry skim milk
1 tablespoon butter
1 teaspoon cinnamon
15 tablespoons warm water (1
   cup minus 1 tablespoon)
½ cup nuts or ½ cup raisins,
   optional

Add dry yeast to the inside container. Add rest of ingredients in the order given. Add raisins or nuts at the additional ingredient signal. After cooling, keep covered in the refrigerator or frozen. Yields 1 loaf.

HOLIDAY AND EUROPEAN
SWEET YEAST BREADS

BASIC MAXI-SWEET DOUGH (REFRIGERATOR)
Divides into Dozens of Sweet Ideas

2²/₃ cups water
½ cup butter
¾ cup shortening
1 cup sugar
2 teaspoons salt

3 packages dry yeast
2 eggs, beaten
10-10½ cups all-purpose flour,
   divided

Heat water, butter and shortening until 120-130°. Use mixer dough hooks or regular beaters to combine sugar, salt, yeast and 3 cups flour in a large bowl. Slowly add liquid ingredients; beat on medium for 2 minutes. Mix in eggs and 1 cup more flour, beating for 3 minutes on high. Add only enough flour to form a sticky, soft dough.

Refrigerate dough overnight or up to 5 days in large, lightly floured, plastic food storage bags, pressing out the air, or a large greased bowl. If necessary punch down refrigerated dough (press out the air). Yields about 5½ pounds.

Variations:

ROLLS, LOAVES AND SQUARES

MAXI-ROLLS: Remove ¹/₅ of refrigerator dough to a lightly floured surface; knead dough until manageable, adding more flour if necessary. Form a 16-inch coil, cutting in 16 pieces; place cut side down on a greased 9-inch round cake pan. For smaller rolls, form in a 24-inch coil, cutting in 24 pieces. Let rise covered, in a warm place, for 1½-2 hours or until light and double in size. Bake at 400° for 12-15 minutes. Yields 16 to 24 rolls.

HONEY ROLLS: Follow directions for Maxi-rolls. Place 24 balls in a 9-inch round pan containing 3 tablespoons butter melted and mixed with ¹/₃ cup honey. After rising, bake at 375° for 20 minutes. Cool in pan a few minutes; invert on serving plate.

SPICY HUNGARIAN ROLLS: Follow directions for Maxi-rolls. Roll 24 balls in the following combined ingredients. Place in a greased 9-inch round pan.

½ cup brown sugar	⅓ cup melted butter
1 teaspoon cinnamon	½ cup chopped nuts
½ teaspoon nutmeg	

Let rise; bake at 375° for 20 minutes. Invert on a serving plate; pour Honey Topping or Vanilla Butter over bread. Double recipe for a 9-inch bundt pan.

> **HONEY TOPPING:** Add enough powdered sugar to thicken ½ cup honey for drizzling over bread.

> **VANILLA BUTTER GLAZE:** Melt 1 tablespoon butter in 1½ tablespoons hot milk; blend in 1 cup powdered sugar and ½ teaspoon vanilla.

CHOCOLATE-COCONUT ROLLS: Spread 16x8-inch rectangle (⅕) of Maxi-Sweet Dough with less than ¼ cup sweetened condensed milk. Sprinkle with 1 square grated, unsweetened chocolate, 2 tablespoons sugar, ¼ cup slivered almonds and ½ cup lightly toasted coconut. Roll as a jelly roll, starting with the long side. Press seam to seal; cut into 16 slices. Arrange, cut side down, in a greased 9-inch round cake pan; let rise until double. Bake at 350° for 20 minutes. While warm, glaze with ¾ cup powdered sugar, 1 tablespoon milk and ¼ teaspoon almond extract.

MAPLE DATE ROLLS: Roll ⅕ of Maxi-Sweet Dough into a 16x8-inch rectangle; brush with melted butter. Cover rectangle with brown sugar mixed with cinnamon; sprinkle with raisins.

Filling:	**Pan Mixture:**
⅓ cup brown sugar	¼ cup chopped pecans
1 teaspoon cinnamon	⅓ cup maple syrup
¼ cup raisins	½ cup chopped dates

Roll as a jelly roll starting with the long side. Press seam to seal; slice into 24 pieces. Place cut side down in a 9-inch round cake pan containing syrup sprinkled evenly with nuts and dates. Let rise until double. Bake at 350° for 20 minutes or until lightly browned. Cool for 5 minutes; invert pan on serving plate. Serve warm.

More Maxi-Sweet Dough Variations:

MILADE'S FRENCH CHOCOLATE RINGS: Divide and roll 2 sections (¹/₅ each) of Maxi-Sweet Dough in 2 (16x8-inch) rectangles. Spread each rectangle with ½ of the following filling ingredients, heated only until chocolate melts and cools to lukewarm.

Filling:

Chocolate Streusel Topping:

1½ cups semi-sweet chocolate
    chips
1 tablespoon instant coffee
²/₃ cup evaporated milk (5-ounce
    can)
¼ cup sugar
1 teaspoon cinnamon

½ cup butter
½ cup all-purpose flour
½ cup granulated sugar
½ cup cup brown sugar, pack
    down
2 teaspoons cinnamon
½ cup semi-sweet chocolate
    chips
½ cup chopped pecans

Roll each rectangle as a jelly roll, starting with the long side. Pinch seam to seal; place seam side down in 2 greased 9-inch bundt pans. Join the two ends together pressing and arranging roll in a continuous, even circle. Cut in butter with flour combined with sugars and cinnamon until crumbly; stir in chips and nuts. Cover rolls with topping; let rise until double. Bake at 350° for 25-30 minutes or until done and the top lightly browned. Cool 5 minutes; cool on wire rack. Makes 2 coffee cakes.

APRICOT-FIG LOAF: Roll ¹/₅ of Maxi-Sweet Dough in a rectangle about ¼-inch thick. Sprinkle ¹/₃ cup chopped, toasted nuts and 1 cup chopped, *plumped dried apricots and/or figs over dough. Starting with the short side, roll as a jelly roll; tuck under ends, placing seam side down in a greased 8½x4½x2½-inch loaf pan. Let rise until double. Bake at 375° for 30-35 minutes. Remove from pan; cool on wire racks. Ice with ½ cup powdered sugar mixed with just enough yogurt (about ¾ tablespoon) to be spreadable and ¼ teaspoon orange extract or cover with apricot preserves.

*Plumped: Microwave dried fruit covered with hot water for 1 minute. Remove from water; drain on paper towels.

SPICY-PRUNE LOAF: Follow Apricot-Fig Loaf directions.   Brush rectangle with melted butter; sprinkle with sugar mixed with spices, topping with nuts and prunes.

½ cup sugar
¼ teaspoon nutmeg
¼ teaspoon mace
½ teaspoon cinnamon

½ cup chopped nuts
½ cup thinly cut, soft dried
    prunes

Roll as a jelly roll, starting with the short side; seal edges and tuck ends under. Place seam side down in a greased 8½x4½x2½-inch loaf pan. Let rise until double. Bake at 375° for 30-35 minutes. Cool on wire racks. Brush with corn syrup; sprinkle with any extra cinnamon-spice sugar or leave plain.

COFFEE CAKE SQUARES

Roll ⅕ of Maxi-Sweet Dough (page 60) to fit a foil lined, greased 15x10x¾-inch jelly roll pan. Choose the desired filling to spread evenly over dough. Cover with topping of choice. Let rise until double. Bake at 350° for 20-25 minutes or until dough layer is done.

Add glaze or topping if indicated. Cut into small bite size squares with a wet serrated knife. When cool, freeze or refrigerate coffee cake squares, sealed air tight with plastic and foil, on baking sheet. Each recipe will yield approximately 60 (1½x1½-inch) squares...(not many servings when all the samples are tasted!)

Perfect for holiday gift-giving and for sweet breads at a coffee. The yield makes the effort well worthwhile. No time for the fillings — use commercial apple, cherry or blueberry fillings.

BAKER'S IDEA: For special "the night before celebrations", for occasions such as horse shows, plays, concerts, etc., decorate each square with a lucky horseshoe design, using Decorator Icing. A "good-luck" square helps chase away the "jitters" before the big production.

APRICOT-CHEESE SQUARES: Spread dough rectangle with Cheese Filling; top with Apricot Filling, spreading evenly. Sprinkle with 1 cup chopped pecans and ¼ cup sugar mixed with ¼ teaspoon nutmeg. Bake as directed. For a variation add ¾ cup toasted coconut to the filling.

PRUNE-SPICE SQUARES: Spread dough rectangle with Jennie's Prune Filling. When baked and cooled, frost with 1 ½ cups powdered sugar, grated orange rind and 2-2 ½ tablespoons orange juice.

CHOCOLATE MARZIPAN SQUARES: Spread dough rectangle with melted butter; Spread top evenly with the Chocolate-Marzipan Filling. Sprinkle with 1 cup chopped almonds. Bake as directed. While warm from baking, glaze with Vanilla Glaze.

FILLINGS, GLAZES AND TOPPINGS

CHEESE FILLING: Cream ingredients until smooth.

1 (8-ounce) package cream
   cheese
½ cup sugar

1 tablespoon milk
1 teaspoon vanilla

APRICOT FILLING: Cover 1 cup dried apricots completely with water; microwave or simmer until soft. Drain apricots. Blend the following ingredients in the food processor:

1 cup drained, cooked apricots
⅓ cup sugar

¼ teaspoon ginger
½ teaspoon cinnamon

JENNIE'S PRUNE FILLING: Combine all ingredients for a thick, but spreadable filling. Jennie often substitutes plumped dates and figs for prunes.

1½ cups stewed prunes, chopped
   and drained
½ cup toasted, chopped pecans

½ cup sugar
½ teaspoon cinnamon

CHOCOLATE MARZIPAN FILLING: Combine all ingredients in food processor until smooth.

2 egg whites
8 ounces almond paste
½ cup cocoa

¾ cup sugar
½ teaspoon almond extract

VANILLA GLAZE: Mix 1½ cups powdered sugar with 3-3½ tablespoons milk, ¼ teaspoon vanilla extract and ¼ teaspoon almond extract until smooth.

LUCKY HORSESHOE DECORATOR ICING: With mixer, beat ¼ cup shortening, 3 tablespoons butter, ½ teaspoon vanilla and 1½ tablespoons milk. Beat in about 2 cups powdered sugar and, if desired, a drop of food color until a smooth, manageable icing forms. Freeze extra icing to make more horseshoes, initials or rosettes on each square. Add 1 tablespoon milk to thin icing for spreading.

TOPPINGS: ½ cup sugar mixed with ¼ teaspoon nutmeg and ¼ teaspoon cinnamon, ¾ cup coconut or 1 cup chopped pecans or almonds.

BLUE RIBBON HOLIDAY BREADS
Win Baking Prizes; Slice Thin for Coffee or Dessert

CHRISTMAS BREAD WREATH: Knead ⅕ of the Maxi-Sweet Dough (page 60) with the following ingredients:

1 teaspoon grated orange peel	¼ cup chopped nuts
¼ teaspoon allspice	¼ cup plumped raisins
½ cup chopped red and green candied cherries and pineapple	

Form fast braids by rolling dough about 4 inches wide by 22 inches long; cut dough in 3 equal strips. Roll slightly with hands to form rolled effect. Braid on a foil lined, greased baking sheet; work ends into braid to form a continuous circle. Let rise until double; bake at 350° until pale brown on edges, about 25-30 minutes. Cool on wire racks. Lightly brush with corn syrup to glaze or use ¾ cup powdered sugar, 1½ tablespoons milk and ¼ teaspoon vanilla. Decorate around wreath with sliced red cherries, as a flower, with sliced green cherries as leaves and candied pineapple and colored citron sliced thin in desired shapes. Makes 1 wreath.

HOSKA: Divide the Christmas Bread Wreath dough in 4 parts for this Czechoslovakian festive braid. Roll first 3 parts into long coils about 12-inches in length to braid. Braid on greased, foil lined baking sheet. Divide last part of dough into 3 pieces. Roll each piece into a coil about 10-inches long. Braid coils. Place small braided loaf on top of larger braid. Tuck ends of braid under loaf to seal. Let rise until double. Bake at 350° for 30-35 minutes. Cool on wire rack. Glaze as Christmas Bread Wreath.

SWEDISH TEA RING: Roll ⅕ of the Maxi-Sweet Dough, Page 60, in a 15x10-inch rectangle; brush with melted butter. Sprinkle with sugar mixed with spices; evenly cover with rest of ingredients.

¼ cup sugar	½ cup chopped almonds and walnuts
½ teaspoon cinnamon	
¼ teaspoon allspice	½ cup sliced, candied red or green cherries
¼ teaspoon nutmeg	

Roll rectangle, starting with the long side, as a jelly roll; place seam side down on a greased, foil-lined baking sheet. Seal ends by pinching together to form a continuous ring. With a knife or scissors cut through the ring, almost to the center. Make slanted cuts about every 1 ¼-inches around the ring. Slightly turn each slice so that the filling shows. Let rise until double. Bake at 350° for 30 minutes. While warm glaze with 1 cup powdered sugar, 2 tablespoons milk and ½ teaspoon almond extract. Yields 1 spectacular ring for Christmas or any special occasion!

ROYAL FRUIT CROWN: Roll ¹/₅ of Maxi-Sweet Dough (page 60) into 1 (21x4-inch) strip. Sprinkle dough with any sugar-spice mixture (save leftover sugar mixtures in marked containers or use sugar and spice for the Spicy-Prune Loaf, page 62). Roll dough, starting with long side, as a jelly roll. Pinch dough together to form a continuous ring; press and pat dough to form an even circle allowing for rising. Glaze crown with beaten egg white.

Plump fruit, covered with hot water, 1 minute in microwave or simmer until soft. Dry on paper towels. Slice thick pieces of citron or candied fruit into thinner slices.

Arrange dried and candied fruit around the circle. Start with large, whole fruits, such as apricots or peaches, placing at the top, bottom and sides. Fill the area around the larger fruit with a pattern of candied pineapple, colored citron, white and dark raisins and nuts. Let rise until double; readjust any fruit displaced by rising. Bake at 350° for 20-25 minutes until light brown on bottom. Readjust or add to any displaced fruit or nuts, during baking, covering all the dough area. Heat ²/₃ cup plum or apple jelly until melted; pour over and carefully brush entire crown. Place back in oven for a few minutes to rewarm jelly if necessary.

Celebrate Christmas or Epiphany! Pretty enough to be a centerpiece and good enough to be the dessert. Leave the wise men as decorations until the 6th of January (Twelfth Day or Epiphany), the coming of the Magi.

CHRISTMAS STOLLEN: Knead ¹/₅ of Maxi-Sweet Dough (page 60) with the following ingredients until well combined.

¼ teaspoon ginger
¼ teaspoon mace
¼ teaspoon cardamom
½ cup chopped, candied fruit
1 tablespoon grated, mixed

lemon and orange peel
½ cup slivered almonds, lightly toasted
¼ cup soft white or dark raisins

Add more flour if necessary; roll dough into an oval, approximately 12x9-inches or form 2 smaller ovals. Spread surface with 2 tablespoons soft butter mixed with ¼ teaspoon almond extract. Fold one long side over almost to the other long side. The top edge will be about ¾ of an inch from the bottom outer edge. Let rise until double on a greased, foil lined baking sheet. Bake at 375° for 20-25 minutes or until a light brown. Cool on wire racks. Brush with ¼ cup soft butter mixed with ½ teaspoon almond extract; sift powdered sugar over entire warm oval. Yields 1 large oval.

The sugar coating depicts snow on this beautiful, fruited German bread. Place on a bed of Easter grass in a colorful box or on cardboard, cover with plastic wrap and tie a festive bow around the packaged bread as a gift.

MELONAS' GREEK NEW YEAR'S BREAD: Knead ¹/₅ of Maxi-Sweet Dough (page 60) with the following:

1 drop anise oil	**¹/₃ cup chopped, toasted almonds**
½ teaspoon ginger	**¼ cup finely chopped candied**
¹/₃ cup white raisins	**ginger**
¹/₃ cup chopped dates	

Smooth into a round ball; let rise until double on a greased baking sheet or in a round container. Cut a cross in the top of the bread. Bake at 350° for 20-25 minutes until light brown. Brush with milk, decorate with almonds and sprinkle with sugar.

John Melonas, an engineer and chef, has been in the restaurant business for 20 years. He is now working with Café 113 in Decatur, Alabama, where he often serves his favorite Greek foods. John's bread is a reminder of thankfulness for the past year and fresh opportunities for the new year.

KRANTZ' CHRISTMAS CAKE

Elegance just between a Danish and a Pastry

1 cup warm milk	**3²/₃ cups all-purpose flour (4 cups**
1 package yeast	**sifted flour)**
1 tablespoon sugar	**1 cup butter or margarine**
¼ teaspoon salt	**4 beaten egg yolks**
½ teaspoon vanilla	**4 egg whites**
	¾ cup sugar

Use a small bowl to dissolve yeast in warm milk; add sugar, salt and vanilla. In a large bowl, cut in flour and butter; mix with egg yolks. Combine with yeast mixture; refrigerate dough sealed air tight in bowl or large plastic bag overnight. Refrigerate covered egg whites.

Allow whites to warm to room temperature; beat until frothy, slowly adding sugar, 1 tablespoon at a time, until stiffly beaten.

Divide dough into 4 equal parts; roll each into a 12x8-inch rectangle. Evenly spread each rectangle with meringue. Arrange chopped nuts and quartered cherries in two rows each to disperse throughout slices. Starting with the long side roll as a jelly roll, not too tightly to prevent splitting. The finished cake will be about 14x4-inches. Cake does not require rising. Bake on a greased baking sheet 20-25 minutes at 350° or until light brown. Cool cakes on wire rack; spread with Butter Frosting (page 68). Top with nut halves. Yields 4 cakes.

BUTTER FROSTING: Blend the following ingredients together.

1 pound powdered sugar   ½ teaspoon vanilla
¼ teaspoon salt   ¼ cup milk

Jim and Ellen Montgomery continue his mother Mildred's tradition of sharing this cake each Christmas with family and friends. A Bostonian immigrant friend brought the recipe from the old country, sharing it with her. The original recipe contained dates and candied fruit.

MARJORIE'S CARDAMOM BRAIDS
Delicate cardamom flavor

2 packages yeast   ½ cup melted butter
½ cup warm water   8-9 cups all-purpose flour
2 cups milk, scalded and cooled   ½ cup sliced almonds
1 cup sugar   ½ cup sugar or crushed sugar
2 teaspoons salt   cubes
1 teaspoon ground cardamom   Egg glaze
4 eggs, slightly beaten

In a large bowl dissolve yeast in warm water. Stir in milk, sugar, salt, cardamom, egg, butter and 4 cups flour. Beat until smooth. Gradually add enough flour to form a stiff dough. Let dough rest for 5 to 10 minutes on lightly floured board. Adding flour as needed, knead dough about 8 to 10 minutes or until smooth. Place dough in greased bowl, turning to coat all sides. Cover and let rise in a warm place until doubled in bulk, about 45 minutes.

On a lightly oiled surface divide dough into 3 portions. Divide each portion into 3 pieces. Roll each piece between palms of hands and oiled surface to form approximately a 10-inch rope. Braid 3 ropes to form a loaf on a greased baking sheet. Seal ends under loaf. Let rise until double, 45 to 60 minutes. Brush loaves gently with 1 beaten egg mixed with 1 teaspoon salt and 2 tablespoons milk; sprinkle with sliced almonds and sugar. After baking for 15 minutes, reapply egg glaze. Bake at 350° for 25 to 30 minutes only until crust is lightly browned and tender, not crisp. Do not over bake! Cool 3 braided loaves on racks.

Marjorie's Finnish mother-in-law shared this recipe for her family's traditional Christmas bread, called Pulla Bread. An anytime treat, Pulla is best served by itself with hot coffee or milk punch.

NANCY'S MILK PUNCH
Fast, Low-Calorie Version of Her Family's Holiday Tradition

6 egg yolks
¾ cup sugar
½ gallon skim milk

2 teaspoons Vanilla or to taste
Nutmeg

Beat yolks and sugar, slowly adding cold milk. Microwave on high for 10 minutes, stirring every 2 minutes or until custard reaches boiling point. Custard will coat the spoon. Do not boil. Add vanilla and serve cold. Place nutmeg in a small container, with a spoon for guests to sprinkle on their serving.

EUROPEAN KUCHEN DOUGH

Kuchen, meaning cake, denotes European hospitality, as more eggs, butter and fruit peel are added for guests and holidays. Any fruits or fillings can be used with a topping of custard, streusel or spicy sugar and nuts.

½ cups water
1 cup milk
1 cup margarine or butter
2 packages dry yeast
½ cup sugar

1½ teaspoons salt
2 teaspoons grated lemon rind
6 cups all-purpose flour, divided
3 eggs

Heat water, milk and butter to 120-130° Fahrenheit. Use mixer dough hooks or beaters to carefully combine undissolved yeast, sugar, salt, rind and 2½ cups flour. Add liquid ingredients; beat on low speed for 2 minutes. Scrape sides of bowl occasionally. Add eggs and 1 cup flour, beating at high speed for 3 more minutes. Stir in enough flour to make a soft dough. Knead dough on a lightly floured surface until smooth, elastic and easily managed. Let rise, top oiled and covered in a greased bowl until double; approximately 1½ to 2 hours. Makes approximately 4 pounds of dough. Refrigerate dough, wrapped in plastic, for a few days or freeze dough if time is limited.

THE KNEADED AND PUNCHED DOWN KUCHEN DOUGH CAN BE USED IN THE FOLLOWING FESTIVE VARIATIONS.

HOLIDAY KUCHEN: Evenly press ¼ of Kuchen dough on the bottom and halfway up the sides of a greased 9-inch round cake pan. Add desired fillings, fresh or canned fruits, sweetened to taste, and toppings. Allow for dough rising until double. Can use Custard or Streusel topping (page 70) on top before baking. Bake at 350° for 35-40 minutes. Mix or match these as a hot or cold coffee treat or as a special dessert.

More Kuchen Variations:

AUSTRIAN APPLE KUCHEN: Press ¼ of Kuchen Dough in bottom and halfway up the sides of a greased 9-inch round cake pan. Brush dough with melted butter; let rise until almost double. Cover top with 2 apples peeled and thinly sliced, overlapped in a circular pattern. Sprinkle ⅓ cup sugar mixed with ¼ teaspoon nutmeg and ¼ teaspoon allspice and ½ cup chopped pecans over top of apples. Cover apples lightly with baking paper or waxed paper for the first 15 minutes. Bake at 375° for 25-30 minutes. Red hots candy sprinkled under apples adds zip to the flavor.

Use cheese and cherry fillings, thick fruit preserves or commercial pie fillings for the Kuchen, Czechoslovakian Kolache buns or Kolache flowers. Any filling used for sweet breads or pastries can be used. Either increase or decrease the filling amount for the amount of dough.

KOLACHE FLOWERS: For forming 3 Kolache flowers, use ¼ of Kuchen dough, dividing into 3 parts. Divide each part into 7 balls. On a greased baking sheet, arrange 2 balls rolled together to form flower center. Place the other 5 balls evenly around the center, touching as petals. Press with fingers or a spoon to form a deep depression in the center of each ball. Brush with melted butter. Form other 2 flowers, allow room for rising. After dough has risen double, reform flower centers and petals if necessary. Fill with a small amount of Almond Cheese Filling and Double Cherry Filling. Bake at 375° for 15-20 minutes or until a pale brown forms on the edges, baking only until done. Remove carefully to cool on a wire rack. Spread with Sour Cream Glaze or sprinkle with powdered sugar.

KOLACHE BUNS: Roll ¼ of Kuchen dough ½-inch thick, cutting with 2-inch or desired cookie cutters, or form into small walnut shaped balls pressing an indention in the center for the fillings. Follow Kolache flower directions for rising and filling. Bake 15-20 minutes at 350° until a pale brown on the edges; do not over bake. Cool on wire rack; drizzle with Sour Cream Glaze, sprinkling with toasted chopped almonds.

TOPPINGS, FILLINGS AND GLAZES

ALMOND-CHEESE CUSTARD TOPPING: Beat 1 (8-ounce) package cream cheese, 2 eggs, ½ cup milk, ½ cup sugar and ½ teaspoon vanilla. Pour over dough and fruit for 1 Kuchen when ready to bake.

STREUSEL: Mix together until crumbly, ¼ cup brown sugar, ¼ cup granulated sugar, ½ cup flour and ½ cup butter. Add ½ cup chopped almonds or 1 teaspoon cinnamon (optional).

ALMOND-CHEESE FILLING: Cream ingredients in food processor until light and fluffy. Makes enough filling for 1 recipe of Kuchen or Kolache.

2 (8-ounce) packages cream cheese	**1 tablespoon milk**
¾ cup sugar	**1 teaspoon almond extract**

DOUBLE CHERRY FILLING: Combine sugar and flour in sauce pan; beat in ¼ cup juice. Stir constantly over medium heat until thick, adding butter and cherries. After mixture is thick, remove from heat; mix in cherry preserves. Enough for 1 recipe of Kuchen or Kolache.

½ cup sugar	**1 tablespoon butter**
2 tablespoons all-purpose flour	**food coloring, optional**
1 (16-ounce) can drained, pitted sour cherries, reserve juice	**1 (12-ounce) jar cherry preserves**

SOUR CREAM GLAZE: Beat 1 cup sour cream with ½ cup powdered sugar and ½ teaspoon almond flavoring until thick and smooth. Add more sugar if needed; refrigerate in an airtight container.

More Kuchen Variations:

BROWN-EYED SUSAN FLOWER BREAD: Divide ¼ of Kuchen dough into 6 balls. Pull dough tops smooth, tucking extra dough under each ball. On a greased baking sheet place 1 ball to form flower's center. Arrange other 5 balls around the center forming flower petals. Allow room for rising until double. After rising bake at 375° for 18-22 minutes until a pale brown; carefully remove to serving plate. Pour Fruit Glaze over entire flower. Smooth glaze on flour center before spreading with chocolate frosting. Spread flower center with chocolate. Cover petals with ¾ cup powdered sugar mixed with 2 tablespoons milk and ¼ teaspoon vanilla. Optional: outline center and petal division with pecan halves.

What an eye opener for an early morning meeting! Serve with hot, steaming coffee and tea. For variety use white chocolate and pineapple preserves.

> **CHOCOLATE FROSTING:** Heat ¼ cup chocolate chips just until melted. Stir until smooth. (microwave on high for 1 minute; stir and microwave again for 30 seconds or until spreadable).

> **FRUIT GLAZE:** Combine all ingredients.

¹⁄₃ cup cherry preserves or strawberry preserves	**1 tablespoon honey**
	¹⁄₃ cup lightly toasted nuts

EUROPEAN FESTIVE NUT ROLL: Roll 3 (¼ sections) of Kuchen Dough (page 69) or 3 pounds of any sweet dough in 3 (16x9-inch) rectangles. Can divide each pound of dough, rolling dough in 6 smaller (13x8-inch) rectangles. Divide and spread filling evenly on each rectangle.

¹/₃ **cup bread or cookie crumbs**	3½ **cups toasted pecans and**
¹/₃ **cup butter**	**walnuts (finely chopped in**
½ **cup whipping cream**	**food processor)**
¾ **cup sugar**	3 **egg whites**
1 **teaspoon salt**	¹/₃ **cup sugar**
1 **teaspoon vanilla**	

Lightly brown breadcrumbs in butter in heavy skillet; add cream, sugar, salt and vanilla. Stir over low heat until combined. Add nuts. Beat egg whites until beginning to form soft peaks. Slowly add sugar; beat until stiff peaks are formed. Fold in cooled crumb-nut mixture. Spread filling evenly on each rectangle; roll each as a jelly roll starting with the long side. Pinch seam to seal; place each roll seam side down on a greased baking sheet, bending as a U shape—a lucky horseshoe shape. Place 2 small rolls on each pan; allow for rising. Let rise until double. Bake at 350° for about 30 minutes until light brown. Let cool; glaze with Ruth's Caramel Frosting. Yields 3 large or 6 small loaves.

This version of Yugoslavian Potica is baked as a tradition by family and friends for the most festive of occasions, such as weddings and anniversaries.

RUTH'S CARAMEL FROSTING

1 **cup brown sugar**	¼ **cup butter**
¼ **cup milk**	**powdered sugar**

Combine sugar, milk and butter in a medium sized saucepan. Bring to a boil over low heat, dissolving sugar. Beat in powdered sugar until desired consistency. Double icing if completely covering Nut Rolls.

EASTER BREADS

HOT CROSS BUNS: This early A.D. spring traditional bread, symboliz-
ing new life, took on new meaning for Christians at Easter. The same "one
a penny, two a penny, hot cross buns" in the nursery rhyme were sold in Old
England only on Good Friday.

Into 3 (¼ sections) European Kuchen Dough (page 69) or 3 pounds of any
sweet dough, knead in the following: ½ teaspoon cinnamon, 2 teaspoons
grated orange rind, 1 cup soft raisins or currants and ½ cup candied fruit
(not always added in the early days). Let rise until double; punch down and
form approximately 40 small buns. Brush buns with 1 egg white beaten
with 1 tablespoon water. Place buns on a large greased baking pan. Use
a knife to mark a cross on the top of the bun. Let buns rise until double in
size. Bake at 350° for 20-25 minutes. Cool on wire rack. Buns can be totally
iced or iced only to form a cross. When icing is dry, carefully wrap and
refrigerate or freeze to prevent drying. Place each bun in a plastic
sandwich bag; tie with ribbon.

Start a family tradition of baking and giving at Easter. Milade Mausoor
wrapped these buns in plastic, placed them in a basket or bag and delivered
them to each friend's door. She rang the bell; walked away watching for the
friend to find the basket. She would call out, "Happy Easter", going on her
way. **Do not leave food unattended!** *My next door neighbors once lost*
their fresh baked bread to our very appreciative German Shepherd dog!!!

ICING: Mix 1-2 tablespoons milk, ½ teaspoon almond flavoring with 1 cup
powdered sugar to form a thick decorator icing. Use decorator tip to form
cross.

EASTER EGG NESTS: Form ¼ of European Kuchen Dough (1 pound;
page 69) into 10 smooth balls, pressing with fingers to form an indented
center. Press flaked coconut around the sides and top of each nest; press
lightly toasted, chopped almond in each center. Place dough in a greased
foil-lined pan with 2-inch sides. Let rise, covered, in a warm place until
light and double. Reshape center if necessary. Bake at 375° until beginning
to turn a pale brown. Do not overcook. Let children form small dough eggs
(allow for rising). Place eggs in pan to rise; bake. When cool, spread with
Decorator Icing (page 64). Fill nests with dough eggs, jelly beans or 1
cooked, dyed egg.

RUSSIAN PASHKA: No time for forming individual buns, use Hot Cross Bun recipe (page 73) forming dough into 6 parts (2 large, 2 medium and 2 small). Roll the 2 largest parts into balls, smoothing the top, tucking under any excess dough. Place each ball on a greased baking pan. Make a ½-inch deep, 2-inch cross on tops of balls. Repeat with 2 medium balls, placing them on top of the first. Place the smallest balls on top of the medium balls, forming 3 tiers. Brush with an egg wash of 1 egg beaten in 1 tablespoon water. Bake at 350° for 40-45 minutes or until brown. Yields 2 Easter breads with 3 tiers representing the Trinity.

Glaze with 1 cup powdered sugar mixed with 1½ tablespoons orange or lemon juice.

EASTER EGG BREAD: Generously grease and flour a small (1½ pound), clean, ham can with rough edges smoothed. Fill ½ full of Bette's Fast Batter Bread dough (page 76) mixed with ⅓ cup each of the following: chopped toasted pecans, chopped candied pineapple and chopped candied cherries or maraschino cherries. Let rise until double. Bake at 375° for 25-30 minutes. Watch! Remove from oven; let stand for 10 minutes before carefully taking off pan. Let bread cool on wire rack. Use appropriate flavoring (¼ teaspoon almond or vanilla) in Decorator Icing (page 64). Glaze or ice total egg; decorate and personalize with a decorator tip or roll in chopped nuts, coconut, colored sugar or colored sprinkles. Place in a basket or plate covered with clean Easter grass.

BAKER'S IDEA: Use this recipe for other festive celebrations. Fill greased and floured oven-proof bowls for baking in a round shape. Decorate as desired.

EASTER BREAD PETS: Form rabbits from ⅕ of the Maxi-Sweet dough (page 60). Divide into 6 to 8 parts, cutting each part in half. Roll each half into a ball; place on a foil lined, greased baking sheet. Pinch off 3 pieces of remaining half of dough section to form a head, 2 long ears and a round tail. Place parts to be added slightly under larger part, gently pressing together. Let rise until double. Glaze with beaten egg white. Bake at 375° only until a light brown and done. Coat again with egg white before removing from oven. Gently remove from pan with spatula. Cool on racks. Tie ribbon around rabbit's neck. Place rabbit in plastic sandwich bag. Carefully refrigerate or freeze on a flat pan. One pound of dough can yield 6 to 8 small rabbits. Vary according to the desired size.

BAKER'S IDEA: Use as table favors at Easter or place in Easter baskets with other yeast bread treats! Yum!

KULICH: Knead ½ of Maxi-Sweet Dough (page 60) until well combined with the following ingredients:

*¼ teaspoon saffron (dissolve in   ½ cup chopped almonds
  1 teaspoon orange juice)   ⅔ cup chopped candied fruit
¼ teaspoon almond extract   ¼ cup raisins
¼ teaspoon vanilla extract   1 teaspoon grated lemon rind
¼ teaspoon lemon extract   1 teaspoon grated orange rind
2 drops anise oil

Grease, flour and fit waxed paper in bottom of 7 (10¾-ounce) soup cans, 3 (1 pound) coffee cans or use any assortment of smaller size cans. Fill cans ½ full. Let rise until dough reaches top of can and begins to form a rounded dome over cans, 1½-2 hours. Bake at 375° for 20-25 minutes, depending on size of can. Use tooth pick or cake tester to check center of bread for doneness. Sides should be a pale, light brown. Cool for 5 minutes and loosen with a narrow, flat spatula. Cool on wire racks.

*Saffron is optional. Saffron was used in breads for the extra flavor and to give a more golden color when eggs were scarce.

ALMOND ICING: Whisk all ingredients; pour over tops of warm bread. Decorate with sprinkles.

1 teaspoon almond flavoring   1¾ cups powdered sugar
2½ to 3 tablespoons milk

Serve the small breads individually or as a large loaf. Remove the top slice and put aside; thinly slice desired bread and replace decorative top until bread is eaten. Traditionally, the most honored guest is often given the iced bread top. Carefully wrap with plastic inside an air tight container; store in refrigerator or freezer.

This Easter Bread, brought to America by Russian immigrants, is a reminder of the tall, rounded domes of the Russian Orthodox Churches. For an edible centerpiece, place different sizes of bread on a clear flat cutting board or clean mirror; surround with clean Easter grass.

YEAST-RAISED SWEET ROLLS, COFFEE CAKES AND LOAVES

BETTE'S SWEET ROLLS
Delicate flavor; doubles easily

1 package dry yeast
¼ cup warm water
¾ cup milk
⅓ cup butter
⅓ cup sugar

½ teaspoon salt
3-3½ cups all-purpose flour, divided
1 egg, beaten

Dissolve yeast in warm water in large bowl. Heat milk and butter just to melt butter; cool to lukewarm (105-115°). Add milk to yeast, sugar, salt, 2 cups of the flour and the egg. Beat soft sponge well; let rise for 2 hours, covered, in a warm place. Mix in only enough flour to form a manageable dough. Knead until smooth on a lightly floured surface. Shape into rolls; cover to rise in a warm place until double. Bake at 400° for 15-20 minutes or until light brown.

BAKER'S IDEA: Use as a base for sweet rolls or coffee cakes. Yields approximately 2 pounds of dough. If not in a hurry, refrigerate dough overnight. Knead dough until smooth before shaping rolls.

BETTE'S FAST BATTER BREAD: Add 1 package dry yeast for a total of 2 packages; increase warm water to ½ cup total. Beat all ingredients with 2 cups or enough flour for mixer beaters or dough hooks to manage beating for 3 minutes. Add enough more flour to form a thick batter. Fill greased muffin pans less then half full. Cover as coffee cakes with fruit or topping. Let rise until double. Bake at 375° 20-30 minutes depending on the size.

JUNE WILSON'S ORANGE ROLLS WITH SOUR CREAM GLAZE
Expect Rave Reviews

SWEET DOUGH:

2 packages yeast
¼ cup warm water
½ cup butter or margarine
⅔ cup hot tap water
1 cup sugar

1 teaspoon salt
⅔ cup evaporated milk (5-ounce can)
5-6 cups all-purpose flour

Dissolve yeast in warm water. Soften butter in hot tap water; mix in sugar, salt and evaporated milk. When cooled to 105-115°, add in the dissolved yeast. Add flour alternately with liquid ingredients to form a sticky dough. Turn into greased bowl, flip over to grease top and let rise until double, about 2 to 2½ hours. Punch dough down.

Divide the dough into three equal parts shaping in balls weighing approximately 1 pound each. Divide each ball in half. Roll each half in a 9-inch circle; brush with butter. Spread filling over butter; press into dough. Divide each circle into 12 pie shaped wedges. Starting with the wide end, roll up each wedge. Place rolls, point side down, touching one another in greased pans. A 9-inch round cake pan holds about 21 rolls. Let rolls rise covered in a warm place 1 to 1½ hours or until double and light to touch. Bake at 375° for 20 minutes or until lightly browned. Glaze rolls while hot. Makes about 72 small rolls or 48 larger rolls.

BAKER'S IDEA: Sweet dough takes longer to rise, but the flavor is worth the time! June lets her dough rise the second time until double. Can refrigerate dough over night; dough will slowly rise in the refrigerator. The next day, remove covered dough to a warm place to rise until light and double original size. Yields approximately 3 pounds of dough.

COCONUT-ORANGE FILLING: Lightly toast coconut in a 250° oven. Watch! Mix coconut, rind and sugar together.

2 cups toasted coconut	**1½ cups sugar**
3 tablespoons grated orange rind	**6 tablespoons melted butter**

SOUR CREAM GLAZE: Beat the following ingredients until smooth.

1 cup sour cream	**½ cup margarine, softened**
1 cup sugar	**4 tablespoons orange juice**

Variations:

JELLY ROLL RECTANGLE: Roll each 1 pound ball into an 8x16-inch rectangle. Brush with melted butter; spread with filling. Roll up each rectangle starting with the long side. Press fingers against the roll to lightly seal roll with each turn. Press to seal edges; place seam side underneath the roll. Reshape the roll if necessary; slice each roll in 24 pieces. Place cut side down in a greased 9-inch round cake pan, paper cupcake liners or muffin pans. Let rise covered in a warm place until double, about 1½ hours. Bake at 375° for 15-20 minutes or until light brown. Pour sour cream glaze over rolls while hot. Yields about 72 rolls.

Served warm this scrumptious confection always brings compliments!

The following variations use June's Sweet Dough, doubled in bulk and punched down. Use Jell Roll Rectangle instructions (page 77) for rolling, slicing and baking. Substitute the following for the coconut-orange filling.

MELT-IN-YOUR-MOUTH CHEESE ORANGE ROLLS: Roll ⅓ (1 pound) of June's Dough (page 76) in a 16x8-inch rectangle; spread with cream cheese mixed with orange extract. Spread with orange rind mixed with sugar. After rolled, sliced and baked, pour ⅓ of sour cream glaze over hot rolls. Yields about 24 rolls.

1 3-ounce package cream cheese, warmed until spreadable	1 tablespoon grated orange rind
¼ teaspoon orange extract	½ cup sugar
	Sour Cream Glaze

NUT-ORANGE ROLLS: Roll ⅓ (1 pound) of June's dough in a 16x8-inch rectangle; brush with butter. Spread with rind mixed with sugar and nuts.

2 tablespoons melted butter	Topping:
1 tablespoon grated orange rind	1½-2 tablespoons orange juice
½ cup sugar	1 cup powdered sugar
½ cup chopped black walnuts or pecans	

After rolled, sliced and baked, pour orange juice combined with sugar over hot rolls. Yields about 24 rolls.

YEAST BREAD CINNAMON ROLLS
Rolls baked close together form a coffee cake

The type of dough will depend on how the rolls will be served. Cinnamon rolls with coffee could require a rich dough, while a tasty sweet bread with supper could be made from a roll dough.

OLD-FASHIONED CINNAMON ROLLS: Use ⅓ (1 pound) of June's recipe (Page 76) or any sweet yeast bread dough. Roll dough in a 16x8-inch rectangle. Combine the following ingredients; spread on rectangle.

¼ cup soft butter	1 tablespoon cinnamon
½ cup packed brown sugar	⅔ cup chopped nuts
¼ cup granulated sugar	

Roll, starting at the long side, as a jelly roll. Press seam to seal; place seam side down. Cut in 24 slices. Place roll, cut side down, in a greased 9-inch cake pan, greased muffin pans or paper lined muffin pans. Let rise until doubled. Bake at 375° for 15-20 minutes or until light brown.

Vanilla Glaze: Combine 1½ cups powdered sugar, 1 teaspoon vanilla and 2-2½ tablespoons milk. Pour over hot baked rolls. Serve warm.

CINNAMON AND CREAM ROLLS: Form the Yeast Bread Cinnamon Rolls. Place rolls, cut-side down, in greased 9-inch round cake pan. Pour ½ cup whole milk or cream mixed with ¼ teaspoon nutmeg and ¼ teaspoon vanilla over rolls. Let rise until double in size, 1-1½ hours. Bake at 375° for 20 minutes. Drizzle tops with Vanilla Glaze.

GLAZED CINNAMON ROLLS: Heat ¼ cup butter, ¼ cup brown sugar and 1 tablespoon corn syrup in a 9-inch round cake pan until butter is melted. Sprinkle ½ cup chopped nuts over the top. Place cinnamon rolls, cut side down, in the pan on top of nut mixture. Let rise until double; bake at 375° for 15-20 minutes or until light golden brown. Cool about 3 minutes. Carefully invert pan on serving dish. Serve warm.

DOUBLE CHOCOLATE CINNAMON ROLLS: Roll ⅓ of June's dough (Page 76) or 1 pound of any sweet dough in a 16x8-inch rectangle. Brush with melted butter; cover with the following combined ingredients:

⅓ **cup brown sugar (packed down)**	**1 teaspoon cinnamon**
2 tablespoons cocoa	⅛ **teaspoon nutmeg**

Roll, starting at the longest side, as a jelly roll. Seal seam; place seam side down. Slice into 24 pieces; place, rolls touching, cut side of rolls on top of the Nut-Sugar coating in the prepared pan. Let rise covered until double in size and light, about 1½-2 hours. Bake at 350° for 15-20 minutes or until light brown. Let cool 3 minutes; carefully invert onto serving plate. Yields 1 coffee cake.

Serve warm or cold. *A must for chocolate lovers!*

NUT-SUGAR COATING: Heat and stir the following ingredients only until melted, on low heat, in a 9-inch pan.

⅓ **cup brown sugar, packed down**	⅛ **teaspoon nutmeg**
1 tablespoon cocoa	**2 tablespoons butter**
1 teaspoon cinnamon	⅓ **cup chopped pecans**

CINNAMON COIL COFFEE CAKE: Divide Bette's dough (page 76) or any 2 pounds of sweet dough in half, rolling each half to a 12x8-inch rectangle. Cut each rectangle into approximately 14 (8-inch) narrow strips or break off pieces of dough to form coils. Dip strips or coils in ½ cup melted butter; roll or dip strips in the following combined mixture.

1½ cups sugar	4 teaspoons cinnamon
½ cup firmly packed brown sugar	1½ cups chopped nuts

Starting in the middle of each greased 9-inch pan, wind the coil around itself. Start the next coil against the end of the first coil until pan is filled. Sprinkle any leftover sugar mixture over the top of each coffee cake. Let rise until double, about 1½ hours. Bake at 350° for 20-30 minutes or until a light brown. Cover cakes with a glaze of 2 cups powdered sugar mixed with 3-4 tablespoons milk and 1 teaspoon vanilla extract. Yields 2 coffee cakes. Serve warm from pan. *A finger licking treat!*

LU'S CHEESE BRAIDS
Delicate Irresistible Bread

1 cup sour cream	Filling
½ cup sugar	16 ounces softened cream
1 teaspoon salt	cheese
½ cup margarine	¾ cup sugar
2 packages yeast	1 egg, beaten
½ cup warm water	2 teaspoons vanilla extract
2 eggs, beaten	Glaze
4 cups all-purpose flour	

Heat sour cream, sugar, salt and margarine just until margarine melts. Dissolve yeast in warm water; mix with egg and cooled ingredients adding enough flour to form a soft dough. Refrigerate covered overnight. Divide dough into 4 sections; roll each into a 12x8-inch rectangle. Beat filling ingredients until smooth; spread evenly on each rectangle. Starting at the long side, roll as a jelly roll pressing seam edge and ends to seal. Place seam side down on a greased baking sheet. To form a fast braided effect cut through curved top edges on both sides of each roll, about 1-inch wide, every 1½-inches. Let rise until double, about 1 to 1½ hours. Bake at 375° for 12-15 minutes. Yields 4 loaves.

GLAZE: Pour 2 cups powdered sugar mixed with 3-4 tablespoons milk and 1 teaspoon vanilla over hot braids.

QUICK CRANBERRIES 'N' CREAM
COFFEE CAKE
Serve for Holiday Brunch or Coffee

1 package dry yeast
¾ cup warm water
4 cups baking mix
1 egg, beaten
½ cup orange marmalade, melted
Filling
8 ounces softened cream cheese

½ cup sugar
1 can whole cranberry sauce,
  drained
2 tablespoons orange rind
⅛ teaspoon lemon extract
¾ cup chopped toasted pecans

Dissolve yeast in water; combine with baking mix (page 121) or commercial baking mix and egg. Knead lightly on a floured surface; divide dough in half. Roll each dough half in a 15x9-inch rectangle; place each rectangle on greased baking sheet. Cover while preparing Coffee Cake filling.

Spread rectangles with combined filling ingredients, leaving a ¼-inch margin. Starting with the long side, roll as a jelly roll, pressing seam edge and ends to seal. Cut through curved top sides of rolls every 1½-inches. Cut for braided effect as Lu's Cheese Braids. If dough is room temperature and light to touch, bake immediately at 375° for 20 minutes or until light brown. Spread marmalade over cake's surface; place back in oven for a few minutes to rewarm marmalade if necessary.

BAKER'S IDEA: Unbaked coffee cakes and dough can be held in refrigerator for up to 24 hours. Before baking coffee cakes from the refrigerator, let stand in warm area 20 minutes or until dough is light. Yields 2 coffee cakes.

WILMA CURTIS' HAWAIIAN BREAD

Endorsed by Athens, Alabama cookbook author, Attie Ming.

²/₃ cup sugar
2 packages dry yeast
1 teaspoon salt
½ teaspoon ginger
¾ cup potato flakes
6½-7 cups bread flour

½ cup butter, margarine or butter
    flavored oil
1½ cups milk (120-130°)
1 cup pineapple juice
2 teaspoons vanilla
3 eggs

Combine sugar, yeast, salt, ginger, potato flakes and 2 cups flour with a mixer or by hand. Mix shortening with milk; beat into dry ingredients. Add pineapple juice, vanilla, eggs and 1 cup flour. Beat for 3 minutes. Add enough flour to form a manageable dough. Knead on lightly floured surface until smooth and elastic. Let rise, covered, in a warm place until double. Divide dough into 3 round loaves; place in 3 greased 9-inch pans or 2 greased, 3 quart ovenproof bowls. Let rise until double. Bake 25-35 minutes at 375°.

BAKER'S IDEA: The Portuguese introduced this special occasion bread to Hawaii. For a little more aloha, add 1 teaspoon grated lemon peel to the batter and press chopped macadamia nuts into loaf tops before rising.

JENNIE'S LEMON BUBBLE BREAD

Light lemon flavored bread — all it needs is a
cup of spiced tea and a good friend.

1 cup milk
½ cup sugar
1 teaspoon salt
¼ cup margarine
½ cup warm water
3 packages yeast
2 eggs, well beaten

5-6 cups all-purpose flour,
    divided
4 tablespoons melted margarine
Topping:
½ cup sugar
¼ teaspoon mace
grated rind of 2 lemons

Heat milk; stir in ½ cup sugar, salt and margarine. Cool to lukewarm. Dissolve yeast in ½ cup warm water; add to cooled milk mixture, beaten eggs and 3 cups flour. Beat until smooth. Add enough flour to make a soft dough. Turn out on a floured board and knead well. Grease top, cover and let rise about 1 hour or until doubled in size. Punch down; flatten dough with hands. Divide dough in half; shape each half into 16 balls. Brush 16 balls with margarine, sprinkling with part of lemon mixture.

Using 2 greased bundt or tube pans, arrange 8 balls in each pan. Divide 16 more balls rolled in butter and sprinkled with lemon mixture into the 2 pans for the second layer. Let rise for 30 to 45 minutes or until double. Bake at 350° for 35 minutes. Yields 2 coffee cakes.

GRANDMOTHER ROSS' RAISIN RUM ROLLS
Unusual Treat with Apple Cider

1 cup milk, heated
½ cup granulated sugar, divided
¼ cup shortening
1¼ teaspoons salt
1 package yeast
1 egg
2½ teaspoons rum flavoring, divided

3½ cups all-purpose flour
2 tablespoons melted butter ¼ cup raisins (or ⅔ cup shredded coconut & ½ teaspoon nutmeg)
1 cup powdered sugar
2 tablespoons hot water

Pour hot milk over ¼ cup sugar, shortening and salt. Cool to lukewarm (105-115°); sprinkle on the yeast to dissolve. Beat until smooth, adding egg and 1½ teaspoons rum flavoring. Add ½ of the flour beating until combined. Cover and let rise until double, about 2 to 2½ hours. Add enough flour to form a manageable dough.

Roll dough into 2 (12x4x½-inch) strips. Brush top with melted butter. Sprinkle with remaining ¼ cup sugar and raisins. Roll from long side. Cut rolls in crosswise slices ¾-inch thick. Place in 3-inch greased muffin pans. Cover and let rise until double, about 45 minutes. Bake at 375° for 15 to 20 minutes. As soon as rolls are removed from oven, drizzle tops with glaze.

GLAZE: Mix 1½ cups powdered sugar, 2-2½ tablespoons hot water and remaining 1 teaspoon rum flavoring. Yields 18 rolls.

RUTH'S MORAVIAN COFFEE CAKE
Loving Sweet Thumb Prints

1 package dry yeast
¼ cup warm water (105-115°)
1 cup unseasoned mashed
  potatoes (can use instant)
1 cup sugar
¼ cup soft butter
¼ cup shortening
1 teaspoon salt

1 cup boiling water or cooling
  potato water
2 eggs
5-5 ½ cups all-purpose flour,
  divided
1 stick butter
½ cup brown sugar

Dissolve yeast in warm water. Mix potatoes, sugar, butter, shortening, salt and boiling water. When potato mixture has cooled, add the yeast mixture. Allow to rise in a warm place until spongy. Add eggs and enough flour to make a soft dough. Let rise until double; punch down. Spread evenly in a greased 12x8x½-inch baking pan.

Make holes in the top with your thumb ⅔'s of the way through the dough. Children would love to help; they may have to use a finger. Fill the holes with pieces of butter and brown sugar. When baking in a large pan, make many holes (40 or more depending on how rich you want the coffee cake). A deeper, but smaller, pan would mean deeper but fewer holes in the cake. Sprinkle extra cinnamon and sugar on the top surface of the coffee cake. Let rise until double, approximately one hour. Bake at 375° for 20 minutes or until light golden brown. Cut into squares; serve warm or cold.

ROCKY ROAD CHOCOLATE BREAD

6½ cups bread flour, divided
1 package dry yeast
⅔ cup instant nonfat dry milk
½ teaspoon salt
½ cup cocoa
½ cup sugar
¼ cup shortening

2 cups water (120-130°)
2 eggs
½ cup slivered almonds, lightly
  toasted
1 cup chocolate chips
¼ cup melted butter

Using mixer, combine 3 cups of the flour, yeast, dry milk, salt, cocoa and sugar in large bowl. Melt shortening in water; mix with dry ingredients. Beat for 3 minutes, adding eggs and gradually more flour until unable to use mixer. Add enough flour to form a manageable dough; knead until dough is smooth. Let rise until double, about 2 hours. Divide dough in half; roll each part into a 9x15-inch rectangle. Brush with melted butter; sprinkle nuts and chocolate chips over dough ¼-inch from edge of dough. Roll from short side of dough pressing edges with each turn.

Pinch seams and ends together, tuck under and place each loaf seam side down in greased 9x5x3-inch pans. Brush tops of loaves with melted butter. Let rise until double or refrigerate, loosely covered with plastic, overnight. If rising in refrigerator, allow dough to warm at least 20 minutes before placing in oven. Dough should be light to the touch and rounded above pan. Bake at 400° for 40-45 minutes until bread sounds hollow. If necessary, cover with foil to prevent over browning. Yields 2 loaves.

GLAZE: Mix 1½ cups powdered sugar, 1 teaspoon almond extract and 2-3 tablespoons milk.

BAKER'S IDEA: This is scrumptious when warm from the oven with a spoonful of glaze on top. Omit the almonds and chocolate chips if a plain loaf is desired. Serve small squares with whipped topping, strawberries and pineapple. For a triple chocolate treat, spread with Chocolate Ganache over the cooled bread instead of a powdered sugar glaze.

BETTY SIMS' CHOCOLATE GANACHE: Melt 12 ounces dark or white chocolate; whisk with 1 cup cold whipping cream until blended and shiny.

YOUR OWN SWEETENED CONDENSED MILK

3 cups instant nonfat dry milk
1½ cups sugar
3 tablespoons butter, melted

¾ cup hot water
1¼ teaspoons vanilla

Blend dry milk, sugar, butter and hot water in blender until smooth. Microwave on high in a large bowl for 2 minutes. Whisk; microwave for 1 more minute; add vanilla. Stores well, when covered in refrigerator; yields about 2 cups of sweetened condensed milk. The commercial brand usually yields 1¾ cups.

BAKER'S HINT: Use this instead of butter to coat sweet breads before sprinkling on fillings. It can be used to thin a glaze. Use in bread recipes as you would the commercial brand. If it thickens in refrigerator, let reach room temperature or add a few drops of milk if necessary.

Make a quick cream sauce to pour over an uncooked 8 to 9-inch pan of yeast rolls, placed close together, using ¼ cup sweetened condensed milk, ¼ cup whole milk or cream and ¼ teaspoon vanilla.

NOTES

SOURDOUGH

MYSTERIOUS SOURDOUGH

"'Gold comes, goes'...'but good sourdough...it goes on forever'"

James A. Michner, *Alaska*

Sourdough starter, attributed to the Egyptians, was for centuries the only method for leavening bread. Using the yeast of the air and fermentation of the flour, they could "start" each new batch of dough, making it rise into light loaves of intricate fruit designs, animal features and classic 1600 B.C. shapes.

Even though America's sourdough, often painstakingly brought from the old country, criss-crossed the mainland from New England to California, American sourdough still conjures up visions of Alaskan prospectors, homesteaders and trappers, often nicknamed "sourdoughs". These romanticized people carried and shared their treasured sourdough pots wherever they camped or lived. The hardy Alaskans' careful handling of their precious sourdough is reminiscent of our modern day sourdough enthusiasts, feeding and affectionately naming their sourdough, Pete or Herman.

My first sourdough starter came from my friend Joy, in Juneau, Alaska. I dutifully carried this dried sourdough treasure for eight years, four moves, and thousands of miles before finally activating it.

Like myself, you may have used time as an excuse or had visions of a mass pouring out the refrigerator door. When the starter (i.e. Herman) was finally used, it was wonderful! After two years of sourdough baking, I froze the starter to take a break. When sourdough was needed for a bread class, the frozen sourdough was thawed, fed and placed in a bowl, at room temperature, until bubbly and ready for use.

If a friend's sourdough starter isn't available, make your own by choosing from a low-in-sugar or a potato-base. Don't be confused with different starters; no one starter is the correct one. Neither are there correct feeders to keep the starter alive and well. Experiment to find the one you like best.

The starter itself depends on feeding, time and capturing the air's natural yeast. This is why your bread may not taste exactly like the San Francisco sourdough bread.

Sourdough baking is very similar to working with yeast dough. Don't think sourdough is that much work! The actual hands on time is short. The long, slow rising of the dough and loaves is done without any effort from you — just a loyal old friend....sourdough.

LOW SUGAR SOURDOUGH STARTERS AND FEEDERS

WILD YEAST SOURDOUGH STARTER

1 cup all-purpose flour **1 cup water**
1 tablespoon sugar, optional

Combine ingredients in a plastic, glass or glazed ceramic container, covered with cheesecloth held in place with a rubber band. Place in a warm place for 1 to 3 days or until bubbly with a pleasant, slightly sour, yeasty fragrance.

Feeder:

1 cup all-purpose flour **1 cup warm water**
1 tablespoon sugar, optional

Feed the sourdough starter flour, sugar and water every 5-7 days; mix until smooth. Let stand 8-10 hours at room temperature until bubbly, gained ½ in size and smells yeasty. Take out the amount needed for baking. Refrigerate unused starter in a clean, loosely covered jar.

Variation:

WILD YEAST, 100% WHOLE WHEAT SOURDOUGH STARTER: Substitute all whole grain flour for the starter and the feeder. Can be substituted in other recipes or make 100% Whole Wheat Sourdough Bread. Freshly ground grain gives the ultimate in flavors.

YOGURT SOURDOUGH STARTER

1 cup low-fat milk (or ⅓ cup nonfat dry milk mixed
 with enough water to form 1 cup milk)
¼ cup low-fat yogurt

Beat milk and yogurt together. Cover with plastic wrap; let stand undisturbed in a warm place until forming a curd as yogurt. This may take 2-3 days. Combine with 1 cup flour and 1 cup warm water in a non-metallic bowl. Use when bubbly, 24-48 hours. Use any feeder to feed or replenish the starter.

FRIEND HERMAN,
YEAST SOURDOUGH STARTER

2 cups all-purpose flour   **1 package dry yeast**
1 tablespoon sugar, optional   **2 cups warm water (105-115°)**

Combine flour, sugar and yeast in a non-metallic bowl; stir in water. Cover Herman with cheesecloth in a warm (80-85°) area. Stir Herman occasionally. Let him stand for 48 to 72 hours or until he gains ½ in size and is bubbly and aromatically yeasty. Use immediately or cover Herman in refrigerator.

Feeder:
1 cup all-purpose flour
1 cup water

Don't forget to feed Herman flour and water every 5-7 days, leaving in a warm place overnight or until bubbly. Take out amount needed. Refrigerate in a clean, loosely covered jar. *Share Herman with another friend.*

After Preparing Sourdough Starter...

When the sourdough starter has become active and bubbly, measure the amount necessary for the recipe. Refrigerate the remaining sourdough starter in a clean jar loosely covered with plastic wrap. Fasten with rubber bands or a canning ring to allow for expansion.

Never leave sourdough starter in a metal container. If baking regularly each week, feed the starter and let stand at room temperature all day or overnight, until bubbly before using.

Starters' flavor and vitality improve with age if used regularly, every 3-5 or 5-7 days. If feeding your sourdough every week without baking, freeze or dry some of the extra starter, share with a friend, or discard some of the starter.

A sourdough starter's dormant yeast cells, forgotten in a refrigerator, will often rejuvenate when fed an equal amount of feeder at room temperature. Test only a small amount to avoid waste.

Starter liquid often separates from the batter and appears dark; stir together before using. Even though sourdough is resilient, remember that a fresh new batch can be made if the color, texture or smell is dramatically changed and questionable. The starch and sugar changing to lactic acid gives the desirable, clean, sour odor and can help prevent harmful bacteria growth.

SOURDOUGH QUICK BREADS

Feed Sourdough; Leave in a Warm Place Until Lively Before Proceeding With Recipe

The following quick breads are easy to make! Use a low-sugar sourdough starter if a sweet product is not desired. Adjust sugar in recipe if necessary.

SPONGE METHOD: A batter is formed using about ¼ of the flour, all the sourdough starter in the recipe and sometimes other recipe ingredients. The faster yeast growth and extra fermentation time adds to the depth of flavor and texture of quick breads and yeast breads.

ALASKAN SOURDOUGH HOTCAKES

1 cup low-sugar sourdough
  starter
2 tablespoons sugar
1 teaspoon salt
1 egg

3 tablespoons cooking oil
whole wheat and all-purpose
  flour
*½ teaspoon baking soda (dissolved in 1 teaspoon water)

Mix starter, sugar, salt, egg and shortening. Dissolve the soda in the teaspoon of water; add to batter. If too thin, add a few tablespoons flour. Keep the batter thin. Heat oiled griddle; pour silver dollar size cakes.

The batter is perfect and the temperature correct when the hotcake spreads a small amount. Bubbles begin to form on the top in a short time. Turn when hotcake is a light golden brown, add a very small piece of butter to each top; quickly transfer to a warm dish. Serve immediately! *Serves 2.*

BAKER'S IDEA: Chopped apples, blueberries, cooked cereal, wheat germ or bran can be added. Freeze extra hotcakes.

* This was part of the original recipe, added to reduce the sourness and to lighten the cakes.

WHOLE WHEAT SOURDOUGH HOTCAKES

HURRIED BAKER: Measure all ingredients ahead, ready to combine in the morning. Whisk room temperature egg white at least to the foamy stage.

SPONGE: Combine all ingredients in a non-metallic bowl; cover and let stand at room temperature overnight or 10-12 hours until light and bubbly.

½ cup whole wheat flour
½ cup all-purpose flour

1 cup low-sugar sourdough
starter
½ cup milk

Mix the following ingredients.

1 egg yolk, beaten
2 tablespoons sugar
3 tablespoons oil

¾ teaspoon baking powder
½ teaspoon salt
¼ teaspoon baking soda
1 egg white, stiffly beaten

When smooth, drop by tablespoonful onto hot, greased griddle. When pancakes are full of bubbles, turn to cook on other side. When light brown, remove to a warm serving plate. Serve hot with butter and syrup.

Variations:

WHOLE WHEAT SOURDOUGH WAFFLES: Spoon batter in hot waffle iron pretreated with non-stick spray or brushed with oil. Bake until lightly crisp, but tender. Makes about 4 (7-inch) waffles. Serve with apples cooked with chopped ham.

WHOLE WHEAT SOURDOUGH BISCUITS: Omit egg; stir in additional flour, about 1 cup. Drop biscuits on greased baking pan or knead a few turns on a floured surface. Cut or pinch off dough, lightly forming biscuits in desired size, or roll out ½-inch thick. Place on greased baking pan; let stand in a warm place for a few minutes or bake immediately. Brush tops with milk, oil or butter; bake at 425° for 10-12 minutes or until a light brown. Makes about 12 (2-inch) biscuits.

SOURDOUGH CRUMPETS

An English muffin's version of a pancake

1 cup sourdough starter
1 tablespoon sugar (omit sugar if
  a sweet starter is used)
¼ teaspoon salt

1 egg
1 tablespoon cooking oil
¼ teaspoon baking soda dissolved in ½ teaspoon water

Beat starter, sugar, salt, egg and oil together; add soda in a large bowl. If necessary, add small amount of flour to form pancake batter consistency. Place covered batter in a warm place until bubbly, 40-45 minutes. Thoroughly grease 3-inch rings (remove top and bottom of tuna cans and smooth edges); heat rings on a greased griddle until medium hot. Pour ¼ cup batter into each ring. When holes have formed on the firm tops, in about 6 minutes, loosen the edges of the crumpet with a knife to remove the rings. Turn crumpets to brown other side. Split crumpets, toast on griddle. Serve with butter and marmalade. Yields about 5-6 crumpets.

SOURDOUGH ENGLISH MUFFINS

Speedy Yeast-Risen Dough

1 package dry yeast
¼ cup water (105-115°)
1¼ cups low-sugar sourdough
  starter
1 tablespoon vegetable oil
2 tablespoons sugar

1 teaspoon salt
¼ cup nonfat dry milk
2½ - 3 cups all-purpose flour
  (could use ½ whole wheat)
cornmeal

Dissolve yeast in water; add starter and oil in a large bowl. Combine sugar, salt, milk powder and enough flour with the sourdough mixture to form a manageable, soft dough. Knead on a floured surface until smooth and elastic, about 5 minutes. Cover and let rise in a warm place until double, about 1 to 1½ hours. Roll the dough ½-inch thick on a cornmeal-sprinkled surface. Cut with a 3-inch floured cutter. Place two inches apart on a baking sheet. Cover and let rise in a warm place just until double, about 30-40 minutes. Place muffins on a lightly greased, preheated medium hot skillet or griddle (300° on an electric skillet). Bake slowly about 10 minutes per side until done throughout. Split muffins in half; toast on each side. Makes about 9 muffins.

For refrigerator rising, place covered, unbaked muffins in refrigerator for 3-12 hours. Finish rising at room temperature for 20 minutes or until light, at room temperature, before baking.

SOURDOUGH MUFFINS

1½ cups all-purpose flour
¾ teaspoon baking soda
½ teaspoon salt
½ cup sugar
¼ teaspoon cinnamon
1 cup low sugar sourdough
  starter (Using Amish starter,
  omit sugar.)

1 egg, beaten
⅓ cup cooking oil
½ cup milk
½ cup chopped dates or raisins
chopped nuts

Combine flour, soda, salt, sugar and cinnamon. Add starter, egg, oil and enough of the milk to form a medium thick batter; mix with dried fruits just until blended. Pour into greased muffin pans. Fill ⅔ full; sprinkle tops with chopped nuts or Streusel Topping. Bake at 400° for 15 minutes. Yields 12 regular size muffins.

SOURDOUGH COFFEE CAKE: Add ¼ teaspoon allspice to the muffin batter; fold in 1 cup drained, canned blueberries or a favorite fruit. Pour into 2 greased 7-inch pans. Sprinkle Streusel Topping over coffee cakes. Bake at 350° for 25-30 minutes. Immediately pour on warm glaze. Yields 2 coffee cakes.

STREUSEL TOPPING: Combine all ingredients until crumbly.

¾ teaspoon cinnamon
¼ teaspoon nutmeg
2 tablespoons butter or
  margarine

¾ cup brown sugar
2 tablespoons all-purpose flour
½ cup chopped nuts

GLAZE: Alternately stir and microwave the following ingredients, on high power, in a large microwaveable container, until mixture comes to a rolling boil (about 2 minutes): ¾ cup sugar, 3 tablespoons milk and 1 teaspoon butter.

SOURDOUGH WHOLE WHEAT BISCUITS

¾ cup whole wheat flour
½ cup all-purpose flour
½ teaspoon salt
½ teaspoon baking soda

1 cup-low sugar sourdough
  starter
2 tablespoons cooking oil

Combine flours, salt and soda; stir in starter and oil. Mix and lightly knead a few times on a floured board. Roll ¼-inch thick; cut 18 (2-inch) biscuits. Bake on a lightly greased baking sheet at 400° for 10-12 minutes or until a light brown.

Variation:

DROP BISCUITS: Omit ¼ cup of the whole wheat flour.

SOURDOUGH CRUNCHY CORNBREAD

3 tablespoons shortening or
  bacon drippings
1 cup coarsely ground cornmeal
1 teaspoon baking soda

½ teaspoon salt
1 cup-low sugar sourdough
  starter
1 cup milk

Melt shortening in a 10-inch iron skillet. Combine meal, soda and salt; mix with all ingredients and melted shortening until combined. Pour thin batter into hot skillet. Bake at 450° for 25-30 minutes. Serve immediately with butter.

AMISH FRIENDSHIP BREAD

Mary Jo Belt, a sourdough baking specialist, and her husband Charles were welcomed to their new home in Homosassa, Florida, by thoughtful neighbors bringing Amish Bread, the starter and the recipe. Enjoy as a dessert or at teatime.

Starter:

1 tablespoon sugar
2 packages dry yeast
1/3 cup warm water

2 cups all-purpose flour
2 cups milk

To prepare the starter, sprinkle sugar and yeast over water to dissolve. Let stand in warm place about 10 minutes (may double in size). Combine flour, milk and yeast mixture in large glass container. Cover loosely with plastic wrap. **DO NOT REFRIGERATE BATTER. DO NOT USE METAL CONTAINER.**

Days 1-2-3, stir or shake.

Day 4, add and stir until blended 1 cup each flour, sugar and milk.

Days 5-6-7-8, stir or shake.

Day 9, add 1 cup each of flour, sugar and milk; stir until blended. Yields 4 cups of starter.

Day 10, pour 1 cup starter into each of 3 non-metal containers with lids. Lids are only for transporting. Give two to friends and keep the third for your new starter. These containers become Day 1 starter once again, following the above directions. Refrigerate or freeze starter if taking a holiday.

To the remaining 1 cup starter, add the following as instructed:

2/3 cup cooking oil
3 eggs
1 cup sugar
2 cups all-purpose flour
1/2 teaspoon baking soda
1 teaspoon cinnamon

1 1/4 teaspoons baking powder
1/2 teaspoon salt
1 teaspoon vanilla
1 cup drained, sweetened purple
    plums, reserve syrup
1/2 cup toasted, chopped pecans

Beat 1 cup starter, oil, eggs and sugar; mix with flour combined with soda, cinnamon, baking powder and salt. Stir in vanilla, plums and nuts only until combined. Pour into 2 (8 1/2x4 1/2x3-inch) greased loaf pans. Bake at 350° for 50-60 minutes or until bread's center top is firm to touch and a cake tester or wooden pick inserted in center top is free of raw batter. Fruit or baked particles sticking does not count. Cool 10 minutes before removing from pans. Good warm or cold as a bread.

Simmer the plum syrup with ½ teaspoon orange or lemon rind. Ladle hot over slices of bread with ice cream or whipped cream as a dessert.

All the variations can be baked in small, greased muffin pans. Bake 10-15 minutes. Watch; should be a light brown color.

Variations:

CHOCOLATE AMISH SQUARES: Substitute ¼ cup cocoa, 1-ounce chopped semi-sweet chocolate and 1-ounce chopped white chocolate for the fruit. Increase the nuts to 1 cup toasted slivered almonds. Can substitute ½ cup chocolate chips for semi-sweet and white chocolate. Serve as a bread or an elegant dessert with fresh strawberries, warm, thick Superb Chocolate Sauce (Page 219) and a topping of cold whipped cream. Bake in a 9-inch square pan to serve in small squares as a brownie.

PEANUT BUTTER AND JAM AMISH BREAD: Substitute ¾ cup chunky peanut butter and 1 cup strawberry jam for the fruit and nuts. *Children's favorite.*

DOUBLE PEANUT BUTTER AND CHOCOLATE AMISH BREAD: Substitute ½ cup peanut butter, ½ cup peanut butter chips and ¾ cup chocolate chips for the fruit and nuts. If desired, substitute ¾ cup peanut butter chips and ¾ cup chocolate chips for the peanut butter. An icing can be added as an option. **YUM!**

PEANUT BUTTER AND CHOCOLATE TOPPING: Optional: Ice small muffins with ½ cup chocolate chips, ½ cup peanut butter chips and 2 teaspoons shortening. Microwave on full power for 1 minute. Stir; microwave 1 more minute or until chips are melted. Mix; dip tops of cool or frozen muffins in icing. Swirl muffins to remove from icing.

PINEAPPLE-CARROT AMISH BREAD: Substitute 1 cup grated raw carrots and 1 cup drained pineapple pieces (8-ounce can) for fruit. Sprinkle tops with coconut. For a real sweet tooth, ice with Cream Cheese Spread (Page 172).

STRAWBERRIES AND CHEESE AMISH MUFFINS: Substitute 1 cup strawberry jam, 1 cup grated sharp cheddar cheese, 1 cup toasted, chopped pecans, 2 tablespoons minced onion and ⅛ teaspoon hot sauce for the fruit. Fill well-greased small muffin cups ½ full. Bake at 375° for 10-15 minutes. *Savor the delicious flavor combination! Excellent addition to a tray of sweet breads.* Bread baked in a loaf tends to crumble.

CHOCOLATE-COCONUT-ALMOND AMISH BREAD: Substitute 2 tablespoons cocoa, 1 cup toasted chopped almonds, 1 cup shredded coconut, 1 cup chocolate chips and 1 teaspoon almond flavoring for fruit, pecans and flavoring. *Chocolate lovers beware!*

FAST METHOD AMISH BREAD: Using a spoon, mix 1 (18.25-ounce) box yellow cake mix and 1 (3½-ounce) package vanilla instant pudding in a large bowl. Beat ½ cup oil, 4 eggs and 1 cup Amish starter; stir into the dry ingredients. Fold in ½ cup drained, chopped maraschino cherries, ½ cup drained pineapple chunks, ½ cup toasted chopped almonds, ½ cup shredded sweetened coconut and ½ cup soft raisins. Stir only until ingredients are combined. Pour into 2 greased and floured 8½x4½x3-inch loaf pans or 3 greased 8-inch round pans. Sprinkle with Streusel topping (page 94). Waxed paper or baking papers on bottom of pans insures easy removal. Bake at 350° for 50-60 minutes for loaf pans, shorter time for smaller pans, about 25-30 minutes.

LOW-SUGAR SOURDOUGH LOAVES

Needs Bubbly, Active Sourdough Starters

ALASKAN NO-KNEAD SOURDOUGH BREAD
An Extra Boost From Commercial Yeast

1 package dry yeast	1½ tablespoons cooking oil
1 cup warm water (105-115°)	1½ tablespoons sugar
½ cup milk	2½ teaspoons salt
½ cup low sugar sourdough starter	4¾ cups bread flour

Dissolve yeast in water; add to milk, starter, oil, sugar, salt and enough flour to form a manageable dough. Place in greased bowl; cover to rise in a warm place (85°) until more than double, about 2 hours. Divide in half on a lightly floured surface; roll each into a 15x10-inch oblong. Beginning at wide side, roll up tightly and seal edges; place seam side down on greased baking sheet. Let rise a little more than double, about 1½ to 2 hours. Make diagonal cuts with a sharp knife, ⅛-inch deep, 2-inches apart, across loaf tops. Brush loaves with 1 egg white beaten with 1 tablespoon of water. Bake at 400° for 10 minutes, 350° for 15-20 minutes or until light brown with a hollow sound when tapped. Cool on wire rack. Yields 2 loaves.

CALIFORNIA STYLE SOURDOUGH FRENCH BREAD

Kneaded Plus Commercial Yeast; no Shortening Added

1 tablespoon sugar	1 cup low-sugar sourdough
1 package dry yeast	starter
½ cup warm water	3-4 cups bread flour
2 teaspoons salt	3 tablespoons cornmeal

In mixing bowl, dissolve sugar and yeast in water; mix in the salt, starter and 1 cup of the flour to form a sponge. Let sponge stand in a warm place until bubbly; add enough flour to form a soft dough. On a lightly floured surface, knead for 8-10 minutes or until smooth and elastic. Let rise in warm place until double, about 2 to 2½ hours.

Punch dough down; flatten into 2 rectangles. Roll each as a jelly roll, pressing down to seal with each turn. Place seam side down on greased baking sheet sprinkled with cornmeal. Let rise until double, about 1½ to 2 hours. Make 3 diagonal slashes across bread. Brush or mist with water. Place pan of hot water in oven. Bake at 400° for 10 minutes, lowering temperature to 350° for 15-20 minutes more. Brush with water over top of bread halfway through cooking. Remove when bread sounds hollow when tapped and is a light brown. Cool on wire rack. Makes 2 small loaves.

Variations:

RYE AND WHOLE WHEAT SOURDOUGH FRENCH BREAD: Substitute ½ cup rye flour and ½ cup whole wheat flour for the bread flour in the sponge. After adding the sponge, beat in ½ cup rye, ½ cup whole wheat and enough bread flour to form a manageable dough for kneading, about 1 cup.

Form one round loaf by flattening and shaping risen dough into a ball. Smooth top surface by tucking extra dough under the ball. Yields one round loaf.

OATMEAL SOURDOUGH FRENCH BREAD: Substitute ½ cup old-fashioned oats in the sponge only.

100% WHOLE WHEAT SOURDOUGH BREAD
No extra fat or sugar added

1 package dry yeast
½ cup warm water
3-4 cups whole wheat flour,
  preferably fresh ground, keep
  refrigerated

1½ teaspoons salt
1 cup Wild Yeast 100% Whole
  Wheat Sourdough Starter

Dissolve yeast in water; add 1½ cups whole wheat flour, salt and starter. Let stand until bubbly and light. Mix in enough flour to form a manageable dough for kneading. Knead on a lightly floured surface for 10-15 minutes until smooth and elastic. Let rise, covered, in a warm place until double.

Flatten into a rectangle; fold over, pressing edges and ends to seal. Turn under ends to fit a greased 9x5x3-inch greased loaf pan or form to fit a 9-inch round pan. Let rise in a warm place, covered, until light and double, about 3-7 hours. Dough will rise to top of loaf pan. Place a pan of hot water in the oven. Bake at 350° for 25-30 minutes or until bread sounds hollow when tapped. Remove bread from pan; cool on wire rack.

BAKER'S IDEA: When reheating bread, butter top or brush with an egg white beaten with 1 tablespoon water. Bake at 350° until hot.

This delicate, pure whole grain flavor and hearty bread calls for homemade butter, if your diet approves. Blend ½ pint whipping cream and salt, to taste, in blender with 4 ice cubes until a creamy butter forms. Children can shake the cream in a plastic jar until butter forms if time permits.

Yum! Reminder of the wooden churn of days past....

HURRIED BAKER:

As whipped cream forms quickly compared to the butter (takes about 20 minutes for the butter), let children spread whipped cream on their bread.

SWEET SOURDOUGH STARTERS, FEEDERS, LOAVES AND ROLLS

Breads made without commercial yeasts or leavenings must have bubbly, active sourdough starters. Do not attempt these breads without feeding your starter; let stand in a warm place for 6-8 hours.

BAKER'S RESUCE FOR IMPROPERLY RISING SOURDHOUGH BATTERS OR DOUGHS: Dissolve 1 package dry yeast in 2 tablespoons warm water; knead into dough, adding extra flour as necessary. For instant bread, pinch off small balls of dough, roll thin and bake on a greased griddle as flat bread. Bread already baked, which did not rise, can be thinly sliced, toasted and served as crackers.

BAKER'S HINT: Decatur's Sherry Tunstill, a creative sourdough baker, substitutes sourdough starter for half the liquid in her favorite recipes for that sour, tangy sourdough flavor.

POTATO SOURDOUGH STARTER

1 package dry yeast
½ cup warm water
2 tablespoons sugar

2 cups warm water
2 ½ tablespoons all-purpose flour

Dissolve yeast in water; mix in sugar, water and flour. Place in a lightly covered quart jar at room temperature. Do not shake or stir for 5 days. Feed with Mary's Potato Sourdough Feeder (page 102) the fifth day.

LOWELLA'S SOURDOUGH FEEDER

Milk-type Feeder for Sourdough Starters; Works with Friend Herman Starter or Your Own Starter

1 cup warm milk
½ cup sugar

1 cup all-purpose flour

Add all ingredients as a feeder to any type sourdough starter; beat until smooth. Let stand, covered, overnight in warm place until bubbly. Remove starter needed for recipe. Refrigerate the remaining starter in a loosely covered jar.

LOWELLA NEEDHAM'S SOURDOUGH BREAD
Use Friend Herman Starter and the Milk-type Feeder

½ cup corn oil
1 cup starter (use Lowella's
   feeder (page 101) for increas-
   ing amount of starter)

½ cup sugar
1 tablespoon salt
1⅓ cups warm water
5½ - 6 cups bread flour

Mix oil, starter, sugar, salt and warm water. Gradually mix in flour; knead well until smooth and elastic. Turn into large greased bowl. Oil top and sides of dough. Cover with plastic wrap; let rise overnight. In the morning punch down dough. Divide into 3 parts; knead each well on floured surface until smooth. Place each portion in a greased 9x5x3-inch bread pan; brush with oil. Cover and let rise 6-12 hours, in a warm place, until double in size. Dough should reach top of pan. Bake at 350° for 30 minutes or until done. Remove from pans; cool on wire racks. *Light and flavorful reminder of potato sourdough without the potatoes.*

Variation:

WHOLE WHEAT SOURDOUGH BREAD: Substitute 2 cups whole wheat for 2 cups white flour. Use ¼ cup less sugar.

MARY'S POTATO SOURDOUGH FEEDER
Contains no flour

¾ cup sugar
3 tablespoons instant potatoes

1 cup warm water

Add all ingredients every 5-7 days to feed your favorite, bubbly, active sourdough starter or the Potato sourdough starter. Mix well; let stand out of refrigerator all day or all night until bubbly and light. After each feeding, freeze some starter, give a cup of starter to a friend or make bread. Refrigerate remaining starter in a loosely covered jar.

MARY JO'S FAVORITE POTATO
SOURDOUGH BREAD

Potatoes lend a depth of flavor and lightness. Sylvia, Ann, Sally and Peggy, expert breadbakers in Decatur, Alabama, use different combinations such as ¼ cup less sugar or 1½ cups starter and 1 cup water to the recipe.

Try experimenting with this according to your own family's taste and dietary needs.

½ cup sugar
¼ cup corn oil
1 tablespoon salt

1 ½ cups warm water
1 cup potato sourdough starter
    (page 101)
6 cups bread flour

In a large bowl combine sugar, oil, salt, water and starter. Mix in the flour gradually to form a soft manageable dough. Place in a very large greased bowl; turn dough over to oil top. Cover; let rise in warm place overnight or 8 to 12 hours until more than doubled in size. Punch down and knead 12 to 15 times. Form into 3 large loaves for 9x5x3-inch bread pans or into 2 large and 2 smaller loaves. Cover and allow to rise in a warm, draft-free place for 6-12 hours or until more than double in size. A warm day may cut the time. Dough will round to the top of pan. Bake at 350° for 25-30 minutes. Cool bread on a rack; brush bread with melted butter. Yields 3 loaves.

Before you say, "I don't have time," look at Mary Jo's scheduling. She feeds her starter in the morning, lets it stand at room temperature until bedtime when she mixes the dough. The dough rises overnight and the next morning she kneads the dough, forms the loaves and allows the bread to rise while she is at work. While she is preparing supper, the bread bakes. Yummy! What a fragrant welcome home for her husband.

Variations:

WHOLE WHEAT POTATO SOURDOUGH BREAD: Substitute whole wheat flour for 1 to 2 cups of bread flour; knead until smooth and elastic before forming into loaves.

CINNAMON-RAISIN POTATO SOURDOUGH BREAD: Roll out dough for loaf pan into a ½-inch thick rectangle. Brush with melted butter and sprinkle with a cinnamon and sugar mixture. Add a sprinkling of raisins and chopped nuts, about ½ cup each, depending on your mood. Roll up the dough, tucking under ends and placing seam side down in the greased loaf pan. Sprinkle top with cinnamon and sugar. It may take 10 minutes longer to bake this bread. This is a "Grandchildren's favorite" according to some of my cooking buddies. Cinnamon or "sticky" rolls can be formed using yeast bread fillings.

SPEEDY POTATO SOURDOUGH BATTER BREAD: No time for kneading or long rising? Dissolve 1 package yeast in ½ cup water. Add dissolved yeast to batter, adding only enough flour, about 5-5 ½ cups, to form a thick batter. Beat ingredients until batter dough pulls away from sides of bowl; allow batter to rise, covered, until more than double, about 2 hours. Beat batter down with a spoon; pour into greased pans or greased oven-safe bowls. Allow to rise until more than double, about 2-6 hours.

POTATO SPONGE

Economical and Easy Sourdough Effect

⅓ cup instant potatoes   1 package yeast
4 cups water   1 tablespoon sugar

Combine ingredients in a quart jar. Leave in a warm place uncovered or covered with cheese cloth for 8 hours or overnight. Yields 4 cups. *Potato Sponge will keep a week covered in the refrigerator. If desired, divide recipe using only ¼ or ½ of Sponge at a time.*

POTATO SPONGE BREAD

Makes 4 loaves or 8 dozen rolls

⅔ cup sugar   ½ cup cooking oil
1 tablespoon salt   4 cups Potato Sponge
10½ - 11 cups bread flour

Combine sugar, salt and 3 cups of flour, in a large bowl, with mixer. Add oil and Sponge. Beat until smooth; beat 2 cups more flour into mixture. Add flour and mix by hand when too difficult for mixer. Knead dough on floured surface until smooth and elastic. Let rise, covered, overnight or about 6 hours in a warm place until light and triple in size. Punch down; let rest for 10 minutes. Cut into four parts for loaves of bread. Press evenly into greased 9x5x3-inch bread pans or form into rolls. Let rise covered in a warm place until double and light, about 3-3 ½ hours. Bake 30-35 minutes at 375° or until brown and bread sounds hollow when tapped. Again brush melted margarine over bread. Bake rolls at 400° for 15-20 minutes or until a light golden brown.

SALT-RISING BREAD

STARTER

1 cup milk   ½ cup whole grain cornmeal
1 tablespoon sugar   1 teaspoon salt

Heat the milk and stir in the sugar, cornmeal and salt. Place this in a jar in an electric skillet or crock pot with hot water in it. Maintain the temperature around 105-115° for 7-12 hours or until it shows fermentation. You can hear the gas escaping when it has fermented sufficiently. The bubble foam, which forms over the starter, can take as long as 24 hours. Do not go on with the bread-making until the starter responds.

The cornmeal must contain the inner germ of the corn and a constant, warm temperature must be maintained for the starter.

SPONGE

2 cups lukewarm water	2 cups all-purpose flour
2 tablespoons sugar	½ teaspoon baking soda
3 tablespoons shortening	

In a medium-sized bowl add water, sugar, shortening and flour to the starter. Beat the sponge thoroughly. Put bowl back in the water to maintain an even 105-115°. Cover and let rise until light and full of bubbles. This will take 2½ to 3 hours. Dissolve ½ teaspoon soda in 1 tablespoon water; combine with sponge.

Extra flour for sponge: Approximately 6½ cups flour

Stir 5 ¼ cups flour into the sponge; knead in more flour as necessary. Knead the dough for 10 minutes or until smooth and manageable. Cut dough into 3 parts. Shape dough and place in three greased 9x5x3-inch pans. Place covered pans in warm water or uncovered pans in a warm oven with a bowl of hot water, maintaining a temperature of 85°. It will take approximately 5 hours for the bread to rise 2 ½ times the original size. The bread will round to the top of the pans. Bake at 375° for 10 minutes, change to 350° for 20 minutes or until a light golden brown.

Can dry salt rising culture! Save ¼ cup of a successful sponge; before adding the soda, pour into a saucer, cover with cheesecloth and allow to dry. Store dried flakes in plastic in a cool, dry place or freeze until needed for salt rising bread. Dissolve in the new warm starter; continue with recipe. Will give a flavor boost. As the starter ferments, the unusual salt-rising smell appears. *This is not an easy bread to make.* It is tricky, but worth the effort for one who loves that very different, pungent smell of salt-rising bread.

The bread is named salt-rising because the starter and batter were kept at a warm temperature by placing the bowl in warm salt. What a treat toasted and buttered! This bread brings back cozy, warm, childhood memories. Salt-rising is a flavor that would be difficult to imitate.

DEAR ADVENTURESOME BAKER,

Don't forget the feeder, time and temperature variables with sourdough or dough relying only on a starter. Air conditioning, heating (even a wood burner) and weather conditions affect the starter. Don't give up; keep working with "Herman" or borrow some starter from a friend who bakes every week. You may become famous in your own time by keeping the art and legend of sourdough alive.

NOTES

QUICKBREADS

QUICK BREADS

Quick to Mix, Quick to Cook and Quick to Eat

Quick breads rely on fast-rising agents — baking powder, baking soda and buttermilk, air and steam. The shortening and sugar are often creamed (beaten until light, incorporating air), eggs are beaten (adding more volume), dry ingredients are added alternately with the wet ingredients. Ingredients can be mixed by hand or the electric mixer.

The fastest mixing is with the food processor, which yields a more compact product as it does not incorporate as much air as creaming by hand with the mixer. Use time as a factor for equipment decisions, as the flavors remain the same. If food processor is used, process **only** until the desired consistency, using the steel blade. **DO NOT OVERMIX. Watch the heat** from the motor for delicate doughs such as biscuits. Freeze shortening to compensate for heat.

Adjust and watch cooking time when using smaller or unusual pan sizes. Small pans help speed baking, yielding more loaves for sharing.

Test for doneness by inserting a wooden pick or cake tester in the center; tester can have an oily look, but should be free of batter. Do not over cook bread as it tends to be dry. Breaks or cracks in the baked top crust are characteristic of many quick breads.

Refrigerated quick breads wrapped air tight in plastic and foil can be stored for days; freeze for 3 months wrapped in plastic wrap with foil covering or in freezer bags. Label!

The Biscuit Method combines all dry ingredients, cutting in the shortening with knives, pastry blender, spoon, fingers, mixer or food processor. Stir lightly and quickly to combine liquid and dry ingredients. Knead dough on a lightly floured board using a few light strokes. **Over handling and too much flour will toughen biscuits.** Pat and roll out biscuits cutting ¼ to 1-inch thick. Use standard cutters, cookie cutters, jars, lids, cans or cut with a knife.

For thinner, crispy biscuits, place further apart on baking pan and for soft, thicker biscuits with softer sides, place closer together. Low-fat biscuits will tend to be more crisp.

Place biscuits on a greased baking pan, slip into a plastic bag to keep tops from drying and hold for 2 to 3 hours in the refrigerator. Pop them in the oven in time for hot biscuits when the family is seated. The flavor and rising **will be enhanced!**

Freeze leftover biscuits. Cut in half, buttered and toasted in the oven, they taste like a rich cracker. Biscuits can be frozen on the baking pan before baking. After freezing, store in freezer bags. Defrost biscuits 30 minutes before using.

BISCUITS, DUMPLINGS AND SCONES

BETTY'S MIAMI YEAST BISCUITS

Refrigerate until needed

1 package dry yeast	2 tablespoons sugar
¼ cup lukewarm water	1 teaspoon baking soda
5 ½ cups all-purpose flour	1 cup shortening or cut shorten-
1 tablespoon baking powder	ing to ¾ cup cooking oil
2 teaspoons salt	2 cups buttermilk

Dissolve yeast in warm water. Thoroughly mix flour with baking powder, salt, sugar and soda in a large bowl; cut in shortening until a coarse meal texture. Add in yeast combined with buttermilk, to form a soft dough. Stir until the mixture cleans sides of the bowl. If using immediately, knead lightly and roll or pat on a floured flat surface. Roll to about half the desired thickness of the finished biscuits. Can keep unused dough, covered in the refrigerator, up to 5 days. Bake on a greased baking sheet in a cold oven set on 450° for 10-12 minutes or until light brown. **NO RISING NECESSARY BEFORE BAKING,** but allow cold dough to warm slightly before baking. Dough rolled ½-inch thick yields 3 dozen, 2-inch, biscuits.

BAKER'S IDEA: Biscuits dipped in melted butter or margarine are similar to some of the popular fast food biscuits.

BAKING MIX REFRIGERATOR YEAST BISCUITS

1 package dry yeast	6 cups baking mix (page 121)
1⅓ cups warm water	

Dissolve yeast in warm water in a large mixing bowl until blended; add baking mix. Stir just until dough leaves sides of bowl. Knead lightly, a few turns, in bowl, using more flour if necessary. Cover and refrigerate. Will keep one week in refrigerator; take out as much dough as needed. Roll dough ½-inch thick; cut in desired size. Place on a lightly greased pan; let rise 25 minutes in a warm place. Bake for 10-15 minutes at 425°. Fast bake by placing in pre-heating oven. Yields 3 dozen, 2-inch, biscuits.

MOTHER'S LITE WHOLE WHEAT BISCUITS

Nutritious, Crunchy and Crisp

1 cup whole wheat flour
2/3 teaspoon baking soda
½ teaspoon baking powder
½ teaspoon salt

1 tablespoon cooking oil
½ cup buttermilk
2 tablespoon all-purpose flour, if
  roll-out biscuits

Thoroughly combine all dry ingredients; add oil and buttermilk. Mix together until a sticky ball forms. Drop by tablespoons onto greased flat, heavy baking pan, or roll out on a lightly floured board using all purpose flour.

I like to shape the dough by hand or cut with a knife into 6 biscuits. Place on a heavy, greased baking sheet and bake at 425° for 15-20 minutes. Yields 6 biscuits.

AUNT MARY'S FAMOUS LOW-FAT
WHOLE WHEAT BISCUITS

1 cup whole wheat flour
¼ teaspoon salt
2 teaspoons baking powder

¼ teaspoon baking soda
½ tablespoon shortening
½ cup milk

Mix the flour, salt, baking powder and soda together; mix in the shortening and milk. Knead lightly on a floured surface. Press dough into ¼- to ½-inch thickness; cut with a 1-inch biscuit cutter. Place on a greased, shallow pan. Lightly press a small lump (about ¼ teaspoon) of butter on top of each biscuit. Bake at 450° until brown. Makes about 10, 1-inch, biscuits.

These biscuits have been eulogized. Before eating whole-grain goodies was in vogue, Aunt Mary served her early morning visitors these hot "make your day better morsels". She always had butter and homemade blackberry jam on the table. In her 90's she still enjoyed munching on these; another example of whole-grain "good for yous".

WINK OF AN EYE BISCUITS

½ - ¾ cup self-rising flour
½ cup sour cream or yogurt

Combine flour and enough cream for a soft dough. Gently knead a few turns on a floured surface or sprinkle surface with wheat germ, sesame seeds or poppy seeds. Pat out desired thickness, about ⅜-inch; cut in 12 squares. Brush tops with melted margarine, milk or butter-flavored cooking spray. Bake on a greased baking pan at 450° for 12-15 minutes until a light golden brown. Yields 12 biscuits.

For a lighter biscuit, beat whipping cream and fold into flour.

LOW-FAT BAKER: Use low-fat sour cream or yogurt.

CAROLYN'S BEATEN BISCUITS

Double recipe for a crowd

3½ cups all-purpose flour
1½ tablespoons sugar
½ teaspoon salt

½ teaspoon baking powder
½ cup lard
⅔ cup skim milk

With a food processor's steel blade, combine flour, sugar, salt and baking powder; process lard, cut in pieces, until cornmeal consistency. Add only enough milk through the feed tube to form a soft, but not sticky, ball of dough. Freeze dough for 30 minutes or refrigerate overnight. Divide dough in half; process one-half at a time for 2 minutes. Roll ¼-inch thick on a lightly floured surface; cut with a 1 ½-inch or 2-inch biscuit cutter. Pierce biscuit with fork tines; place on ungreased baking sheet. Bake at 375° for 20-25 minutes. Makes 3 dozen.

If making by hand, cut in lard with dry ingredients. Add milk until a soft ball of dough forms. Beat in a rhythm with a mallet, folding over as dough is beaten. This takes a steady 30-45 minutes.

Carolyn Sparks shows her love for Southern foods as she fills these biscuits with sliced country ham for their traditional Kentucky Derby celebrations. For brunches, picnics and snacks split leftover biscuits to butter and toast. Good keepers stored in airtight containers. They are addictive!

FLAVORFUL BUTTER BISCUITS

2 cups all-purpose flour	5 tablespoons butter (room
1 tablespoon baking powder	temperature)
½ teaspoon salt	¾ cup milk

Mix the flour, baking powder and salt; cut in butter until a coarse meal texture. Stir enough milk into mixture for a ball to form. Knead a few turns on a lightly floured surface. Roll out ½-inch thick; cut into desired shapes. Cook on a slightly greased baking sheet at 425° for 10-15 minutes or until light golden brown. Yields 12 (2-inch) biscuits.

Variation:

CHEESE SWIRLS: On a lightly floured surface, roll prepared Butter Biscuit dough to an 18x18-inch square. Spread surface with softened butter; sprinkle on the cheese, cayenne pepper, thyme and paprika.

3-4 tablespoons softened butter	½ teaspoon dried, crushed thyme
½ cup grated Parmesan cheese	½ teaspoon paprika
¼ teaspoon cayenne pepper	

Roll as a jelly roll, pressing seam to seal. Place seam side down, cutting in 12 slices. Push up, underneath the slice of roll to slightly raise top of swirl; place in greased muffin pans. Yields 12 muffins. Serve with a salad or roast beef.

SANDY'S ALABAMA CHOCOLATE BISCUIT GRAVY

Chocolate Gravy is a special tradition in Sandy's family. After the biscuit is buttered, the chocolate is spooned on the biscuit. Have to try, to believe how good!

¼ cup all-purpose flour	1½ cups milk
1 cup sugar	½ teaspoon vanilla flavoring
2 tablespoons cocoa	

Mix flour, sugar and cocoa in heavy sauce pan. Slowly stir in milk until smooth. Heat the mixture on a medium low temperature until a medium thick sauce forms. Stir constantly, add vanilla flavoring. Serve hot.

BETTE HANEY'S SOUTHERN STYLE BISCUITS

A most sought after recipe on "Cooking with Bette", WBRC TV's Morning Show from Birmingham, Alabama.

3 cups self-rising flour
1½ teaspoons baking powder
½ cup cold lard (refrigerator cold for hand mixing, freeze for food processor)

3 tablespoons cold or frozen butter or margarine
1-1¼ cups buttermilk
½ cup melted butter or margarine melted butter

Combine flour and baking powder. Cut in lard and butter or margarine until cornmeal consistency, using pastry blender, finger tips or food processor.

If using food processor, remove processed dry ingredients. Stir in enough buttermilk to form a slightly sticky dough; let stand for 5-10 minutes while flour absorbs moisture. Knead a few times on a lightly floured surface; roll dough ½-inch thick. Cut with a floured cutter or glass; dip in melted butter. Bake at 425°, on an ungreased pan, in the center of the oven for 12-15 minutes, until a light golden brown and done throughout. Yields 18 delicate, company biscuits using 2 ¼-inch biscuit cutter.

HURRIED BAKER: Shape "cat's head biscuits", the size of a cat's head, by hand.

Heat leftovers at 400° for 5 minutes. Split, buttered and toasted, these are a delicacy.

Bette's gastronomic roots started early with her father's love of cooking. Her ease of presentation and generous sharing of culinary arts have inspired her friends and viewing audiences.

RUTH SHIRLEY'S FANCY OR PARTY BISCUIT DOUGH AND FAVORITE APPLE DUMPLINGS

Between a Pastry and a Biscuit

PARTY BISCUIT DOUGH: Thoroughly mix flour, salt and baking powder in a medium bowl. Cut in shortening. Add milk all at once and stir until moistened. Roll ¼-inch thick, cut as desired, and bake at 400°. For Apple Dumplings, cut dough in 5-inch squares.

2 cups all-purpose flour
1 teaspoon salt
2 teaspoons baking powder

¾ cup shortening
½ cup milk

FILLING: Core, peel and slice 6 apples. Combine ½ cup sugar with 1 teaspoon cinnamon. Arrange apples on each square, sprinkling with sugar and cinnamon; fold corners toward center. Arrange dumplings in a greased 11x8x2-inch baking dish. Pour syrup over dumplings. Bake in moderate oven (375°) 35 minutes. Serve hot with ice cream. Makes 6 to 9 dumplings.

Don't expect any leftovers from this recipe!

SYRUP: **Simmer** sugar, water and spices until syrup consistency; add butter.

2 cups sugar
2 cups water
¼ teaspoon cinnamon

¼ teaspoon nutmeg
¼ cup butter

MOTHER MARLOWE'S BANANA FRIED PIES: Cut banana in half lengthwise; cut in half crosswise to form 4 chunks of banana. Roll biscuit dough ½-inch thick, cut with a 2-inch cutter. Roll biscuits to a ¼-inch thick circle. Place banana on ½ of dough; add 1 tablespoon butter and 1 tablespoon sugar. Fold other half of dough over and seal edges by crimping with a fork. Fry in a small amount of oil for 6 minutes on each side, or until brown. Makes 8 pies with 2 bananas. *An all-age favorite!*

MAW DePOYSTER'S 2 in 1
BISCUIT AND DUMPLINGS

"Skillet Biscuits"

1½ cups self-rising flour	¾ cup buttermilk
¼ cup oil	2 tablespoons oil for pan

Mix flour with oil and buttermilk. Turn out on a floured board. Roll or pat dough down to ¼-inch thick. Cut out biscuits. Pour oil in a 9x1¼-inch pan or Maw's favorite, a 9-inch iron skillet. Place biscuits in oil and turn biscuit upside down to coat both sides. Bake at 425° for 10-15 minutes. Yields 9 (2-inch) biscuits.

Variation:

DUMPLINGS: Add a beaten egg to the above recipe. Roll out the dough; cut in strips. Add a few strips of dough at a time to simmering broth. Add enough strips of dough to rise and cover surface. Cover pan; cook until done.

Maw makes her chicken broth from a stewed hen. Remove chicken from bones, adding to broth and dumplings.

IMOGENE'S QUICK DUMPLINGS

½ cup self-rising flour	2-4 tablespoons water or broth
1 tablespoon shortening	2 quarts chicken broth

Combine flour and shortening. Slowly add liquid to form the desired dough. If needed, add more liquid for drop dumplings and more flour for roll-out dumplings. Roll dough less than ¼-inch thick, cut in strips and add to simmering broth or ease soft dough by spoonfuls into simmering broth. Simmer, covered, for 15-20 minutes until done. If doubling recipe, cook only one layer of dumplings at a time, removing cooked dumplings.

Imogene Ford's mother returns the cooked dumplings to the simmering liquid with a can of chicken gravy and cooked chicken pieces. *Don't bother to call folks for dinner. They will have their bowls in hand!*

GRANDMOTHER CARTER'S CORNMEAL DUMPLINGS

No shortening added

1 cup cornmeal
1½ cups boiling broth
1 teaspoon sugar
¾ teaspoon salt (omit or decrease according to broth)

1 egg
red pepper pod
2 quarts broth

Gradually add cornmeal to hot broth in a medium bowl; stir until thick mush. Add sugar and salt. Cool to lukewarm, beat in egg and chill in refrigerator. Drop by rounded tablespoons onto floured surface; roll into small balls, dredging with more flour if needed. Ease into simmering liquid with a red pepper pod. Cover; cook slowly for 15 minutes or until done. (Quick method): Add more cornmeal; spoon into simmering broth. Lightly sprinkle with freshly grated black pepper and paprika.

Grandmother used turnip green pot liquid cooked with country ham or the liquid left from cooking a cured ham. Try liquid cooked with a "tired of eating ham" bone with meat left on it. I use chicken broth and add pieces of chicken for a chicken and dumpling soup. Season to taste.

ANNETTE'S MATZO BALLS

Her Food Remedy for a Virus or Flu siege

2 large eggs
2 tablespoons oil
½ cup matzo meal, unbleached
Kosher matzos (an unbleached
cracker bread made from wheat
flour and water)

1 teaspoon salt, (if meal is un-
salted)
2 tablespoons chicken broth

Beat eggs and combine with oil in a medium bowl; add matzo meal, salt and chicken broth. Refrigerate for 10-20 minutes. Form dough into 1-inch balls or cut into dough with a tablespoon. Slip dough into 1½ quarts simmering chicken broth; cover pot and simmer for 25-30 minutes until matzo balls are done. For a lighter more savory matzo ball, separate the eggs, adding 1 teaspoon dried parsley, ½ teaspoon dill and ½ teaspoon thyme to the beaten yellows. Beat the whites until stiff; fold into all the ingredients.

FLAKY DROP BISCUITS

Fast and Creative

2 cups self-rising flour   **¼ cup cooking oil**
¼ teaspoon baking soda   **¾ cup buttermilk**

Combine flour and soda in a medium mixing bowl. Measure oil and buttermilk together; mix into dry mixture. Drop by spoonfuls onto a greased baking sheet. Bake at 425° for 10-15 minutes or until a light brown. Yields 12 (2-inch) biscuits.

The irregular shape is part of the character of these speedy jewels. Can smooth tops of biscuits with wet hands.

Variations:

FRIED DROP BISCUITS: Cook by spoonfuls in hot 375° oil. When light brown, turn to cook other side. Drain; serve warm.

CRUNCHY WHOLE GRAIN COATING: Whole grain flours such as rye flour with caraway seeds, coarse ground cornmeal, steel cut oats, wheat germ, bran, crushed dry cereals or seeds can be sprinkled on the work surface to coat the drop biscuit dough. Lightly knead the dough a few turns, adding more flour as necessary. Cut with a flour dipped, serrated knife, biscuit cutter or shape by hand.

HERB DROP BISCUITS: Mix in the following crushed, dried herbs: 1 tablespoon parsley, 1 teaspoon dill weed, 1 teaspoon rosemary, ¼ teaspoon onion powder and ⅛ teaspoon garlic powder. Brush tops of biscuits with melted butter before cooking.

SAUSAGE DROP BISCUITS: Mix in 1 cup cooked, drained and crumbled sausage.

CHEESE DROP BISCUITS: Add ⅔ cup shredded sharp cheddar to the dough. Lower oven temperature to 375°.

BACON CRUNCH DROP BISCUITS: Save your left over bacon; crumble and store bacon in the freezer. Add ½ cup bacon bits to the dough.

Crush fried pork skins, from the snack section of the grocery store, discarding any hard pieces. Sprinkle pork skin crumbles on the work surface for kneading the biscuit dough a few turns, adding more crushed pork skins. Cut dough in squares with floured knife.

SWEET POTATO OR PUMPKIN BISCUITS

Fall Special

2 cups baking mix (page 121)   1 teaspoon grated orange rind
¼ cup sugar   ¼ cup butter or margarine
¼ teaspoon cinnamon   ¾ cup cooked, mashed sweet
¼ teaspoon nutmeg   potato or pumpkin
¼ teaspoon salt   milk

Combine baking mix, sugar, spices and salt in a medium bowl. Mix in orange rind, butter and sweet potato or pumpkin. Add a little milk or more baking mix if needed to make a soft drop dough. Drop by rounded tablespoons onto a lightly greased baking sheet. Brush biscuits with milk; smooth tops of biscuits. Bake at 400° for 10-15 minutes. Makes about 20 small biscuits.

BAKER'S HINT: If a less sweet biscuit is needed, substitute firmly packed brown sugar for the granulated sugar.

CARROT-ZUCCHINI SCONES

Quick Supper Bonus

2 cups baking mix (page 121)   ⅛ teaspoon salt
1 cup grated, unpeeled zucchini   cold water
  and/or peeled carrots

Combine mix, vegetables and salt; add a small amount of water if needed, to form dough into a ball. Flatten to a circle on a floured surface. Cut in pie shaped wedges; place on a greased baking sheet. Bake at 400° about 15 minutes or until light brown. Yields about 12 wedges.

Use your garden bounty for this colorful, tasty bread. A clever way to add more vegetables to your meal.

BREAKFAST AND TEA SCONES

QUICK CINNAMON SCONES

Yogurt Rich

2 cups baking mix	1 cup yogurt
¼ cup light brown sugar	¼ cup raisins
1½ teaspoons cinnamon	½ cup chopped nuts

Combine baking mix, sugar and cinnamon; mix in yogurt, raisins and nuts. Drop by spoonfuls on a greased baking pan. If desired, sprinkle tops with more nuts. Smooth tops with wet hands. Bake at 375° for 15-20 minutes. Spoon Nutmeg-Vanilla Glaze over warm biscuits. Yields 12 scones.

NUTMEG-VANILLA GLAZE: Combine 1 cup powdered sugar with ¼ teaspoon nutmeg, 1 teaspoon vanilla and 2-3 tablespoons milk.

HILDA'S YORKSHIRE SCONES

¾ cup all-purpose flour	1 egg, slightly beaten
¼ cup sugar	2 tablespoons milk
¼ teaspoon salt	⅓ cup seedless raisins or
1½ teaspoons baking powder	chopped pitted dates
¼ cup butter or margarine	

Combine flour, sugar, salt and baking powder. Cut in the margarine until mixture resembles coarse meal. Mix in the egg and milk until a soft dough forms. Lightly knead in raisins using more flour, if needed. Pat the dough into a circle, ¼ to ½-inch thick. Cut into wedge shapes or cut in desired shape. Bake at 425° on a lightly greased baking sheet for 12 to 15 minutes. Yields 6 wedges.

Pass the butter and orange marmalade, or serve with a bowl of Lemon Curd (page 120) for afternoon tea. For a variation, try Wheat Scones (page 120).

Close your eyes and dream of tea and scones in Merry Ol' England. The missing touch will be MeMe Dupes' friend Hilda's English accent.

LEMON CURD: Use blender or food processor to chop peel and combine all ingredients.

¾ cup sugar
1½ lemons' yellow peel or grated peel

¼ cup lemon juice
3 eggs
½ cup melted butter

Microwave on high for 4 intervals of 30 seconds each in a large microwaveable bowl. Thoroughly beat the ingredients with a whisk after each interval. Cooking time is 2 minutes. Repeat the same process one more time, whisking all the curd at each 30 second interval. The total cooking time for the recipe will be 4 minutes, or until curd thickens. Cool and serve with sweet quick breads, biscuits or pastries.

Variation:

WHEAT SCONES: Use ½ whole wheat flour and ½ all-purpose flour.

SCOTCH OATCAKES

1½ cups all-purpose flour
1 teaspoon salt
½ teaspoon baking soda
¾ cup shortening

1½ cups oats
½ cup sugar
cold water

Mix flour, salt and soda together. Cut in the shortening with 2 knives or a pastry blender. Combine the flour-shortening mixture with the oats and sugar. After mixing the dry ingredients together, make a well in the center. Slowly add enough cold water (about ¼ cup, adding less than ½ cup total water) to form a stiff dough. Form into a ball and press the dough on a lightly floured board to a 8x8-inch square. Cut into 16 (2-inch) squares. If a crisper version is desired, roll dough about ¼-inch thick. Bake in a 350° oven for 15 minutes or until a light brown around the edges; serve hot. Yields 16 squares.

When served these short bread-type scones for breakfast in Nova Scotia, Ruth and David Shirley could purchase the recipe for a quarter — quite a bargain! Add spicy, flavorful preserves or a zesty soup with a salad. Brighten breakfast with seasonal cookie cutters. For a "real top of the morning" St. Patrick's Day, I use a shamrock cutter, sprinkling unbaked tops with green sugar.

Variation:

WHOLE GRAIN SCOTCH OAT CAKES: Substitute ¼ cup rye flour and ¼ cup whole wheat flour for ½ cup of all purpose flour. The total combined flours will be 1½ cups.

HOMEMADE BISCUIT OR BAKING MIXES

Baking mixes are time- and money-saving short cuts for quick breads. Choose your own amount and type of ingredients. The whole grains will produce a heavier, but very flavorful, nutritious product. Commercial or homemade baking mixes can be used in all the recipes.

ALL-PURPOSE HOMEMADE BISCUIT OR BAKING MIX

Calcium and Protein Boost

7½ cups all-purpose flour
1 cup instant nonfat dry milk
¼ cup sugar
1 tablespoon salt

¼ cup baking powder
1¼ cups solid vegetable shortening (does not need refrigeration)

Sift flour, dry milk, sugar, salt and baking powder together in a large bowl. Cut in shortening until the mixture resembles coarse meal. Use pastry blender, low speed setting on the mixer or the food processor. Store in an airtight container in a cool place. When measuring the mix, pile lightly in a cup and level with a knife. Yields about 10⅔ cups.

Substituting self-rising flour for all-purpose flour, omit salt and baking powder.

Variations:

WHOLE WHEAT BISCUIT OR BAKING MIX: Substitute whole wheat flour for ½ of all-purpose flour in homemade baking mix.

WHEAT AND OATS BISCUIT OR BAKING MIX: Change flour to 3¾ cups all-purpose flour, 2 cups whole wheat and 1¾ cups quick oatmeal.

BAKING MIX BISCUITS

½ to ⅔ cup milk
3 cups baking mix

Combine mixture in a medium bowl, stirring until dough is blended. Knead in the bowl or on a floured surface for a few turns. Roll or pat ½-inch thick. Cut with floured cutter. Yields 18 (2-inch) biscuits. Bake at 425°, 15-20 minutes. Yields 14 (2-inch) biscuits.

BAKER'S IDEA: Use half and half cream, whipping cream, yogurt or sour cream in the place of milk for a special taste treat. Substitute a carbonated lemon or lime drink or carbonated water for the liquid; yields a light biscuit.

Variations:

CORNELL BISCUITS: Add 1 teaspoon wheat germ and 1 tablespoon soy flour in each 1 cup measurer; lightly spoon the baking mix, made with dry milk, over the top. If using commercial baking mix, add 1 tablespoon dry milk to each cup. Research nutritionist Dr. McKay urged home bakers to enrich all their breads, cakes, cookies and pastry products with this formula. Nutritional boost for family oldsters and youngsters.

BISCUIT BREAD STICKS: Pinch off dough; roll between hands to form a 6-inch bread stick. Brush on egg white wash (1 egg white beaten with 1 tablespoon water). Sprinkle with your favorite topping or roll the bread in a topping before baking. Try creole seasoning, sesame seeds, poppy seeds, coarse salt, lemon-pepper, millet seeds, crushed barley pearls or oregano and garlic-onion salt for toppings.

SPEEDY CINNAMON COFFEE ROUND: Prepare biscuit dough; pat out, ¼-inch thick, on floured surface. Cut into 6-inch long narrow strips. Melt ½ cup butter in a 9-inch round, oven-proof baking dish or pan. Dip strips in butter; roll in ¼ cup brown sugar, ¾ cup granulated sugar, 2 teaspoons cinnamon and ¾ cup chopped nuts. Place dough in center of pan, coiling dough around center until pan is filled. Cover with any extra sugar mixture. Bake in 375° oven for 15-20 minutes until light brown. Pull apart or cut into individual servings while warm. A glaze of ¾ cup powdered sugar, 1½-2 tablespoons milk and ½ teaspoon vanilla extract is optional. A fast, easy version of the yeast Cinnamon Coil Coffee Cake (page 80).

SPEEDY STICKY CINNAMON ROLLS: Roll out baking mix biscuit dough on a baking mix floured board ¼-inch thick. Spread the following combined and creamed ingredients on the dough.

2 tablespoons butter	**1 teaspoon cinnamon**
¹/₃ cup brown sugar	**½ cup raisins, optional**

Roll dough as a jelly roll. Place seam side down. Cut ¼ to ½-inch thick slices. Combine the following ingredients in a 9x2-inch round cake pan.

¼ cup butter	**1 tablespoon corn syrup**
¼ cup brown sugar	**¹/₃ cup chopped nuts, optional**

Heat pan until butter is melted; stir ingredients. Place cinnamon roll slices in pan, cut side down. Bake at 375° for 12-15 minutes or until a light brown. Carefully invert on serving plate.

For plain cinnamon rolls, place rolls, cut side down, in a greased pan. While warm, drizzle with a powdered sugar glaze.

BAKING MIX DROP BISCUITS

2 cups baking mix
²/₃ cup milk

Mix milk and mix to form a sticky dough. Drop by spoonfuls on a cookie sheet. Bake at 425° for 10-15 minutes. Yields 12 (2-inch) biscuits.

Variations:

DOWN SIDE-UP BISCUIT PIZZA: In a greased 9-inch square pan, add 1 cup cooked sausage, ham or chicken spread with 1 cup thick pizza sauce and sprinkle with a covering of chopped green pepper, onions, celery and mushrooms. Evenly spoon thinner biscuit dough over top. Use only 1 cup baking mix to ²/₃ cup milk and 1 egg. Bake at 425° for 15-20 minutes or until ingredients are hot and topping is light brown. Sprinkle 1 cup shredded mozzarella cheese over top when almost done.

FRUIT DROP BISCUITS: Combine 1 cup peeled, finely chopped apples and 1 teaspoon grated orange or lemon rind.

VEGGIE DROP BISCUITS: Add 1 cup finely chopped, drained vegetables cooked until crunchy tender. Mix or match carrots, squash, zucchini, onions, green, yellow or red bell peppers, parsley, green beans, pimento pepper or ¼ jalapeno pepper for a little zip. Sprinkle biscuit dough tops with celery salt.

MINTED DROP BISCUITS: Microwave 1 cup finely chopped, peeled apples with 1 tablespoon finely chopped mint leaves in a covered container until hot. Cool slightly; add to dough. Great with lamb or Indian curry. Serve around a dish of mint jelly.

CURRIED CHEESE DROP BISCUITS: Add ½ teaspoon curry powder, ½ cup chopped chutney and ⅔ cup grated sharp cheddar cheese to dough. Serve with fruit salad or baked chicken salad.

SOURDOUGH DROP BISCUITS: In place of milk add ⅔ cup non-sweet sourdough starter.

WHOLE-GRAIN QUICK BREADS

HEALTHY AND HEARTY

These robust breads can be tested for doneness with a wooden pick or cake tester in the center; the toothpick should be free of batter. Serve warm; cut in wedges or squares.

If you are just beginning to cultivate a taste for whole-grains, substitute half whole wheat flour and half all-purpose flour for the whole wheat flour in the recipe.

WHEAT-BRAN ROUND

Satisfying and Nutritious

½ cup whole wheat flour
½ cup all-purpose flour
1 cup bran cereal (bran buds-not flakes)
3 tablespoons wheat germ
¾ teaspoon baking powder

½ teaspoon baking soda
½ teaspoon salt
3 tablespoons sugar
3 tablespoons butter or margarine, melted
½ cup buttermilk

Combine both flours, cereal, wheat germ, baking powder, soda, salt and sugar in a medium bowl; mix in melted shortening and buttermilk. Spoon into a greased 8-inch pan or iron skillet. Smooth top surface with the back of a spoon dipped in water. Bake in a 375° oven for 25 minutes or until done.

Makes 4 to 8 wedges, size depends on how hearty the appetite! Cut open left over bread to use for creamed turkey or dishes requiring rice as a base.

A family favorite on a cold day, served hot from the oven with a bowl of vegetable soup.

APPLESAUCE OATMEAL BREAD

1½ cups all-purpose flour
1 teaspoon baking powder
1 teaspoon baking soda
1 teaspoon salt
1 teaspoon cinnamon
½ teaspoon nutmeg
⅔ cup brown sugar

2 eggs, beaten
1¼ cup sweetened thick
 applesauce
1½ cups uncooked quick oats
¾ cup raisins
½ cup chopped nuts
⅓ cup melted shortening

Mix together the flour, baking powder, soda, salt and spices in a large bowl. Combine with brown sugar mixed with eggs and applesauce. Stir in oats, raisins, nuts and melted shortening. Pour batter into 2 greased 8x4x2-inch loaf pans. Bake at 350° for 1 hour. Yields 2 loaves.

A "stick to the ribs" breakfast bread - surely beats a bowl of plain oatmeal.

GRANDMOTHER CARTER'S LOW-FAT GRAHAM BREAD

Her 1870's quick supper bread

½ teaspoon salt
2 tablespoons sugar
½ teaspoon baking soda
½ teaspoon baking powder

2 cups whole wheat flour or
 graham flour
2 tablespoons shortening
1 egg, beaten
1 cup buttermilk

Combine salt, sugar, soda, baking powder and flour in a medium bowl. Melt shortening in a 9-inch baking pan—Grandmother used an iron skillet. Stir egg and buttermilk into dry ingredients only until moistened. Mix in the melted shortening; quickly pour the batter into the hot pan. Bake at 400° for 20 minutes until crusty. Yields 8 wedges.

BAKER'S IDEA: Serve as a "hearty" breakfast bread or a change from cornbread. Vary with nuts, raisins or seeds, up to 1 cup. Split, butter and toast leftovers.

ANN'S IRISH SODA BREAD

Light in Calories, Heavy in Nutrition

2 cups whole wheat flour	½ teaspoon salt
½ cup all-purpose flour	¾ cup buttermilk
½ teaspoon baking soda	

Combine flours, soda and salt in a medium bowl. Mix buttermilk with dry ingredients. Knead lightly, smoothing and forming an 8-inch round. Cut a cross in the top; bake on a greased heavy pan for 25 minutes at 400° or until done.

This is an authentic, favorite Irish family recipe straight from the "Emerald Isle."

RUTH'S BAKED BROWN BREAD

No shortening added
That is correct! No steaming needed with this Brown Bread!

1 cup all-purpose flour	½ teaspoon baking soda
3 tablespoons sugar	2 cups low-fat buttermilk
2 teaspoons baking powder	1 cup molasses
2 cups whole wheat flour	1 cup raisins
1 cup bran cereal (bran buds, not flakes)	

Combine flour, sugar, baking powder, whole wheat flour and 100% bran cereal in a large bowl. Dissolve soda in buttermilk. Slowly stir molasses and buttermilk-soda mixture into mixed dry ingredients. Add raisins. Pour batter into 2 greased 8 ½x4 ½x3-inch pans. For easy slicing, Ruth uses an 11x13-inch pan. Bake at 350° for 40-45 minutes. Yields 2 loaves.

BAKER'S IDEA: Delicious with cream cheese, as a traditional brown bread for sandwiches or plain with salads and soups. Served with tea on a boat trip in Ireland.

DAWN'S STEAMED BROWN BREAD

No shortening added

1 cup raisins
2 cups bran buds cereal
2 cups low-fat buttermilk
2 tablespoons molasses

1 cup sugar
2 cups all-purpose flour
2 teaspoons baking soda
½ teaspoon salt

Soak raisins for about 15 minutes in hot water or microwave for one minute. Drain and absorb excess moisture with paper towels. Mix bran and buttermilk in a large bowl; add molasses, sugar and flour combined with soda and salt. Stir in the raisins. Grease and flour the inside of 5 (10 ¾ ounce) soup cans. Place batter, evenly divided, into the cans, covering tops with foil crimped to the sides. Place cans in a large pot on a rack with 1-inch of water. Cover pot; simmer for 2 ½ hours. Remove cans from water; let stand about 10 minutes. Remove bread from cans. Yields 5 loaves.

Have a bowl of Boston Baked Beans on hand with a salad for a special meal.

Slice cold with plain cream cheese or add minced pineapple and toasted coconut to sweeten the cheese.

What a full of energy after school snack! Homework won't be so bad after a power lift from this bread.

ANN GEBHART'S GOOD MORNING
BANANA HEALTH BREAD

No Sugar Added

1 cup all-purpose flour
1 cup whole wheat flour
1 tablespoon baking powder
5 very ripe bananas

8 ounces low fat vanilla or plain
    yogurt
2 eggs, beaten
¼ cup oil

Combine flours and baking powder. Mash bananas with the yogurt; add with eggs and oil. Mix all ingredients until moistened; pour into a greased 8x8x2-inch pan. Bake at 350° for 25-30 minutes. Test with a wooden pick to check for doneness.

Would you believe, Ann threw together this original as she ran out the door for her before breakfast jog. Breakfast was ready to take out of the oven when she returned. For those who are not "morning people", bake in the afternoon for the after school and after work hungry crew. A slice of this bread and a glass of skim milk made my nutritionist friends smile.

IRENE'S WHEAT AND BARLEY BREAD

Unusual, Nutty Flavor

1¹/₃ cups hot milk
²/₃ cups crunchy wheat and barley
cereal
3 tablespoons margarine
²/₃ cup sugar

1 egg
2 cups all-purpose flour
1 tablespoon baking powder
1 teaspoon salt

Pour milk over cereal and margarine; let stand until cool. Beat the sugar and egg in a medium bowl until light; mix in the flour combined with baking powder and salt, alternately with milk mixture. Bake in an 8x5x2-inch greased loaf pan at 350° for approximately 1 hour. When cool, seal in plastic wrap. Cut in thin slices for breakfast or lunch.

MAIN COURSE BAKING MIX QUICK BREADS
BREADS TO BUILD-A-MEAL-AROUND

BALANCE WITH "VEGGIE" SOUP AND FRUIT SALAD

ONION-CHEDDAR TOPPED QUICK BREAD

Great addition to roast beef or pork!

2 cups baking mix
1 tablespoon minced parsley
½ teaspoon rosemary
¹/₈ teaspoon black pepper
²/₃ cup milk
1 cup chopped onion
3 tablespoons chopped green
bell pepper

2 tablespoons butter or margarine
1 egg
½ cup whole milk, evaporated
milk or light cream
1½ cups sharp cheddar cheese

Combine mix, herbs, spice and milk. Spread dough in a greased 8x11x2-inch casserole, or a 9-inch square pan, depending on the thickness desired. Lightly saute the chopped onion and bell pepper in the butter. Beat egg with milk, combining with the onion mixture. Spread over the dough. Bake at 400° for 20-25 minutes, depending on thickness. A few minutes before bread is done, sprinkle with sharp cheddar cheese. Serves 6.

Hurried Baker: Add all the ingredients together. Bake, cut in small squares, and serve for a buffet supper.

PIZZA BREAD

Favorite for all ages

2 tablespoons oil
1 egg
2/3 cup milk
1 teaspoon worcestershire sauce
2-4 drops hot pepper sauce

2 cups baking mix
1/4 cup minced onion
2 teaspoons oregano
1/2 teaspoon dried basil
1 tablespoon chopped parsley

Topping:

1 cup sliced ripe olives or pimento stuffed green olives - mix or match
2 cups shredded mozzarella cheese or thinly sliced cheese

Beat oil, egg, milk and sauces; combine with baking mix, onion, oregano, basil and parsley in a medium bowl. Press the dough to fit a 12-inch greased pizza pan. Bake for 10 minutes at 400°; remove from oven.

Sprinkle bread with olives; cover with cheese. Bake for 10 extra minutes or until bread is baked and cheese is melted. Yields 6, 2-inch, slices.

OWEN'S ZUCCHINI SUPPER CAKES

Eat Your Cake and "Veggies" too!

1/2 cup baking mix (page 121)
1/4 cup grated Parmesan cheese
1/4 teaspoon salt
1/4 teaspoon pepper

2 large eggs, lightly beaten
2 cups coarsely grated or finely
    chopped zucchini
Butter or margarine

Mix baking mix, cheese, salt, and pepper; stir in eggs and zucchini until mixture is moist. Cook small cakes on a buttered medium hot griddle until brown on both sides. Serve hot. Makes 8-10 pancakes. *Hide leftovers in the refrig' — delicious snack.*

Owen is a dedicated, prize winning chef, but specializes in Texas-Mexican foods in his Del Cocinero Restaurant in Decatur, Alabama.

Variation:

HERB SUPPER CAKES: Add 1/4 cup fresh, chopped herbs, such as parsley, thyme or rosemary and 2 tablespoons grated onion. Can use 1 tablespoon dried, crushed herbs and 1½ teaspoons dried minced onions instead of fresh herbs.

MEXICAN CHEESE SUPPER BREAD

Crunchy on the Outside; Soft on the Inside

2½ cups baking mix (page 121) | 2 eggs, beaten
2 cups salsa sauce | 1 cup grated cheddar cheese

Stir baking mix, sauce, eggs and cheese just until combined. Pour ingredients into a well-greased 8x8x2-inch baking container. Bake at 375° for 30-40 minutes. Yields 8 servings. A wooden pick inserted in bread should be batter-free when bread is done. Can be served sliced or spooned as a spoon bread.

Adds color and extra protein to a vegetable supper.

CHEESE HERB SUPPER BREAD

2½ cups baking mix | ¼ teaspoon onion powder
1 teaspoon dried, crushed dill weed | ⅛ teaspoon garlic powder
2 teaspoons dried, crushed parsley | 2 eggs, beaten
¼ teaspoon dry mustard | 1 cup milk
  | ½ cup grated cheddar cheese
  | ½ cup cottage cheese

Combine baking mix, herbs, mustard, onion and garlic. Stir in eggs, milk and cheeses, just until combined. Pour ingredients into a well-greased 8x8x2-inch baking container. Bake at 375° for 30-40 minutes or until wooden pick inserted in bread is batter-free. Bread will be a soft texture on the inside. Cut in squares or serve with a spoon. Yields 8 servings.

HURRIED BAKER: Bake in the microwave following manufacturer's directions; sprinkle with more cheese on top when **almost** firm. Watch, as this bakes quickly. It will take approximately 12-15 minutes on medium-high power. Rotate dish ¼ turn after 10 minutes.

I like to start baking in the conventional oven and finish baking in the microwave oven. Let stand a few minutes before serving.

ROSE'S GREEK OLIVE BREAD

Moist and Cheesy...Served Warm

2 tablespoons instant potato
flakes
1 (5-ounce) can evaporated milk,
warmed
1 tablespoon margarine
1 cup sour cream or yogurt
1 egg

2 cups baking mix (page 121)
¼ teaspoon garlic powder
1 tablespoon instant, dry, minced
onion
1 cup Monterey Jack cheese
1 cup drained, pitted sliced ripe
olives

Mix potatoes with milk and margarine in a large bowl; beat in sour cream
with egg. Stir in baking mix combined with garlic powder and onion only
until moist. Fold in cheese and olives; spread in greased 10-inch iron
skillet. Bake at 375° for 30-35 minutes or until a pale brown. Serve hot.
Yields 6 wedges.

MARA'S FRESH CORN AND HERB BREAD

Individual cakes or one skillet of unique flavors

1 egg
²/₃ cup milk
1 tablespoon cooking oil
½ cup whole wheat flour
½ cup all-purpose flour
1 cup fresh or drained, canned
corn kernels
½ cup grated jalapeno cheese
½ cup chopped onions

2 tablespoons each fresh parsley
and cilantro (coriander plant
leaves)
or substitute fresh thyme
½ cup cooked, crisp, crumbled
bacon
¹/₈ teaspoon black pepper
2 tablespoons cooking oil

Beat egg, milk and oil in a medium bowl; combine with flours. Add corn,
cheese, onions, parsley, cilantro, bacon and pepper. Heat oil in a 10-inch
iron skillet; mix into batter. Form corn cakes to fry individually or pour
mixture into hot skillet to bake at 400° for 15-20 minutes, or until a light
golden brown.

*Serve a hot, golden brown cake or slice with a medley of fresh vegetables or
a cold salad plate.*

*Mara, a gourmet cook and native Californian, keeps informed on the latest
in nutritious and gourmet foods. Both are featured in her bread!*

CORNBREAD

Cornbread is a universally loved, nutritious bread. There are as many different names and methods to prepare cornbread as there are regions of the country. Are you eating a hoe cake developed from cooking on a hoe over embers, journey cake for traveling, johnny cake, corn dodgers or corn pones? The extensive variations go from hot water cornbread or Indian fry bread to a cake-like cornbread sweetened with molasses or sugar.

The corn itself varies with the coarseness of the grind and the color: yellow (Northern), white (Southern) and blue (Southwest Indian). A coarsely ground or finely ground meal alters the texture of the final product from coarse to smooth. Except for esthetics, the color does not change the finished product — an unbelievable statement, worth fighting over, by folks from each of these areas.

Cornbread can be baked in any container, but the old-fashioned, well seasoned iron skillet is still a favorite. Speed the cooking process by melting the shortening in an iron skillet in the oven or on top of the stove. Pour and mix the melted shortening into the batter; immediately pour the batter into the hot skillet to be placed back in the hot oven. This process forms a crispy crust much prized by Southern cooks.

Ruth remembers Grandmother Carter in East Tennessee making her individual corn dodgers by patting each one in shape, molding them in her hands until they were smooth, slightly rounded little cakes. They would hold their shape in a hot oiled skillet on top of the stove. When golden brown on both sides, they were served with butter.

My Dad remembers his mother and grandmother in Virginia scooping up a handful of cornbread mixture and letting it fall back and forth between closed palms using a rocking motion to shape the pone. He and his brothers and sisters would make a special request for "egg bread", knowing that the egg made the bread more moist and rich.

No problem with leftovers in that time. Cold cornbread was delicious when crumbled in a bowl, adding cold milk and a sprinkling of sugar. Voilà! Your own corn cereal! This is my Dad's favorite late night and after fishing snack.

AUNT GRACE'S INDIVIDUAL CORN PONES

½ cup cornmeal
1 pinch of baking powder

¼ cup boiling water plus 2
  tablespoons

Mix cornmeal, baking powder and enough boiling water to form a soft mixture. When cool enough to handle, wet hands and form cakes. Fry in a small amount of oil until golden brown on both sides.

Aunt Grace Edwards Dalton was still making these to go with her supper when she was 93. Cornmeal must be even healthier than we thought! The small recipe was just enough for her dinner.

DYANN'S SCALDED CORN CAKES

1 quart boiling water
2 teaspoons salt

2½ cups cornmeal

Add salt to boiling water. Gradually stir in cornmeal. Remove from stove and cover pan; let mixture stand until cool. Separate the mixture in portions smaller than an egg. Flatten and fry in deep fat or pan fry in hot skillet, turning once.

BAKER'S LOW-FAT IDEA: Corn cakes can be placed in a hot greased skillet for 15 minutes in a 425° oven. Serve these golden brown cakes with fresh vegetables.

MOTHER'S CORNBREAD

Ingredients were added by memory and never written on paper.

2 tablespoons oil
1 cup self-rising cornmeal

1 egg
¾ cup buttermilk

Heat oil in an 8-inch skillet. Combine cornmeal with egg beaten in buttermilk. Mix in hot oil. Pour immediately into hot pan. Bake at 425° for 15 minutes or until brown.

RIVERDALE MILL'S CORNBREAD

Fresh Water Ground Cornmeal

1½ cups cornmeal - Use at least
  ½ of the coarse water ground
  cornmeal, if available.
2¼ teaspoons baking powder
¼ teaspoon salt

1 egg
1 cup milk
2 tablespoons margarine or
  bacon drippings

Mix cornmeal, baking powder and salt together; add in beaten egg and milk. Melt margarine in an 8-inch iron skillet. Add melted margarine to the batter; pour batter in hot skillet to bake at 400° for 20 minutes. Serve hot.

HURRIED BAKER: Hungry folks ready to eat before bread is done? Whip out the greased skillet to heat; when hot, pour batter into silver dollar cornbread pancakes. When light brown, serve as an appetizer or as a meal accompaniment.

Variation:

CRACKLING CORNBREAD: Add 1 cup finely chopped cracklings.

CRUNCHY CORNBREAD

Almost like eating individual corn pones, without the work

3 tablespoons bacon drippings or
  shortening
1 cup coarsely ground cornmeal

1 teaspoon baking soda
½ teaspoon salt
2 cups buttermilk

Melt shortening in a 10-inch iron skillet.

Combine meal, flour, soda and salt; add buttermilk and melted shortening. Stir or lightly whisk out large lumps. Pour cornbread batter in hot skillet. Bake at 475° for 20-25 minutes or until done. This thin batter will form a golden brown crust; double recipe for a thicker bread. If top isn't brown soon enough, turn on broiler for a few minutes. Watch! Serves 4.

CORNBREAD SALAD
Freeze leftover cornbread; save for salads

2 cups chopped tomatoes
  (about 4)
1 green pepper, chopped
1 onion, chopped
2 stalks celery, chopped
½ cup chopped dill or homemade
  sweet pickles

12 slices bacon, crisply cooked
  and crumbled
1 cup mayonnaise
8-inch skillet cornbread,
  crumbled, or cornbread muffin
  mix (8½ ounce)

Combine tomatoes, green pepper, onion, pickles and bacon. Drain off excess juice, about ⅓ cup; add to mayonnaise. Add cornbread to vegetables; toss gently. Layer ½ of cornbread mixture in a bowl; spread with mayonnaise mixture. Repeat layers. Cover and chill for 3 hours or overnight. Sprinkle top lightly with paprika. Makes 8-10 servings.

Mitchell Diggs, who was Food Editor for the Birmingham Post Herald, used this recipe and variations of cornbread salads as a feature story...just in time for those luscious summer tomatoes.

BAKER'S IDEA: Good side dish for barbecue or burgers. Try adding chopped broccoli flowerets for a change.

MEXICAN CORNBREAD SALAD: Reduce mayonnaise to ½ cup, add 2 (15-ounce) cans drained, mixed/matched kidney or pinto beans, 2 cups grated jalapeno or cheddar cheese, 1½ cups salsa and 1½ cups sour cream or plain low-fat yogurt. Omit pickles.

Evenly crumble ½ of cornbread in a large bowl, layering with kidney beans and ½ of combined chopped vegetables mixed with salsa; sprinkle with ½ of bacon and grated cheese and cover with ½ of mayonnaise mixed with sour cream. Top with rest of cornbread mixed with drained pinto beans and continue layering of ingredients, adding the remaining sour cream mixture last. Garnish with seeded and sliced jalapeno peppers or cover top with raw onion rings from thinly sliced sweet onions. Use your imagination and available fresh vegetables to create this filling salad. Serves 9 to 10.

Leftovers with juices spooned over a layer of shredded mixed greens (spinach and lettuce) forms another meal.

Mexican Cornbread Salad makes a filling and colorful salad. Substitute good quality, low-calorie sour cream, mayonnaise or cheese if desired.

BAKER'S IDEA: Add 1 tablespoon fresh cilantro and/or parsley. Fresh tomatoes can be omitted, canned corn can be substituted or added with beans. For a taco-type salad, using cornbread instead of nachos, add 1 cup cooked, drained ground beef instead of the bacon; serve salad on a layer of chopped lettuce.

CORNBREAD MAIN DISH CASSEROLES

AUNT MARY'S COMPANY CORNBREAD

¾ cup yellow or white cornmeal
1 cup all-purpose flour
3 teaspoon baking powder
1 teaspoon salt

2 tablespoons sugar
2 eggs beaten
1 cup milk
¼ cup melted shortening or cooking oil

Mix together cornmeal, flour, baking powder, salt and sugar. Beat eggs and milk; add to dry ingredients with shortening, melted in skillet, mixing only until moistened. Bake in a greased, hot 10-inch iron skillet or heavy pan at 400° for about 20 minutes until light brown. Yields 8 to 10 wedges.

Variations:

HAM AND CHEESE CORNBREAD DINNER: Add the following ingredients; bake in a well-greased 2 quart casserole, about 30 minutes at 400°. Serves 4 to 6.

1 (17 ounce) can cream style corn
  (2 cups)
1½ cups cooked ham, cubed
6 ounces swiss cheese cubed or
  shredded

¼ cup chopped green onions
½ cup chopped bell pepper

GRITS CORNBREAD: Use those leftover grits. Substitute 1 cup cooked grits for 1 cup flour. Add 1 cup sharp cheese and ⅛ teaspoon cayenne pepper for an extra protein and flavor boost. Serve plain or with creamed ham and vegetables or creamed eggs.

RICE CORNBREAD: Substitute ¾ cup cooked rice for 1 cup all-purpose flour.

BAKER'S IDEA: Split leftover cornbread; top with Chicago Chili (chili with beans and meat), fresh-chopped green onions and grated cheddar cheese.

Serve the following spoon breads or casserole breads with a spoon or spatula.

RUTH'S SPOON BREAD

A Southern Classic — worth every minute of preparation

1½ cups milk	1 teaspoon salt
½ cup yellow cornmeal	2 teaspoons sugar
2 tablespoons all-purpose flour	3 egg yolks, beaten
3 tablespoons butter	3 egg whites, stiffly beaten

Heat milk; slowly add cornmeal mixed with flour, stirring well. Cook about 5 minutes over low heat until mixture thickens. Stir constantly to prevent lumping. Remove from heat and beat until smooth; add butter. When cool, add salt, sugar and beaten egg yolks. Just before baking, beat the egg whites until stiff; fold whites into the cooled cornmeal mixture. Pour into a buttered 9x3-inch casserole. Place casserole in a pan containing hot water. Bake in a 350° oven for 45 minutes, until set with a soft, pudding-like texture. Serve hot directly from the casserole, using a large spoon. Pass the butter! Serves 4.

PEEPIE'S MEAL-IN-ONE SPOON BREAD

Prepare enough for seconds

1 cup cornmeal	1 tablespoon sugar
4 cups whole milk	1 teaspoon salt
3 egg yolks	Black pepper to taste
¼ cup chopped onions	3 egg whites, stiffly beaten
¼ cup celery	

Cook cornmeal and milk to a mush. Beat in egg yolks, onions, celery, sugar, salt and pepper to cooled cornmeal mixture. Fold in the egg whites. Pour into a greased 3-quart baking dish; bake at 350° for approximately 1 hour or until set as a pudding. Serves 6. Serve with butter.

Peepie's guests serve themselves from a pottery baking casserole. She adds a platter of cooked sausage, fruit salad and dessert for her appreciative and most fortunate guests.

JALAPENO CORNBREAD CASSEROLE

3 eggs beaten
1 cup milk
1 package (8½-ounce) corn
  muffin mix
1 onion, finely chopped

1 (4-ounce) chopped chili peppers or jalapeno peppers
1 (17-ounce) can creamed corn
½ cup cooked, crumbled bacon
2 cups grated cheddar cheese,
  divided

Beat eggs and milk in a large bowl; add rest of ingredients and 1 cup cheese. Stir to blend. Bake in an 8x11½x2-inch casserole dish. Bake at 375° for 35 minutes or until a soft consistency which holds its shape. Sprinkle remaining cheese over the top. Serve hot. Serves 5 to 6, adding salad and fruit.

DILLY CORNBREAD

Calcium Boost

3 eggs
⅓ cup milk
½ cup cottage cheese
1 (8½-ounce) package corn
  muffin mix

1 teaspoon dry dill weed
2 tablespoons finely chopped
  onion

Whisk eggs in a medium bowl with milk and cottage cheese; combine with mix, dill and onion just until combined. Bake in a greased 8x8-inch pan, 8-inch skillet or 1½ quart casserole, at 400°, for 15-20 minutes. Serves 4.

Variations:

DILLY BROCCOLI CORNBREAD: Add 1 (10-ounce) package frozen chopped broccoli, thawed and drained. Bake 25-35 minutes. Batter will be set with a soft spoon bread consistency.

DILLY TURNIP GREEN CORNBREAD: Add 1 (10-ounce) package frozen, chopped turnip greens, thawed and drained. Add 10 slices crisply cooked and crumbled bacon. Bake as Broccoli Cornbread.

Does this sound Southern? Disguised veggies!

SPEEDY DOUBLE CORN SPOON BREAD

1 (8½-ounce) box corn muffin mix   ½ cup melted margarine
2 eggs beaten   1 (17-ounce) can cream style corn
1 (8-ounce) carton sour cream,   ¾ cup grated cheese
    yogurt or cottage cheese,
    blended in blender

Mix all ingredients in the order given. Pour into a greased 2-quart casserole. Bake at 350° for 50-60 minutes.

To make this a one-dish meal, add ½ cup cooked chopped meat, ground sausage, hot dogs or ham. Sprinkle ½ cup grated cheese on the top as bread comes from the oven.

BAKER'S IDEA: Add some zip to the casserole with one pod green chili and 1 green pepper, seeded and chopped. Serves 6 to 8.

Use a 2-quart, rectangular, oven-proof glass casserole to cut the baking time. When beginning to brown, place in microwave to finish cooking. Watch! The microwave takes a very few minutes.

Add a finger food salad: celery and carrot sticks with apple and tomato wedges on spinach leaves.

MAMA ADA'S CORN LIGHT BREAD

Mary Jo's grandmother, Ada Buchanan, baked this bread when she started housekeeping eighty years ago. This mild flavored bread amplifies the crunchy, sweet flavor of the ground corn.

2 cups cornmeal   ⅓ cup shortening
½ cup all-purpose flour   ⅓ cup sugar
½ teaspoon salt   2 cups buttermilk
1 teaspoon baking soda

Mix the cornmeal, flour, salt and soda together in a medium bowl. Add melted shortening and sugar to the cornmeal mixture, stirring in the buttermilk until combined. Pour into a greased 9x5x3-inch loaf pan. Bake at 375° for 45-60 minutes. Serve hot with butter. Yields 1 loaf.

The original recipe used a little less than ½ cup lard.

YOUR OWN CORN MUFFIN MIX
Can Substitute for 3 Packages of 8½-ounce Corn Muffin Mix

2 cups + 1 tablespoon all-pur-
    pose flour
2 cups coarse, yellow cornmeal
²/₃ cup shortening

¾ cup sugar
2 tablespoons baking powder
1½ teaspoons salt

Combine flour, meal and shortening with a spoon or pastry cutter; mix in sugar, baking powder and salt. Keep mixture sealed in a cool place.

Variation:

CORN MUFFINS: Add 1 beaten egg and ⅓ to ½ cup milk to 1¾ cups Corn Muffin Mix just until combined. Bake at 400° for 12-15 minutes in 12 greased small muffin pans. Yields 12 small muffins.

BAKER'S IDEA: Substitute 1¾ cups mix for 1 (8½-ounce) package corn muffin mix.

GOLDEN CORN STICKS OR MUFFINS

1 cup boiling water
1 cup self-rising cornmeal
½ cup milk

2 tablespoons oil or melted butter
1 egg, beaten

Oil corn stick pans with approximately 1 ½ teaspoons oil brushed over each section. Place pans in oven to heat just before using.

Combine water with cornmeal in a medium bowl. Add milk, oil and egg. Mix well and pour into hot, oiled iron corn stick pans or in greased muffin pans. Fill pans half full with batter. Use a ladle or spoon. Bake at 475° for 18-20 minutes until golden brown. Yields 16 corn sticks or 12 muffins. Serve hot.

BRAN CORN STICKS OR MUFFINS

3 tablespoons margarine or
    shortening
2 tablespoons sugar
1 egg, beaten
1 cup milk

¾ cup bran buds cereal
½ cup cornmeal
1 cup self-rising flour
1½ teaspoons baking powder

Cream shortening and sugar in a medium bowl; add egg, milk, bran and cornmeal. Combine flour and baking powder; mix with milk mixture only until blended. Pour into hot, well-greased pans, filling only half full. Bake at 400° for 18-20 minutes or until light brown. Makes 24 corn sticks or 12 muffins.

MARY Q'S HUSH PUPPIES

A Flavorful Feast with Husband Zeke's Cooked Fresh Fish

1 cup self-rising cornmeal
1 onion, chopped, about ½ cup

milk

Mix cornmeal, onions and just enough milk (about ½ cup) to hold dough together. Ease by spoonfuls into 375° oil, deep enough to cover; brown on both sides. Center should be done.

HURRIED BAKER: Add enough milk to make a pancake like batter. Pour by tablespoonfuls onto a hot greased griddle. Turn to lightly brown both sides.

MAW'S HUSH PUPPIES

1 egg
1 cup milk
1 cup self-rising corn meal

1 cup baking mix
1 cup chopped onion

Beat egg with milk in a medium bowl; combine with cornmeal and baking mix. Fold in onions; form into walnut-shaped balls. Cook in 375° oil, deep enough to cover, until light golden brown and cooked in center. Drain on paper covered pans.

Pass the fish and feast!!

Variations: The perfect addition to a vegetable dinner.

HUSH PUPPY BREAD: Add 3 tablespoons margarine, melted in a 10-inch heavy pan or iron skillet, 1 teaspoon dill and 2 tablespoons parsley. Blend only until combined. Pour into prepared hot pan. Bake at 400° for 25-30 minutes or until a light golden brown. Butter top of bread; serve hot. Vary with 1½ cups grated cheese sprinkled over hot bread.

Make a full meal with fish, carrot-cabbage-cole slaw and mixed fresh fruit. *The puppies are guaranteed not to bark.*

CHEESE HUSH PUPPY BREAD: Cover baked, hot bread with 1½ cups grated cheddar cheese or jalapeno cheese.

SAUSAGE-CHEESE HUSH PUPPY BREAD: Add ½ pound sausage or sliced sausage links, cooked and drained. After baking, cover with 1½ cups grated cheddar cheese.

Vegetable soup and a fruit salad makes this a balanced meal. Just call, "come and get it".

WAFFLES AND PANCAKES

More than breakfast fare...

Supper often includes waffles and pancakes. Add Canadian bacon and baked fruit to the mouth-watering aroma from the steamy waffle iron.

Make batter ahead to save time before the meal, adding more liquid if too thick. Usually for a light pancake, a thinner, smaller amount (not over ¼ cup) of batter works best.

Can use less shortening in the batter when pre-treating the griddle and waffle grids with cooking spray or lightly brushing with oil.

For interest and variety, add small amounts of chopped fruits or vegetables to a favorite batter. Top the hot cooked pancakes and waffles with fresh fruit or frozen, thawed fruit, applesauce with a dash of cinnamon or fruit-flavored yogurt.

FAVORITE ALL-PURPOSE WAFFLES

Choose a special variation

2 egg whites
2 egg yolks
1 cup all-purpose flour
½ teaspoon baking soda

½ teaspoon salt
3 tablespoons melted butter or oil
1 cup buttermilk

Beat egg whites in mixer bowl until soft peaks form; beat in yolks on low speed until blended. Combine flour mixed with soda and salt alternately with oil mixed with buttermilk. Pour batter in a pre-heated waffle iron baking as usual, or vary waffles by sprinkling a choice of grated cheese, chocolate chips, chopped pecans, cooked sliced sausages or cooked crumbled bacon over the batter. Close lid to bake until a medium or crisp doneness. Yields 4 (7-inch) waffles.

BAKER'S IDEA: For lighter waffles, fold combined ingredients into stiffly beaten egg whites. For richer, sweeter waffles, add 2 tablespoons sugar and substitute sour cream for buttermilk.

Variation:

WHOLE WHEAT WAFFLES: Substitute whole wheat for ½ of all-purpose flour.

RAE'S OAT-BRAN WAFFLES: Substitute oat bran for ½ of all-purpose four. Fold combined ingredients into stiffly beaten egg whites.

FOUR GRAIN WAFFLES OR PANCAKES

A Healthy Winner

1¼ cup whole wheat flour
¼ cup buckwheat flour
¼ cup millet flour
¼ cup barley flour
½ teaspoon salt
1 tablespoon baking powder

2¾ cups buttermilk, more buttermilk may be needed for a medium thick batter
2 eggs, beaten
¼ cup cooking oil

Combine the flours with salt and baking powder in a medium bowl; stir in buttermilk beaten with eggs and oil. Add more buttermilk as necessary to form a pourable batter for the waffle iron or griddle. Ladle batter into hot waffle iron. Serve crisp and hot. Yields 8 (7-inch) waffles.

Reduce shortening to 2 tablespoons for pancakes. Cook on a hot, lightly greased griddle. Brown on both sides.

Variations:

Use any combination of whole grain flours; mix or match as desired. Rye and whole wheat would be a winning combination.

OATMEAL WAFFLES AND PANCAKES

Light and Nutritious

1 cup oats, quick variety
¾ cup all-purpose flour
2 tablespoons sugar
1 teaspoon baking powder
½ teaspoon baking soda

½ teaspoon salt
2 egg yolks
1½ cups buttermilk
3 tablespoons margarine, melted
2 egg whites

In a large bowl, stir together oats, flour, sugar, baking powder, soda and salt; stir in egg yolks beaten with buttermilk and margarine. Fold in stiffly beaten egg whites. Bake in hot waffle iron. Yields 4 (7-inch) waffles.

Reduce margarine to 2 tablespoons for pancakes; bake on hot, oiled griddle.

BAKING MIX WAFFLES AND PANCAKES

WAFFLES AND PANCAKES: Combine ingredients; pour in hot waffle iron or on a hot griddle. Yields 4 (7-inch) waffles and 12 pancakes.

1½ cups baking mix
2 teaspoons sugar
2 tablespoons oil, waffles only

1 egg, beaten
1⅓ cups milk

CAMPER PANCAKES: Combine ingredients; thin batter as needed with water. Yields 6 small pancakes.

1 cup baking mix
1 egg

¾ cup water

CAMPER PEANUT BUTTER PANCAKES: Add 3 tablespoons crunchy peanut butter to the ingredients.

BUTTERMILK GRIDDLE CAKES
Hearty!

2 cups all-purpose flour
1 teaspoon baking soda
½ teaspoon salt
1 tablespoon sugar
2 eggs, well beaten

2 cups buttermilk
2 tablespoons melted shortening
1 chopped tart apple or sweet-
    ened berries (about 1 cup),
    optional

Mix together flour, soda, salt and sugar in a large bowl; combine with eggs, buttermilk and shortening. Stir in fruit. Bake on hot griddle. Serve with butter and warm apple syrup. Makes about 18 griddle cakes.

Variations:

SAUSAGE GRIDDLE CAKES: Fold ½ cup cooked and drained sausage into batter.

CLAM GRIDDLE CAKES: Omit fruit. Drain 1 (6.5-ounce) can minced clams; reserve liquid. Omit sugar; increase melted shortening to ¼ cup. Substitute up to half clam liquid for half of the buttermilk. Fold clams into batter with 1 teaspoon onion flakes. Serve with Peggy's Cocktail Sauce (page 214) or salsa and sour cream or nonfat yogurt with a sprinkling of crumbled, crisp cooked bacon.

BAKER'S IDEA: Flavorful, unusual Saturday brunch.

RICE GRIDDLE CAKES
Save Leftover Rice; No Fat added

¾ cup all-purpose flour
1 tablespoon sugar
2½ teaspoons baking powder
½ teaspoon salt

2 eggs, beaten
½ cup milk
1 cup drained, cooked rice

Combine flour, sugar, baking powder and salt in a medium bowl; stir in eggs beaten with milk and rice. Drop by spoonfuls on a hot greased griddle. Turn when tops are bubbly; lightly brown on both sides. Yields 12 small pancakes.

With a few revisions, the Rice Griddle Cake recipe can be a fried Speedy New Orleans Calas, found in the doughnut section.

Variation:

RICE WAFFLES: Add 3 tablespoons melted butter to the Rice Griddle Cake recipe. Proceed with the waffle iron directions. Makes 4 (7-inch) waffles.

BREAD CRUMB PANCAKES
Thrifty and Nutritious

1 cup dry bread crumbs or ²/₃ cup
 cooked leftover cereal
²/₃ cup all-purpose flour
2 teaspoons baking powder
2 tablespoons sugar

½ teaspoon salt
1 ½ cups milk
2 tablespoons butter
1 egg, beaten

Combine bread crumbs, flour, baking powder, sugar and salt in a medium bowl; mix in milk, butter and egg. Pour on hot griddle; turn when bubbly to barely brown other side. Serve hot with butter and syrup. Yields 12 pancakes.

Variations:

SPICY FRUIT BREAD CRUMB PANCAKES: Add ½ teaspoon cinnamon and ⅓ cup raisins or other soft, diced, dried fruit to the batter.

BACON OR HAM BREAD CRUMB PANCAKES: Add ½ cup cooked, crumbled bacon or ½ cup finely chopped, cooked ham to the batter.

YVONNE'S WHOLE WHEAT PANCAKE MIX
Start a Hearty, Healthy Morning!

2 cups whole wheat flour
2 cups all-purpose flour
1 teaspoon salt
1½ cups rolled oats (optional)

2 tablespoons baking powder
½ cup wheat germ
2 tablespoons sugar

Combine all ingredients; refrigerate mix in a sealed plastic bag.

YVONNE'S WHOLE WHEAT PANCAKES: Whisk 3 tablespoons cooking oil, 1 egg and 1 cup milk; mix in 1 ⅓ cups Yvonne's Pancake Mix. Pour batter on hot oiled griddle. When bubbles form, turn pancakes. Bake until light brown. Serve immediately with fruit and yogurt. Yields about 12 pancakes.

YVONNE'S WHOLE WHEAT PUMPKIN PANCAKES: Combine 1 ½ cups Yvonne's Pancake Mix with the following ingredients:

¼ teaspoon ginger
¼ teaspoon cinnamon
¼ teaspoon nutmeg
1½ cups milk

1 egg, beaten
2 tablespoons cooking oil
½ cup drained pumpkin pulp

Cook on hot oiled griddle. When bubbles form, turn to brown on other side. Serve with hot sliced apples, baked with maple syrup, and whipped topping. Yields about 16 pancakes.

Yvonne Hogland's pre-school classes loved munching on these as a fall treat, but her family requests these nutritious pancakes all year.

BUTTERMILK CORNMEAL HOTCAKES

1½ cups cornmeal
½ cup all-purpose flour
1½ teaspoons salt
1 teaspoon baking soda

2¼ cups buttermilk
3 tablespoons melted butter
2 eggs

Combine cornmeal, flour, salt and soda; mix with buttermilk, beaten with butter and eggs. The batter should be a thick cream consistency. Spoon 2 tablespoons of mixture on hot lightly-oiled griddle or frying pan. Cook until light golden brown; turn once to lightly brown other side. Yields about 18 pancakes.

Pour on hot blackberry or blueberry syrup, complete with the real fruit. For a quick Sunday night supper, spoon undiluted, hot cream of chicken soup combined with chopped chicken, celery, onion, green pepper and 1 teaspoon curry powder over the pancakes. Sprinkle tops with cheese.

RIVERDALE MILL'S BUCKWHEAT PANCAKES

Hearty Breakfast for Champions

1 cup buckwheat flour	½ teaspoon salt
1 cup whole wheat flour	1 package dry yeast
1 teaspoon baking powder	2 eggs
½ teaspoon baking soda	2 cups milk

Combine flours, baking powder, soda, salt and dry yeast in a large bowl. Mix in eggs beaten with milk until smooth, forming a thin batter. Refrigerate overnight. Add more liquid if needed; bake on a hot greased griddle. Serve with butter and sorghum. Yields 18 pancakes.

Riverdale Mill is a unique mill dating back to 1858. The J. L. McCoy family is currently restoring and operating the mill out of Knoxville, Tennessee. Buckwheat can also be found in many grocery and health food stores.

HURRIED BAKER: Omit yeast and add 1 more teaspoon baking powder. Can cook immediately!

BARBARA ANNA'S BAKED APPLE PANCAKE

Treat Yourself to Brunch

Pancake:	**Filling:**
½ cup all-purpose flour	1 tart apple, sliced (¼-inch)
⅓ cup milk	1 tablespoon brown sugar
2 large eggs	**Topping:**
1 tablespoon sugar	1 teaspoon lemon juice
⅛ teaspoon nutmeg	2 tablespoons powdered sugar
3 tablespoons butter	

Combine flour, milk, eggs, nutmeg and sugar in blender. Melt butter in a 9-inch oven-proof skillet; combine butter with blender ingredients. Arrange apple slices in bottom of skillet; return to oven until butter is hot and begins to sizzle. Pour egg mixture over apples; sprinkle brown sugar on top. Bake at 425° for 15-20 minutes or until puffy and a light golden brown.

Sprinkle with lemon juice and powdered sugar. Serve with marmalade or syrup. A feast for one. Serving two? Add sausage, cheese grits, and coffee. Barbara Ann Straker serves this anytime-of-the-day delight at her home in beautiful La Jolla, on the ocean in Southern California.

ALL-PURPOSE CRÉPE
Do not use batter for one hour
Add elegance to Hors d'oeuvres, Salads, Entrees and Desserts

3 eggs
1½ teaspoons sugar, optional for
 non-sweet crépes
⅛ teaspoon salt

1½ cups milk
2 tablespoons butter
1½ cups all-purpose flour

Use blender or food processor to beat all ingredients until smooth. Let the batter stand for several hours or overnight before cooking the crépes. Brush a crépe or omelet pan or small skillet with vegetable oil or melted butter; heat until hot, not smoking. Test proper griddle heat by sprinkling on water from wet hands; water will sizzle at proper temperature. Add about two tablespoons batter. Move the pan to coat with the batter. When crépe is set (about one minute), turn it over by gently moving a spatula under the crépe. Cook on other side approximately ½ minute. Place the crépe on a towel, stack to use or place between waxed paper to freeze. Makes approximately 30 (5½-inch) crépes. Don't be discouraged if your first crépes are not perfect thin, white, pancake-like crépes. All the crépe will not show unless it is a flat sandwich crépe.

Variations:

SILVER DOLLAR CRÉPES: Increase milk about ¼ cup to make a thinner batter. Pour small amount of batter on hot, greased griddle to form a 3 or 4-inch crépe.

MEAT CRÉPES: Add cheese with cooked sausage, a spicy hotdog or any thick meat or seafood filling. Spoon about 1 tablespoon of filling at the lower end of crépe; roll the crépe, placing seam side down. Cut crépes in small pieces or use silver dollar size crépes. Serve crépes cold or hot with a salad. Bake chicken or seafood crépes with a cheese or cream sauce to serve hot. Crépes with a sauce can be prepared in the morning. Refrigerate until time to bake for dinner. Bake at 350°until hot, about 15 - 20 minutes.

SANDWICH CRÉPES: Place an 8-inch crépe on each individual serving plate, spread with salad dressing, adding flat lettuce leaves, sliced tomatoes and thin-sliced chicken. Cover with another crépe, spread with horseradish sauce layered with thin-sliced roast beef and thin sliced swiss cheese. Add another crépe, spread with salad dressing adding thin-sliced cheddar cheese and strips of crisply cooked bacon. Top with another crépe. When served, spoon hot cheese sauce or cold Thousand Island dressing over the sandwich. Garnish with sweet onion rings and olives. Serve with a knife and fork.

BACON-CHEESE CRÉPES

Prepare ahead; bake before serving

½ pound sharp cheddar cheese, grated
½ cup cooked, chopped, crisp bacon or cooked, chopped ham
1 small onion, finely chopped
1 green pepper, finely chopped
2 teaspoons brown, spicy mustard, optional
½ teaspoon worcestershire sauce
3 tablespoons mayonnaise
20 (5½-inch) crépes

Combine all ingredients in a medium bowl. Divide filling into 20 parts. Place filling evenly across lower end of crépe; roll up the crépe. Place seam side down on greased baking pan. Bake in a 375° oven only until cheese melts, about 15-20 minutes. Cut crépes in 3 pieces if serving as hors d'oeuvres. Serve with a honey mustard sauce.

CHERRY CHEESE CRÉPES

Impressive do-ahead dessert

Sauce:

2 tablespoons butter
2 tablespoons all-purpose flour
2 (1 pound) cans pitted dark sweet cherries in heavy syrup
½ cup granulated sugar
1 teaspoon lemon juice

Filling

1 tablespoon milk
1 (8-ounce) package cream cheese
1 teaspoon almond extract
½ cup powdered sugar
1 recipe crépes
whipped cream

Melt butter, stir in flour over low heat until smooth. Add syrup from cherries, sugar to taste and lemon juice. Cook until thickened; add cherries.

Beat filling ingredients until smooth. Place a tablespoon of filling evenly across lower end of crépe; roll up crépe, placing seam side down. Heat crépes; serve hot with heated cherry sauce. Top with whipped cream.

POPOVERS

Steam Does the Rising — Low in Fat
Almost a crépe batter in a muffin pan

2 large eggs
1 cup milk
1 tablespoon melted butter or
  cooking oil

1 cup all-purpose flour
¼ teaspoon salt

Combine all ingredients in blender or mixer until smooth and bubbly. Fill generously greased oven-proof custard cups, popover pans or muffin pans ½ full of batter. Heavy, greased metal pans can be heated in the oven before adding batter to speed baking. Bake at 400° for 15 minutes; to prevent falling while baking, do not open oven door. Lower temperature to 375°; bake 15-20 minutes longer. Can check on popovers the last few minutes. Light golden brown popovers hold their shape after popping over. If not served immediately, make a slit with a knife for steam to escape. Makes 6 muffin size popovers.

Serve with fresh fruit butter or cut off top and fill with eggs or meat. Can sprinkle tops with powdered sugar when served plain if desired.

FRUIT BUTTER: Combine, in the blender, ¼ cup strawberries or other fresh fruit, 1 stick softened butter and enough powdered sugar for desired sweetness and consistency. Chill and serve.

Variations:

WHOLE GRAIN POPOVERS: Use ½ whole wheat flour and ½ all-purpose flour.

CHEESE OR MEAT POPOVERS: Add ¼ cup Parmesan cheese or ½ cup cooked, well-drained and chopped ham, beef or pork.

This is a great addition to a "veggie" or salad plate.

YORKSHIRE PUDDING: Use popover recipe. Refrigerate batter until beef roast is done. Pour 2-3 tablespoons meat drippings in a greased 9-inch round pan; pour batter into pan. Bake at 400° for 30 minutes or until pudding is puffed and brown on top and bottom. Extra beef juice can be poured over the pudding when served if desired. Cut into squares; serve immediately with beef.

MUFFINS

All Ages Delight in these Flavorful Bites

Call them muffins or gems, named for old fashioned fluted muffin pans, they are in step with today's fast pace.

Usually the dry ingredients are mixed separately from the liquid ingredients before combining them. Add beaten liquid ingredients all at once, stirring just until moistened. Over mixing causes a tough, heavy muffin. Do not beat! The batter is supposed to be a little lumpy. Lumps disappear in baking.

Unless using paper-lined muffin cups, generously grease muffin pans, grease and flour or coat with baking spray. Fill prepared muffin pans ⅔ full. Hold spoon close to the middle of muffin pan, pushing dough off spoon with a flat knife or use a measuring cup with a pouring lip. Muffin batter, as sweet quick breads, should be moderately thick, not too thick or thin. Fill empty muffin cups about ½ full of water in a partially filled muffin pan.

Regulate serving size by baking small or regular muffins. The small size muffin eats and bakes faster - this way you can sample more varieties! Don't forget to shorten the baking time. Test for doneness by the light brown color and a wooden pick inserted in muffin center being batter free. If muffins stick, loosen around the pan edge with a knife. Serve hot or cool on wire racks. Freeze on a baking sheet; wrap in plastic or foil to store in plastic freezer bags. Thaw for snacks, meals or gifts.

When baking muffins ahead to freeze for a special event, cook only until done. Place back in muffin tins to thaw and reheat. Taste like freshly baked muffins!

Let's start with the muffins used mainly at mealtime.

MEALTIME MUFFINS

QUICK DILLY HERB MUFFIN ROLLS

1 cup self-rising flour
1/8 teaspoon garlic powder
1/2 teaspoon onion flakes
3/4 teaspoon dill seeds

1/2 teaspoon parsley
2 tablespoons Parmesan cheese
1/3 cup butter
3/4 cup yogurt

Combine flour, 4 dried herbs and cheese in a medium bowl; mix in butter and yogurt only until moistened. Fill small, greased muffin pans 2/3 full. Bake at 375° for 12-15 minutes. Yields about 1½ dozen small muffins.

Variation:

Richer Herb Roll: Substitute ½ cup sour cream for the ½ cup yogurt.

QUICK SOUR CREAM GEMS

2 cups baking mix

1½ cups sour cream or plain
    yogurt

Combine baking mix and sour cream. Fill greased small muffin pans 2/3's full. Bake at 400° until a light brown. Brush surface with melted butter if desired. Yields 2 dozen.

BRAN MUFFINS, ETC. ETC. ETC.
Refrigerate Covered Batter 3-4 Weeks

3/4 cup cooking oil
2 cups boiling water
6 cups shreds of 100% wheat
    bran cereal, divided
5 cups all-purpose flour

5 teaspoons baking soda
1½ teaspoons salt
4 eggs
2 cups sugar
1 quart buttermilk

Place oil, boiling water and 3 cups of bran in a bowl while measuring other ingredients. In a large bowl, combine flour, soda and salt. Beat eggs and sugar until light; add eggs, buttermilk and bran mixture to the flour, stirring until moistened. Mix in remaining 3 cups of bran only until combined. fill greased muffin pans 2/3's full; bake for 15-20 minutes at 400°. Yields approximately 14 cups batter and 64 muffins.

Not so many muffins unless you bake at midnight, as the aroma draws folks to your kitchen. Refrigerate extra batter for fresh hot muffins. Freeze baked muffins, in plastic bags, to serve later; thaw when there is no time to bake.

ETC. ETC. ETC. - Now for the fun! Substitutions and Variations follow for the total recipe.

Charlotte's Oatmeal Bran Muffins: Substitute 2 cups quick cooking oats for 2 cups of bran added to the oil and water.

Fig-Nut Bran Muffins: Add 1 cup chopped nuts and 1 cup chopped, dried or fresh figs.

Raisin Bran Muffins: Add 1 or 2 cups raisins.

Molasses Bran Muffins: Add ½ cup molasses.

Honey Bran Muffins: Add ½ cup honey.

The following additions are for **1¼ cups batter,** yielding 6 regular size muffins or 12 small muffins. Bake regular muffins 15-20 minutes and small muffins for 10-12 minutes.

Apple-Cinnamon Bran Muffins: Add ½ cup finely-chopped, peeled apples tossed in a mixture of ¼ teaspoon cinnamon and 2 tablespoons sugar.

Blueberry Bran Muffins: Add ⅓ cup blueberries.

Banana Bran Muffins: Add ¼ cup mashed bananas.

Raisin Bran Muffins: Add ¼ cup raisins.

Date Bran Muffins: Add ¼ cup chopped dates, sprinkled with powdered sugar to help separate them.

Surprise Muffins: Add different ingredients to each individual muffin batter. For example, add 3 slices of banana, a few blueberries, raisins, date pieces, chopped apples to different muffin cup sections. Allow for these additions in filling pans with batter; do not exceed ⅔'s full. Good children's project!

THE WHOLE BOX BRAN MUFFINS
Hurry-Up Muffins

4¹/₃ cups all-purpose flour
1½ teaspoons salt
5 teaspoons baking soda
2 cups sugar
¾ cup cooking oil

4 eggs
1 quart buttermilk
1 box raisin bran flakes cereal
 (15-ounce)

A similar recipe to "Bran Muffins Etc. Etc. Etc.", adding raisin bran flakes instead of the shreds of wheat bran cereal with boiling water.

In a large bowl, combine flour, salt and soda. Beat sugar, oil and eggs until light; add with buttermilk to the flour mixture, mixing just until moist. Stir in bran flakes only until combined. Refrigerate batter or fill greased muffin pans ²/₃'s full. Bake at 400° for 15 minutes. Yields about 3 dozen muffins.

HEALTH OATMEAL MUFFINS
Low-Fat

¼ cup wheat germ
¾ cup whole wheat flour
1 cup all-purpose flour
1 teaspoon baking powder
1½ teaspoons baking soda
½ teaspoon salt
²/₃ cup sugar
2 cups quick cooking oats

2 cups buttermilk
2 eggs, beaten
½ cup molasses
¼ cup cooking oil
²/₃ cup raisins
²/₃ cup chopped nuts
²/₃ cup toasted sunflower seeds

Mix wheat germ, flours, baking powder, soda, salt, sugar and oats in a large mixing bowl. Stir in buttermilk combined with eggs, molasses and oil just until moistened. Fold in the raisins, nuts and seeds. Pour into greased muffin pans, filling ²/₃'s full; bake at 400° for 20 minutes. Yields about 3 dozen muffins.

What a "full of energy" after school snack! Homework won't be so bad after a power lift from this bread.

HAVE-IT-YOUR-WAY SAVORY MUFFINS

Bite-Size Yums

2 cups baking mix (lightly spoon into cup)
1 egg
¾ cup milk

Beat egg and milk in a medium bowl; add baking mix stirring only until moistened. Variations can be added to the batter — choose a favorite or experiment. Add ingredients to small, well-greased muffin pans. Bake at 400° for 12-15 minutes until a pale brown. Yields 24 small muffins.

Variations:

SURPRISE OLIVE-PECAN MUFFINS: Cover bottom of each small greased muffin section with chopped pecans; cover with 2 chopped, pimento stuffed, Spanish olives. Add batter almost to the top; top raw batter with a pecan half.

Total recipe: Add ¾ cup chopped pecans and ½ cup chopped olives, filling muffin pans ²/₃'s full.

BACON-CHEESE MUFFINS: Cover bottom of each small greased muffin section with finely crumbled, crisply cooked bacon; cover with a layer of grated cheddar cheese. Add batter almost to the top.

Total recipe: Add ½ cup crumbled bacon and ¾ cup grated cheese to the total batter, filling muffin pans ²/₃'s full. Drained, crumbled, cooked sausage and chopped cooked ham can be substituted for the bacon.

GREEN CHILIES AND CHEESE MUFFINS: Cover bottom of each small greased muffin section with drained, chopped, mild, canned green chilies; cover with a layer of grated cheddar cheese. Add batter almost to the top.

Total recipe: Add ½ cup chilies and ¾ cup grated cheese to the total batter, filling muffin pans ²/₃'s full.

POPCORN MUFFINS
Recycle the Leftover Popcorn!

1½ cups baking mix (page 121)
1 tablespoon brown sugar, packed down
¾ cup chopped, popped popcorn*

1 egg
¾ cup milk
⅓ cup crunchy peanut butter

Combine baking mix, sugar, and popcorn in a medium bowl; add egg beaten with milk.Stir in peanut butter,mixing only until moistened. Fill small greased muffin pans, approximately ¾ full. Bake at 400° for10-12 minutes, until pale brown. Yields 24 small muffins.

*Chop only fully popped corn with food processor; discard any hard pieces.

BASIC SWEET MUFFINS

GRANDMOTHER CARTER'S OLD FASHIONED DROP CAKES

After eating a delicious blueberry muffin in a Birmingham, Alabama gourmet restaurant, I tried duplicating the muffin. After much work, I accidentally discovered my Grandmother's recipe written on an old grocery list. Eureka... I had rediscovered that same wonderful muffin.

½ cup margarine
1½ cups sugar
2 eggs
1 cup milk
1 teaspoon vanilla extract

¼ teaspoon lemon extract
2 or 3 drops coconut extract
½ teaspoon salt
4 teaspoons baking powder
2 ¾ cups all-purpose flour

Cream shortening and sugar until light and smooth in a large bowl; beat in eggs, milk and extracts. Mix together salt, baking powder and flour; add to creamed mixture just until moistened. Fill greased muffin pans ⅔'s full. Bake at 400° for 15-20 minutes. Yields 18 muffins.

Variations:

Applesauce muffins: add one teaspoon applesauce in center of each unbaked muffin batter in muffin pans.

Blueberry Muffins: Fold 1½ cups frozen, thawed and drained blueberries into the batter before pouring into muffin pans.

Ol' Fashioned Flavor Touch: Fold 1½ teaspoons grated orange or lemon rind and 1 teaspoon freshly grated nutmeg into batter.

Old Fashioned Sugar Topping: ¼ teaspoon freshly grated nutmeg (may substitute dried ground spice) mixed with 3 tablespoons granulated sugar. Sprinkle on top of muffin before baking.

BLACK WALNUT BLUEBERRY MUFFINS
Delightful flavor Contrast — Walnuts and Blueberries

2½ cups all-purpose flour
¾ cup sugar
1 tablespoon baking powder
½ teaspoon salt
½ cup butter
¾ cup chopped black walnuts

2 eggs
1 cup milk
1 teaspoon vanilla
1½ cups fresh or frozen blueberries

Combine flour, sugar, baking powder and salt in a large bowl; cut in the butter until cornmeal consistency. Add chopped nuts. Beat eggs with milk and vanilla ; combine with the flour mixture only until moistened. Gently fold blueberries into the batter. Pour batter into greased muffin pans filled ⅔'s full. Bake at 400° for 20 minutes or until a light golden brown. Yields 18 muffins.

FOOD PROCESSOR ORANGE MUFFINS
Fast with a food processor and small muffin pans for baking.

1 cup sugar
2 eggs
4 tablespoons margarine
1 whole orange, thin skinned
¾ cup raisins, white or dark
¼ cup nuts, small pieces

1 cup buttermilk
½ teaspoon vanilla flavoring
1 teaspoon almond flavoring
½ teaspoon baking powder
1 teaspoon baking soda
2½ cups all-purpose flour

Blend sugar, eggs and margarine in blender or food processor. Add one orange, cut in sections with seeds removed, and raisins. Thoroughly chop; add nuts to chop, leaving in small pieces. Combine processed ingredients with buttermilk and flavorings. Mix baking powder, soda and flour together in a large bowl; stir in remaining ingredients only until moistened. Spoon into greased muffin pans, filling ⅔'s full. Bake at 375° for approximately 20 minutes for standard size muffins or until light brown. Makes approximately 18 regular size muffins or 36 small muffins.

FAST-BAKING MIX MUFFINS

HOT CROSS MUFFINS
No time for traditional yeast Hot Cross Buns?

2 cups baking mix
¼ cup sugar
¼ teaspoon nutmeg
¼ teaspoon mace
2 beaten eggs

¾ cup milk
3 tablespoons oil
½ teaspoon grated orange rind
¼ teaspoon grated lemon rind
½ cup soft or plumped raisins

Combine baking mix, sugar and spices in a large bowl; stir in remaining ingredients only until moistened. Fill greased muffin pans ⅔'s full. Bake in 400° oven for 15-20 minutes or until a light brown. Cool; brush tops with light corn syrup. Make a powdered sugar icing cross on top of each muffin when cool. Yields 12 muffins.

Let children help make these for sharing with friends and neighbors at Easter! Pop in plastic sandwich bags; tie with colored ribbon.

QUICK CRANBERRY MUFFINS
Makes 2 dozen small muffins

½ cup sugar
2 tablespoons margarine
1 egg
1 cup milk

1 cup chopped raw cranberries
2 cups baking mix
½ teaspoon grated orange rind

Combine sugar, margarine, egg and milk in food processor; add cranberries only to chop in pieces. In a large bowl, stir all ingredients with baking mix only until moistened. Fill the greased muffin pans ⅔'s full. Bake at 400° for 15-20 minutes. Yields 12 muffins.

Can substitute 1 cup whole cranberry sauce for raw cranberries and the sugar in this recipe.

EASY PEAR MUFFINS

Use canned or fresh fruit

1 cup baking mix
¼ cup sugar
¼ teaspoon nutmeg
⅛ teaspoon cinnamon
¼ teaspoon ginger
⅓ cup liquid (could be juice from
fruit or a compatible fruit juice)

1 beaten egg
¼ teaspoon orange or lemon
rind, grated
¾ cup chopped, drained pears or
peaches

Combine mix, sugar and spices in a medium bowl; stir in remaining ingredients only until moistened. Fill greased muffin pans ⅔'s full. Bake at 400°, for 15-20 minutes, until light golden brown. Yields 6 muffins.

FAST SPICY-PLUM MUFFINS

Muffins needed; keep baby food on hand!

1 cup baking mix
½ cup sugar
½ teaspoon allspice
¼ teaspoon cinnamon
¼ cup oil

2 eggs, beaten
1 (6-ounce) jar junior baby food,
plums
½ cup chopped nuts
⅓ cup raisins

Combine baking mix, sugar and spices in a medium bowl; stir in remaining ingredients only until moistened. Pour into greased small muffin pans filling ⅔'s full. Bake at 375° for 20 minutes until a light golden brown. Yields 36 small muffins.

APRICOT-ORANGE MUFFINS
Yields 40 Flavorful Bite-size Yums

²/₃ cup orange juice
1½ tablespoons oil
1 egg
¹/₃ cup sugar
2 cups baking mix

¹/₃ cup chopped, toasted pecans
¹/₃ cup plumped, chopped dried
   apricots
¹/₃ cup apricot preserves

Whisk juice, oil, egg and sugar in a large bowl; stir in remaining ingredients only until moistened. Pour into well-greased muffin pans, filling a little less than ½ full. Bake at 400° for 15-20 minutes or 10-12 minutes for small size muffins. While hot in pan, pour 2 teaspoons sauce over regular size muffins and 1 teaspoon sauce over small muffins. Yields 20 muffins.

BAKER'S IDEA: Can substitute apricot nectar for water and juice in sauce and in muffin batter. Apricot preserves can be spooned over hot muffins while in the pan instead of the sauce.

LIQUID ORANGE SAUCE: Combine in a large microwavable bowl ¹/₃ cup frozen orange juice, thawed, ²/₃ cup water and ¾ cup sugar. Stir and microwave on high for 2 minutes or until sugar melts. Refrigerate extra sauce for pancakes or french toast.

APPLESAUCE BREAKFAST PUFFS
Add to a Good Morning!

¼ cup sugar
1 teaspoon cinnamon
½ cup applesauce
¼ cup milk
1 egg

2 tablespoons cooking oil
2 cups baking mix
3 tablespoons chopped, peeled
   apples
Melted butter

Beat sugar, cinnamon, applesauce, milk, egg and cooking oil in a large bowl; add baking mix and apples stirring only until moistened. Fill greased small muffin pans ½ full. Bake at 375° for 10-12 minutes or until a pale brown. Dip tops in spicy topping. Yields 48 small puffs.

BAKER'S IDEA: Vary topping by substituting powdered sugar for granulated sugar. Toss warm muffins in powdered sugar and spices.

SPICY TOPPING: Combine 1 teaspoon ground cinnamon and 1 cup granulated sugar.

SALLY LUNN MUFFINS
Delicate base for strawberry short cake

These colonial quick muffins are a version of the English Sally Lunn bread found in the yeast bread section. Wouldn't Sally Lunn, who legend says, sold these buns on the streets of England, be pleased that we are still making her bread for toast or tea?

¼ cup butter or margarine
½ cup sugar
2 beaten eggs
2 cups all-purpose flour

¾ cup milk
½ teaspoon salt
1 tablespoon baking powder

Cream butter and sugar in a large bowl; beat in the eggs until light and thickened. Beat in the milk. Mix in the flour combined with salt and baking powder only until moistened. Fill greased muffin pans ⅔'s full; bake at 400° for 15-20 minutes or until a pale brown. Yields 1 dozen.

For a lighter, more authentic effect, separate the eggs, beating only the yellows with the sugar. Beat the whites separately until stiff; fold in the batter until combined. Can bake in greased small bread pans. Bake at 375° for 25-30 minutes or until a wooden pick inserted in center is batter free. Cool on wire rack. Cut baked, fragile bread with a serrated bread knife.

REFRIGERATOR GINGER MUFFINS
Batter keeps 3 weeks covered and refrigerated

¾ cup margarine
1 cup sugar
4 eggs
1 cup molasses
1 cup buttermilk (can use sour
   cream)
4 cups all-purpose flour
1 teaspoon baking powder

2 teaspoons baking soda
½ teaspoon salt
¼ teaspoon nutmeg
3 teaspoons ginger
¼ teaspoon cinnamon
⅔ cup nuts
¾ cup raisins

In a large bowl, cream butter and sugar; beat in eggs, molasses and buttermilk. Combine flour with baking powder, soda, salt and spices; mix with the creamed mixture, only until moistened. Fold in nuts and raisins. Fill greased muffin pans ⅔ full. Bake at 400° for 15-20 minutes. Yields 3 dozen.

My Virginia Great-Grandmother would say, "Ginger cakes or muffins aid digestion!"

STRAWBERRY JAM MUFFINS
Old Fashioned Flavor

²/₃ cup margarine or shortening
1 cup sugar
2 eggs
1 teaspoon vanilla
1 cup strawberry jam (blackberry jam or apricot preserves)
1 cup buttermilk
2½ cups all-purpose flour

1 teaspoon salt
1 teaspoon baking soda
1½ teaspoons baking powder
½ teaspoon cinnamon
¼ teaspoon cloves
¼ teaspoon allspice
¼ teaspoon nutmeg
¼ teaspoon mace

In a large mixer bowl, cream the shortening and sugar; beat in eggs, adding the vanilla, jam and buttermilk. Combine flour with salt, soda, baking powder and 5 spices; add to the creamed mixture. Stir just until moistened. Fill greased muffin pans ²/₃ full. Bake at 375° for 15 minutes until light brown. Yields 1½ dozen muffins.

To glaze, spread extra preserves over hot muffins before removing from pan.

For a sweet treat, ice with Ruth's Caramel Frosting (page 72).

CANDY BAR MUFFINS
A Flavor Winner!

2 cups all-purpose flour
½ cup sugar
2 teaspoons baking powder
½ teaspoon salt
2 tablespoons cocoa
1 egg

1 cup buttermilk
¼ cup oil
½ teaspoon vanilla
3 regular size candy bars (chocolate covered nougate) or 2 (2.24 ounce) size

Thoroughly mix flour, sugar, baking powder, salt and cocoa; combine with egg beaten with buttermilk, oil and vanilla just until moistened. Break or chop candy bars into small pieces, folding into batter. Pour batter in greased muffin pans. Evenly distribute candy in the pans. Bake at 400° for 15-20 minutes. Yields 12 muffins.

ICE CREAM MUFFINS

Could this be having your cake and eating it too?
These are for children!

1 cup softened ice cream (whatever flavor your heart desires;
not diet ice cream)

½ teaspoon vanilla extract
½ teaspoon almond extract
1 cup self-rising flour

Mix ice cream with extracts in medium bowl; combine with flour only until combined. Fill paper lined or greased muffin pan ⅔'s full. Bake at 400° F. for 15-20 minutes. Yields 6 muffins.

Use specialty ice creams for the holidays. For the 4th of July, add ¼ cup chopped maraschino cherries and ¼ cup chopped blueberries. Swirl baked tops in white icing; add a small American flag.

Variation:

ICE CREAM CONE MUFFINS: Press folded strip of foil around small cake cones to stabilize cones in small muffin pans. Fill cones ⅔'s full with batter. Bake until a wooden pick inserted in center is batter free, about 20-25 minutes at 350°. Swirl top with a vanilla powdered sugar icing.

THE APPLE MUFFIN OR BREAD

Jump Start the Day!

½ cup butter
1 cup sugar
2 eggs
¼ cup buttermilk or yogurt
1 teaspoon vanilla
2 cups all-purpose flour
1 teaspoon cinnamon
1 teaspoon baking powder

1 teaspoon salt
1 teaspoon baking soda
2 cups finely chopped apples
½ cup chopped nuts
Topping:
½ cup sugar
½ teaspoon cinnamon

Cream butter and sugar in a large bowl; beat in eggs with buttermilk and vanilla. Stir in the flour combined with cinnamon, baking powder, salt and soda only until moist. Fold in apples and nuts; spoon into greased bread pans or greased muffin pans. Sprinkle batter with combined topping. Bake at 375° for 20-25 minutes for small loaves. Muffins bake at 400° for 15-20 minutes. Yields 18 muffins.

BAKER'S HINT: Food processor makes quick work of the chopping and creaming.

QUICK TEA BREADS AND COFFEE CAKES

Tea Breads are delectable and irresistible plain or filled with fruits, vegetables or seeds. Doneness can be tested in the middle of the bread with a wooden pick or cake tester being free of batter when removed. Pieces of baked fruit or chocolate sticking to tester do not count. The bread is usually done when the center of the loaf is firm to touch, the fragrance of the bread fills the room and the top of the bread is a light brown. Take out immediately. When the bread is visibly pulling away from the sides or the color is too dark, the bread is overly done. If this happens, remove from the pan as quickly as possible to cool on a rack. Allow sweet breads to remain in the pan for a few minutes if possible. Steam helps removing from the pan and cooling helps strengthen the loaf structure.

Use any small muffin pans for bite size portions and speedy baking. My favorite pans are the small, miniature loaf pans. Grease and flour pans, line with baking paper or coat with baking spray.

Glazes are optional on all breads. Slice thin to add a sweet taste to a meal or coffee, instead of using a dessert. Serve warm or cold.

Frozen sweet tea breads taste fresh from the oven when warmed. When warming with the microwave oven, use the defrost setting for a few seconds. The actual time depends on the size and temperature of the slices, as well as your particular microwave oven. When using microwave's full power, cover with a damp cloth. Revive those not-so-fresh sweet breads by toasting.

Need to lower the shortening content or sugar content of a favorite tea bread? Lower shortening by 1/3 of the total amount. Example: for 1 cup cooking oil (use 2/3 cup oil) or 1½ cups sugar (use 1 cup sugar). If volume or moisture is too low, replace oil removed with equal amounts of yogurt or applesauce. You must add yogurt or applesauce if reducing the shortening by more than 1/3. Plump all dried fruits by covering with hot water; microwave for 1 minute. Drain.

ANDREA'S FRUIT BREAD

Bananas, Strawberries, Peaches or Pears

1½ cups cooking oil
2½ cups sugar
3 eggs
3 cups all-purpose flour
1 teaspoon baking soda
¾ teaspoon salt
½ teaspoon cinnamon

1 tablespoon vanilla
½ cup buttermilk
1½ cups fruit (drained, peeled,
  cut or mashed-whatever is
  appropriate)
1 cup chopped nuts
1 (3½-ounce) can coconut

Beat oil, sugar and eggs in a large mixing bowl. Combine flour, soda and salt; add alternately with buttermilk and vanilla to the egg mixture. Mix in fruit, nuts and coconut. Bake in 3 greased and floured 9x5x3-inch loaf pans. Bake at 375° for about 1 hour or until cake tester is free of batter and the bread a golden brown.

Andrea lives in Tampa where fresh fruits abound, but frozen fruits will do as well.

RUTH'S DATE BREAD

Moist With Fruit

1½ cups boiling water
1 pound dates, chopped
1 teaspoon baking soda
½ cup butter
1 cup sugar

2 eggs
2 cups all-purpose flour
½ teaspoon salt
1 cup nuts, chopped

Pour 1½ cups boiling water over chopped dates and 1 teaspoon soda; cool. Cream butter and sugar in a large bowl; beat in eggs. Add in flour mixed with salt alternately with the cooled date mixture. Combine only until blended; add nuts. Bake in a greased 9x5x3-inch loaf pan at 350° for 45-50 minutes. To prevent over-browning, cover with foil for the last 10 to 15 minutes or until it tests done with a wooden pick inserted in center being batter free.

This yummy Date Bread was Ruth's first cooking adventure as well as her Grandmother Carter's most favorite. Her Grandmother, who lived with the family, was always checking on the little baker...encouraging and sampling. It is very obvious that compliments to the cook will reap rewards...no matter what the age!

CAROLYN KING'S CHERRY-PECAN BREAD
Add Cheer for Christmas or any Day!

¾ cup sugar
½ cup butter or margarine
2 eggs
2 cups all-purpose flour
½ teaspoon salt
1 teaspoon baking soda

1 cup buttermilk
1 cup chopped pecans
1-10 ounce jar maraschino
  cherries, drained and chopped
1 teaspoon vanilla
Glaze, optional

In a large bowl, cream sugar, butter and eggs. Mix together flour, salt and soda. Add flour mixture, alternately with buttermilk, to the egg mixture, mixing after each addition. Stir in nuts, cherries and vanilla until combined. Pour into a greased 9x5x3-inch loaf pan; bake at 350° for 55 to 60 minutes.

Cherry Glaze: mix ½ cup powdered sugar mixed with 1 tablespoon cherry juice.

ORANGE-CRANBERRY BREAD
Holiday Special

1 egg
¼ cup plus 2 tablespoons
  margarine
1½ teaspoons salt
Thinly pared outer rind of ¼
  orange and ½ lemon or grated
  rind of 1 orange

1 cup sugar
¾ cup orange juice
1 cup cranberries
½ cup pecans
2 cups all-purpose flour
1½ teaspoons baking powder
½ teaspoon baking soda

Use a food processor or a blender to blend the egg, margarine, salt, peels, sugar and orange juice; add nuts just to chop. Add cranberries to mixture just to barely chop. Do not blend berries or nuts. Lightly mix the contents of the food processor with the flour combined with the baking powder and soda in a large bowl. Pour batter into a greased 9x5x3-inch loaf pan; bake at 350° for 40-50 minutes. Yields 1 loaf.

Orange Glaze: Mix ½ cup powdered sugar with ½ teaspoon orange extract and 2½ teaspoons milk; glaze cooled loaf.

PINEAPPLE-PECAN BREAD
Delightful Flavor Combination

¾ cup brown sugar
¼ cup margarine
1 egg
2 cups all-purpose flour
1 teaspoon baking soda

½ teaspoon salt
⅓ cup frozen orange juice concentrate thawed
1 cup crushed pineapple
½ cup chopped pecans

In a large mixing bowl, cream sugar and margarine; beat in egg. Mix flour, soda and salt together. Add flour mixture, alternately with the juice concentrate, to the creamed mixture, mixing after each addition. Stir in the undrained pineapple and chopped pecans. Pour batter into a greased 9x5x3-inch loaf pan. Bake at 350° for 50-60 minutes. Yields 1 loaf.

Vanilla Yogurt Sauce: Mix ½ cup vanilla yogurt with 1 tablespoon brown sugar. Serve in a bowl with sliced bread; garnish with whole strawberries.

CHERRY SURPRISE LEMON BREAD
OR MUFFINS
Add a Little Zip to Washington's Birthday!

1 cup margarine
2 cups sugar
4 eggs
½ teaspoon salt
½ teaspoon baking soda
3 cups all-purpose flour

1 cup buttermilk
1 teaspoon lemon extract
1 teaspoon almond extract
Grated rind of 2 lemons
1 cup chopped nuts
1 can cherry pie filling, optional

Cream margarine and sugar in a large bowl; beat in eggs. Mix salt, soda and flour; add alternately with buttermilk and 2 extracts to the creamed mixture. Fold in the grated rind and nuts. Drain as much of the sauce from the cherry pie filling as possible; fold cherries into the batter. Pour the batter into 2 greased 9x5x3-inch loaf pans. Bake at 350° for approximately 1 hour. Yields 2 loaves.

For muffins, drop 2 or 3 cherries in the batter of each muffin section; adjust batter amount to totally fill pans only ⅔'s full. Bake at 400° for 20 minutes.

Lemon Glaze: Glaze bread or muffins with 1 cup powdered sugar mixed with 1 teaspoon lemon extract and 1 to 2½ tablespoons milk.

MEME'S BLUEBERRY BREAD

Keep a Loaf; Share a Loaf

1½ cups brown sugar
½ cup margarine
1 egg
1 teaspoon vanilla
1 cup buttermilk

2½ cups all-purpose flour
1 teaspoon salt
1 teaspoon baking soda
1½ cups blueberries
½ cup nuts

Cream brown sugar and margarine in a large bowl; beat in egg, vanilla and buttermilk. Gradually add in the flour combined with salt and soda. Fold in blueberries and nuts. Pour into 2 greased, 8½x4½x2½-inch, loaf pans; bake 1 hour at 350°.

BUTTER TOPPING: Cream ½ cup granulated sugar with 2 tablespoons butter; smooth icing over loaves.

KEY LIME BREAD

A Light Touch of Florida

2 cups sugar
1 cup butter
4 egg yolks
3¼ cups all-purpose flour
1 teaspoon salt
2 teaspoons baking powder

1¼ cups milk
1 cup chopped pecans
1 teaspoon lime
   or lemon flavoring
grated rind of 2 limes
4 egg whites

Cream the sugar and butter in a large bowl; beat in the egg yolks. Combine the flour, salt and baking powder; add to egg mixture alternately with the milk. Mix in the pecans, flavoring and peel. Beat egg whites until stiff; fold into batter. Pour batter into 2 greased, 9x5x3-inch, loaf pans. Bake at 350° for 50-60 minutes. Yields 2 loaves.

LIME GLAZE: Dissolve ¾ cup granulated sugar in juice of 2 limes while bread is baking. Pour glaze over hot bread in pan allowing glaze to soak into loaves.

KATHRYN'S AVOCADO BREAD

No Shortening Added

2 eggs	¾ cup sugar
½ cup ripe avocado	½ teaspoon baking soda
1 cup buttermilk	1 teaspoon baking powder
1 cup toasted pecans	¼ teaspoon salt
2 cups all-purpose flour	⅛ teaspoon ginger or curry

Combine eggs, avocado (peeled with seed removed) and buttermilk in food processor until smooth. Add nuts, chopping in short on and off motions. Mix flour with sugar, soda, baking powder, salt and spice in a medium mixing bowl. Add processor mixture, stirring only until combined. Pour batter into a greased 9x5x3-inch loaf pan. Bake at 350° for 1 hour or until a wooden pick inserted in the center is clean. *Serve strips of this mild, pale green California bread around a bowl of thick salsa.*

WALDORF SALAD BREAD

Moist with a Delicate Flavor

1½ cups sugar	3 cups all-purpose flour
¾ cup cooking oil	1 teaspoon baking soda
3 eggs	1 teaspoon celery salt
2 cups sliced apples	1 teaspoon baking powder
½ cup celery pieces	½ teaspoon ginger
½ cup pecans or English walnuts	½ teaspoon cinnamon
½ cup raisins, optional	

Mix sugar, oil and eggs in food processor; add apples, celery, nuts and raisins, while chopping with on and off action. Thoroughly mix flour, soda, salt, baking powder and spices together in a large bowl; add in wet ingredients just until combined. Pour into 2 greased and floured 8½x4½x2-inch loaf pans; bake at 375° for 50-60 minutes. Yields 2 loaves.

BAKER'S IDEA: Food processor not available, chop apples, celery and nuts by hand.

GRANDMOTHER HUNTER'S
CANDIED ORANGE BREAD
"Even better the next day"

Joy Gabriel's grandmother from Martinsville, Ohio always made her own candied orange peel or orange marmalade to go in her English Tea Bread. Save the rind from those prized holiday oranges!

CANDIED ORANGE PEEL: Remove as much white membrane from orange rind as possible. Cover peel with water and simmer until tender; drain. Grind or chop in blender, food processor or by hand. Use equal parts of peel, sugar and water. Cook slowly until the syrup is thick. Can be stored in small jars covered with paraffin or frozen. Use for breads or to glaze meats.

1 cup sugar	1 tablespoon baking powder
2 tablespoons cooking oil or butter	3 cups all-purpose flour
	1 cup milk
2 eggs	1 cup candied orange peel
¼ teaspoon baking soda	1 cup chopped, toasted pecans,
½ teaspoon salt	optional

Cream sugar, oil and eggs. Mix soda, salt, baking powder and flour; add alternately with milk to the egg mixture, stirring with each addition until combined. Stir in orange peel and nuts. Pour into 2 greased 8½x4½x2-inch loaf pans. Bake 50-60 minutes at 350°. Makes 2 loaves. If desired, cover tops with Cream Cheese Spread.

HURRIED BAKER: substitute commercial orange marmalade for candied orange peel, orange juice for milk and cover hot loaf with extra orange marmalade.

CREAM CHEESE SPREAD: Beat 1 (3-ounce) package cream cheese with 3 tablespoons butter, ½ teaspoon vanilla and enough powdered sugar to spread easily on bread.

Variation:

AMBROSIA ORANGE BREAD: My family continues to observe an old Virginia Christmas food tradition of fresh ambrosia. Sectioned oranges, grated fresh coconut and cubed fresh pineapple, prepared the day before, are a flavor delicacy. Ambrosia Orange Bread brings back those memories without all the work. Add ½ cup coconut and ½ cup well drained, canned pineapple pieces to the Candied Orange Bread Batter.

LOUISE'S ISLAND TEA BREAD

Louise Oden is a dedicated chef, with a specialty in breads, at the Courtyard Restaurant in Decatur, Alabama

Sweet potato or pumpkin is the surprise in this flavorful, moist, dark bread. This is a home baker's version.

2 cups sugar
1½ cups vegetable oil
5 large eggs
1 package coconut instant
  pudding (3½-ounce)
1 package pistachio instant
  pudding (3½-ounce)
2 cups cooked sweet potatoes or
  pumpkin, (one pound can)
  holds approximately

2 cups all-purpose flour
1½ teaspoons baking soda
1¼ teaspoons salt
¾ teaspoon nutmeg
¼ teaspoon cinnamon
¼ teaspoon ginger
¼ teaspoon mace
¼ teaspoon allspice
²/₃ cup flaked coconut
½ cup toasted, chopped almonds

Cream sugar and oil in a large mixer bowl; beat in eggs, one at a time. Combine with puddings and sweet potatoes or pumpkin; gradually mix in flour combined with soda, salt and 5 spices. Stir in the coconut and almonds. Pour into 2 well-greased and floured, 9x5x3-inch, bread pans. Bake at 350° for approximately 1 hour until wooden pick inserted in center of bread comes out clean. Cool for 10 minutes; remove from pan to cool on wire rack. Makes 2 loaves.

QUICK POPPYSEED-BRAN BREAD

A Super Fast Treat

4 eggs
1 cup water
½ cup oil
1 cup raisin bran flakes
2 tablespoons poppy seeds
1 (18.5-ounce) yellow cake mix

1 (3½-ounce) package instant
  butterscotch pudding mix
½ cup all-purpose flour
¼ teaspoon mace
¼ teaspoon nutmeg
½ teaspoon cinnamon

Beat eggs, water and oil in a large mixer bowl. Slowly mix in bran flakes, poppy seeds, 2 mixes and flour combined with spices. Mix on medium speed just until combined. Pour into 2 greased and floured 9x5x3-inch pans. Bake at 375° for 25 to 30 minutes. Test for doneness with a wooden pick.

Variation:

QUICK POPPY SEED LEMON OR ORANGE BRAN BREAD: Substitute lemon or orange cake mix and lemon pudding mix.

BANANA BREADS

Rescue very ripe bananas by freezing or baking immediately in a fruit bread. Use before the overripe stage as the sugar content changes. If desired, serve breads with Lemon-Banana Sauce.

JO'S BANANA BRAN BREAD
Perfect for a trip or a good morning wake-up.

½ cup sugar
¼ cup shortening
1 egg
1 cup all-bran cereal flakes
 (can use raisin bran flakes)
¼ cup water
1½ cups mashed ripe bananas

1½ cups all-purpose flour
½ teaspoon salt
2 teaspoons baking powder
½ teaspoon baking soda
1 teaspoon vanilla
½ cup chopped pecans

Cream sugar, shortening and egg in a large bowl; stir in the cereal flakes, water and bananas. Mix in the flour thoroughly combined with salt, baking powder and soda. Stir in the vanilla and nuts. Pour into a greased 9x5x3-inch loaf pan. Bake at 350° for 50-60 minutes. Yields 1 loaf.

LEMON-BANANA SAUCE

½ cup mashed ripe bananas,
 about 1 banana
½ cup sugar
1½ tablespoons lemon juice

⅛ teaspoon nutmeg
⅛ teaspoon ginger
½ teaspoon grated lemon rind

Mix bananas, sugar and lemon juice; microwave mixture on high, covered, in a microwaveable bowl for 2½ to 3 minutes. Stir in spices and rind. Spread over loaves or serve with any sweet bread.

QUICK BANANA-NUT BREAD

Light and Creamy Version

1 cup sugar	2 eggs
1 (8-ounce) package cream cheese	2 cups baking mix
	½ cup chopped nuts
1 cup mashed ripe bananas, about 2 large bananas	1 teaspoon vanilla

Cream the sugar and softened cream cheese; combine with bananas and eggs. Can use a blender or food processor. Mix in biscuit mix, nuts and vanilla, by hand, just until combined. Pour into a well greased 9x5x3-inch loaf pan; bake at 350° for 1 hour.

HONEY WHOLE WHEAT BANANA BREAD

Healthy and Tasty Whole Grains

½ cup cooking oil	½ teaspoon salt
²/₃ cup honey	2 teaspoons baking soda
2 eggs	1 cup mashed ripe bananas
½ cup wheat germ	½ cup chopped nuts
1½ cups whole wheat flour	

Mix oil, honey and eggs in a mixing bowl; stir in the dry ingredients, wheat germ, flour, salt and soda which have been thoroughly mixed together. Combine until just blended, adding the bananas and nuts. Bake in a greased, 9x5x3-inch, loaf pan for 50-60 minutes at 350°. Yields 1 loaf.

AUNT MARY'S BANANA BREAD

Delicious Way to Save Bananas

1 cup sugar	2 cups all-purpose flour
½ cup margarine	1 teaspoon baking soda
3 ripe bananas, mashed	¼ teaspoon salt
2 eggs	½ teaspoon vanilla

Cream together sugar and margarine in a medium size mixer bowl; beat in bananas and eggs. Mix together flour, soda and salt; add to batter with vanilla. Pour into a greased and floured 9x5x3-inch loaf pan; bake at 350° for 1 hour. Serve with sauce. Yields 1 loaf.

BANANA-SPLIT BREAD: Fold in the bananas, thin sliced instead of mashed, with ½ cup chopped, toasted pecans, ¹/₃ cup chopped maraschino cherries and ¹/₃ cup chocolate chips for banana split trimmings.

JANIS' BANANA-ORANGE BREAD

Zippy-orange flavor - no sugar, salt or fat added

2 eggs
2 ripe bananas
1 (6-ounce) can frozen orange
 juice
 concentrate
2 cups all-purpose flour
1 teaspoon baking powder

1 teaspoon baking soda
1½ teaspoons spice, cinnamon,
 nutmeg or ginger or a combination
1 cup chopped nuts
1 cup raisins

Blend eggs, bananas and concentrate in blender; stir in flour mixed with baking powder, soda and spice. Mix in nuts and raisins. Bake in a 9x5x3-inch greased loaf pan at 350° for 35 minutes until a light golden brown. Yields 1 loaf. *Even better the next day!*

JO HOSEY'S BANANA PEANUT BUTTER BREAD

Keeps Well

⅓ cup cooking oil
¾ cup creamy peanut butter
¾ cup sugar
2 eggs

1½ cups mashed, ripe bananas
1¾ cups all-purpose flour
2 teaspoons baking powder
½ teaspoon salt
¼ teaspoon baking soda

In a large bowl, cream oil, peanut butter and sugar; beat in eggs and bananas. Add flour mixed with baking powder, salt and soda alternately with banana combination; mix with each addition until combined. Pour batter into a greased 9x5x3-inch loaf pan. Bake at 350° for 55-60 minutes. Yields 1 loaf.

Add 3 tablespoons yogurt for more moisture if using crunchy peanut butter.

PEANUT BUTTER HONEY SPREAD: Cream ½ cup peanut butter and 2 tablespoons honey. Add confectioners sugar if too thin. Serve in a bowl beside bread slices.

VEGETABLE BREADS

CARROT-APPLESAUCE BREAD

You will never guess this delicious flavor secret.

2½ cups all-purpose flour
2 teaspoons baking soda
2 teaspoons cinnamon
½ teaspoon salt
2 cups grated, raw carrots

Beat the sugar, oil, vanilla, applesauce and eggs until light. Stir in flour thoroughly combined with soda, cinnamon and salts only until combined. Bake in 2 well-greased and floured pans at 350° for 50-60 minutes. Yields 2 loaves.

ANNE'S DATE-PUMPKIN BREAD

Freezes and Keeps Well

²/₃ cup shortening
2²/₃ cups sugar
4 eggs
1 pound can pumpkin, about 2
  cups
²/₃ cup water
3½ cups all-purpose flour

2 teaspoons baking soda
½ teaspoon baking powder
1 ½ teaspoons salt
1 teaspoon cinnamon
1 teaspoon ground cloves
²/₃ cup chopped dates or raisins
²/₃ cup chopped nuts

Cream shortening and sugar in large mixer bowl; beat in eggs one at a time on medium speed. Mix in pumpkin and water. Carefully combine flour, soda, baking powder, salt and spices; mix with pumpkin mixture. Stir in the dates and nuts until combined. Pour into 2 greased and floured 9x5x3-inch loaf pans. Bake at 350° for approximately 1 hour. After 10 minutes remove pan; cool loaf on wire rack. Yields 2 loaves.

JOY'S LEMON-CARROT BREAD

Boost for sagging spirits—ol' rabbit never had carrots this good!

3 large eggs
1 cup cooking oil
2 cups sugar
1 medium lemon
2 cups carrot chunks
½ teaspoon cinnamon

3 cups all-purpose flour
1½ teaspoons salt
1 teaspoon baking soda
1 teaspoon baking powder
½ teaspoon nutmeg

Cream eggs, oil and sugar in the food processor; add lemon cut into quarters, removing seeds, stem and any excessive white portion of skin. Process the peeled, sliced carrots until finely chopped. In a large bowl, mix flour with salt, soda, baking powder and spices; combine with the processed ingredients. Pour into 2 greased and floured 9x5x3-inch loaf pans. Bake at 350° for about 1 hour. Glaze while hot with lemon spread. Yields 2 loaves.

BAKER'S IDEA: Can use blender or grater in place of food processor.

LEMON SPREAD: Combine 1 cup powdered sugar with the juice of ½ lemon,adding milk, if necessary, for spreading.

Variation:

ORANGE AND NUT CARROT BREAD: Omit lemon from Joy's Lemon Carrot Bread; add 2 teaspoons grated orange rind and 1 cup chopped nuts. Decrease sugar to 1½ cups.

EVELYN'S ZUCCHINI BREAD

Extra Zucchini Made Scrumptious

3 eggs
1 cup vegetable oil
1½ cups sugar
2 teaspoons vanilla
2 cups all-purpose flour
¼ teaspoon baking powder
2 teaspoons baking soda

3 teaspoons ground cinnamon
1 teaspoon salt
2 cups zucchini, peeled and
  grated
1 cup raisins
1 cup chopped nuts

Beat eggs until light; add oil, sugar and vanilla, beating until creamy. Mix together flour, baking powder, soda, cinnamon and salt; combine with egg mixture. Mix in zucchini, raisins and nuts. Pour into 2 greased 8x4x2-inch loaf pans. Bake at 375° for one hour. Let cool 10 minutes before removing from pan. Makes 2 loaves.

SAVORY SPINACH BREAD

Impress the Lunch Bunch

1½ cups sugar
¾ cup cooking oil
3 eggs
1 (10-ounce) package frozen,
   thawed, drained spinach
⅓ cup crisp, cooked and drained
   bacon

½ teaspoon minced onion
½ average size orange
3 cups all-purpose flour
1 teaspoon baking soda
1 teaspoon onion salt
1 teaspoon baking powder
¼ teaspoon nutmeg

Mix sugar, oil and eggs in the food processor; add spinach, bacon, onion and orange, cut in sections. Combine with on and off action until chopped. Thoroughly mix flour, soda, salt, baking powder and nutmeg together in a large bowl; stir in processed ingredients just until combined. Pour into 1 greased and floured 9x5x3-inch pan. Bake at 375° for 50-60 minutes. Yields 1 loaf.

BAKER'S IDEA: if a food processor is not used, use chopped spinach; chop other ingredients by hand. *Tantalizing flavor combination!*

COFFEE CAKES

CRUNCHY APPLE COFFEE CAKE

2 cups peeled, finely chopped
   tart apples
¾ cup sugar
¼ cup brown sugar
1 cup all-purpose flour
¼ cup wheat germ
1 teaspoon baking soda

¼ teaspoon salt
¼ teaspoon nutmeg
¼ teaspoon cinnamon
2 eggs
2 tablespoons molasses
½ cup cooking oil
½ cup crunchy wheat and barley
   cereal

Combine apples with sugars in a large bowl; let stand while combining the flour, wheat germ, soda, salt and spices. Beat the eggs, molasses and oil into the apple mixture; mix in the dry ingredients and the cereal until combined. Pour into a greased 8-inch square pan. Bake at 350° for 40-45 minutes. Cut in squares or narrow strips as bread.

Serve with coffee or for dessert with Helen's Orange Sauce (page 185) and Ice Cream.

BISHOP'S BREAD

Invite someone important; not just for Bishops!

3 eggs
1 cup sugar
1 teaspoon almond extract
1 cup all-purpose flour
¼ teaspoon salt
1 teaspoon grated lemon rind

1 cup chopped dates
½ cup chopped toasted almonds
½ cup chopped black walnuts
1 (6-ounce) package chocolate
chips

Use mixer to beat eggs with sugar and extract, in a medium bowl, until creamy. Mix in flour combined with salt. Stir in rind, dates, nuts and chips. Pour into a well-greased 9x5x3-inch loaf pan or a greased 9-inch, round, ovenproof serving container. Bake at 300° for 40-50 minutes. Test with wooden pick for doneness. After 10 minutes, remove pan; cool loaf on rack. Cut into thin slices or small wedges. Yields 1 loaf.

Variation:

BISHOP'S SHORT BREAD COFFEE CAKE: Add ⅓ cup butter to beat with eggs and sugar. Serve from container or line container with greased foil.

SUGAR PLUM COFFEE CAKE

A Favorite: Moist and Spicy

1 pound prunes
2 cups sugar
½ teaspoon nutmeg
½ teaspoon cloves
1 teaspoon cinnamon
1 teaspoon salt

¾ cup shortening
2 eggs
1 cup whole wheat flour
1 cup all-purpose flour
2 teaspoons baking soda

Add just enough water to cover prunes for soaking overnight; pit and chop prunes, measuring 2½ cups of prune pulp and juice mixture. Simmer chopped prunes, prune liquid, sugar, spices, salt and shortening for 5 minutes; cool the mixture. Beat the eggs in a large mixer bowl; combine with the cooled prune mixture and the flours mixed with soda. Pour into 2 greased 9-inch cake pans. Bake at 300° for 1 hour. Serve warm or sliced cold. Freezes well. Yields 2 cakes.

Cut in squares and serve warm with orange sauce, whipped topping or ice cream for coffee or as a dessert.

ISABELL'S POPPY SEED COFFEE CAKE
Light and Unusual; Calls for a Party!

4 egg whites	¼ teaspoon salt
1 cup margarine	¼ cup poppy seeds
1½ cups sugar	1 cup buttermilk
4 egg yolks	1 teaspoon almond extract
2½ cups all-purpose flour	Topping:
1 teaspoon baking soda	½ cup sugar
1 teaspoon baking powder	1 teaspoon cinnamon

Beat the egg whites until stiff; set aside. With mixer, in a separate large bowl, cream the margarine and sugar, beating in the egg yolks; mix in the flour combined with the soda, baking powder, salt and seeds alternately with the buttermilk and extract. Fold in the egg whites; pour ½ of the batter in a greased tube pan. Combine sugar and cinnamon; sprinkle ½ of the topping over the batter. Cover with the rest of the batter; sprinkle with the remaining sugar topping. If desired, cut through with a knife to give a marbling effect or leave the sugar mixture in layers. Bake at 350° for 60 to 65 minutes. *Vary size with different pans.*

CAROLYN'S BLUEBERRY SPICE COFFEE CAKE

¾ cup margarine	1 teaspoon vanilla extract
1½ cups sugar	2 cups blueberries
4 eggs	Filling:
3 cups all-purpose flour	½ cup brown sugar
1½ teaspoons baking powder	2 tablespoons all-purpose flour
¾ teaspoon baking soda	⅛ teaspoon ginger
½ teaspoon salt	¼ teaspoon nutmeg
1 cup sour cream	¼ teaspoon cinnamon
1 teaspoon almond extract	

With mixer, cream margarine and sugar in large bowl; beat in eggs. Add in flour combined with baking powder, soda and salt alternately with the sour cream and extracts; mix until combined. Pour ⅓ of batter into a greased, floured bundt or tube pan. Sprinkle ½ of the blueberries and ½ of spice filling over the batter. Repeat layers; top with last ⅓ of batter; bake at 350° for 55-60 minutes. Cool on rack, upside down, for 10 minutes; gently remove from pan to finish cooling. Pour glaze over warm coffee cake.

ALMOND GLAZE: Whisk 1½ cups powdered sugar, 2-3 tablespoons milk, ½ teaspoon each, vanilla and almond extracts until smooth.

DATE COFFEE CAKE WITH CHOCOLATE NUT TOPPING

Scrumptious Flavor Combination

1 cup chopped dates (8-ounce package)
1½ cups boiling water
1 teaspoon baking soda
½ cup shortening
1 cup sugar
2 eggs

1¾ cups all-purpose flour
¾ teaspoon baking soda
¼ teaspoon salt
Topping:
1 cup chocolate chips
½ cup chopped nuts
½ cup sugar

Combine dates, boiling water and 1 teaspoon soda; let cool. Cream shortening and sugar in a large mixer bowl; beat in eggs until light. Mix flour, combined with additional soda and the salt, into the egg mixture alternately with the cooled date ingredients. Pour into a greased and floured 13x9x2-inch casserole or pan. Combine topping ingredients; sprinkle over top of batter. Bake at 350° for 30 minutes. Yields 24 (2-inch) squares.

Put on the coffee; call your friends.

RUTH'S RUSSIAN FRUIT COFFEE CAKE

Colorful Brunch Addition

Pastry:
½ cup butter
½ cup sugar
2 egg yolks
1¼ cups all-purpose flour

Topping:
2 cups fresh fruit, peeled and
   sliced apples, blueberries,
   plums, kiwi or apricots.
Sweeten and cook dried fruit.
¼ cup sugar

Cream butter and sugar in medium bowl; beat in egg yolks. Add flour lightly mixing until smooth. Pat with fingers over bottom of a 9-inch cake pan; chill until firm. Cover with fruit; sprinkle top with sugar. Bake at 375° for about 20-30 minutes or until crust is a light brown. Yields 8 servings.

BAKER'S IDEA: For fruit too beautiful to cook, bake crust; spread with 3-ounces softened cream cheese beaten with ½ cup powdered sugar and ½ teaspoon vanilla. Add rows of fresh fruit.

TOFFEE CANDY BAR COFFEE CAKE

Dark, Moist and Delicious

2 cups all-purpose flour
1 cup brown sugar, packed down
½ cup granulated sugar
1 teaspoon baking soda
½ teaspoon salt
⅔ cup margarine
1 egg

1 teaspoon vanilla
1 cup buttermilk
6 (1.2-ounce) chocolate covered
  toffee bars
½ cup nuts, chopped

Mix flour, sugars, soda and salt in large bowl; cut in margarine. Save ½ cup of this mixture for topping. Beat egg and vanilla into buttermilk; mix with the flour mixture until combined. Pour batter into a greased and floured 13x9x2-inch pan. Use a food processor or a blender to crumble the candy. Combine the candy, nuts and saved flour mixture; sprinkle evenly over batter. Bake at 350° for approximately 25 minutes. Cool in pan; cut in squares. Yields about 32 (1½x1½-inch) squares. *Perfect sweet for a picnic or a buffet supper.*

QUICK TOFFEE BAR COFFEE CAKE

Yummy Baking in the Fast Lane

1 (18.5-ounce) yellow cake mix
1 package butterscotch instant
  pudding
1 cup sour cream
2 eggs
⅔ cup cooking oil

Topping
½ cup chopped nuts
½ cup saved cake mix
6 (1.2-ounce) chocolate
covered toffee bars
½ cup flaked coconut

Remove ½ cup cake mix for topping; mix rest of cake mix, pudding, eggs, sour cream and oil in a large mixer bowl. Pour into greased and floured 13x9x2-inch pan. Crumble toffee in a blender or processor. Sprinkle combined topping evenly over batter. Bake at 350° for approximately 25 minutes. When cooled, cut in squares. Yields about 24 (2-inch) squares.

TIME-SAVING JEWISH CHEESE COFFEE CAKE

Serve a Crowd for Brunch

*1 cup cottage cheese
3 eggs
½ cup cooking oil
½ cup water
1 teaspoon vanilla extract
1 teaspoon almond extract

¼ teaspoon cinnamon
¼ teaspoon ginger
1 (18½-ounce) yellow or lemon
   cake mix
1 (3½-ounce) vanilla, coconut or
   lemon instant pudding mix

*Process in blender for finer crumb, optional.

SUGAR AND SPICE STREUSEL TOPPING: Combine the following until crumbly:

½ cup brown sugar, packed
½ cup granulated sugar
½ teaspoon nutmeg
½ teaspoon cinnamon

1 cup chopped pecans or
   almonds
½ cup all-purpose flour
½ cup margarine

Whisk cottage cheese, eggs, oil, water and flavorings until blended. By hand, stir spices, cake and pudding mixes together in a large bowl; add liquid ingredients stirring **only** until combined. Pour batter into 2 greased 9-inch or a 13½x9½x2-inch greased, glass casserole or pan; cover batter with Streusel topping. Bake at 350° for 50-60 minutes. Test doneness with a wooden pick inserted in middle of cake being batter free. Do not overcook, as this coffee cake should be dense and moist. Let cool in container before cutting. Yields more than 50 squares, 1½x1½ inches. *Try different flavors of cake and pudding mixes for the desired color, flavor effect. Fill any size greased foil pan a little less than ½ full of batter to allow for the topping. Take to a friend or neighbor....don't tell them all your ingredients.*

RUTH'S FAVORITE GINGERBREAD

Fragrant Memories

½ cup shortening
½ cup brown sugar
1 egg, beaten
1 cup molasses
2½ cups all-purpose flour
1½ teaspoons ginger

¼ teaspoon nutmeg
1 teaspoon cinnamon
1 teaspoon baking soda
½ teaspoon salt
½ teaspoon baking powder
1 cup boiling water

Cream shortening and brown sugar in a large mixer bowl, beating in the egg and molasses. Mix in the flour combined with spices, soda, salt and baking powder alternately with boiling water. Pour into a greased 8-inch square pan. Bake at 350° for 40-50 minutes. Test with a wooden pick in center of bread for doneness. Yields 6 servings.

Serve hot or cold — plain with whipped cream, caramel dressing or hot orange sauce with ice cream.

Variations:

RUTH'S FAVORITE APPLE GINGERBREAD: Add 1 cup peeled and finely chopped apples to the batter.

PANCAKES AND WAFFLES: Pour ¼ cup batter on hot, oiled griddle or pour batter on preheated waffle iron.

HELEN'S ORANGE SAUCE

1 cup sugar
1 tablespoon all-purpose flour
Juice of 1 orange (about ½ cup)

1 cup boiling water
½ cup butter

Mix sugar and flour in a heavy saucepan; stir in juice and boiling water. Cook over medium heat, stirring constantly. Simmer until thickened; mix in butter. Serve hot over gingerbread.

GRANDMOTHER CARTER'S CARAMEL DRESSING

1 cup granulated sugar
1 cup brown sugar

2 teaspoons all-purpose flour
1 cup water

Combine first three ingredients in a quart-size sauce pan; gradually add water, stirring after each addition. Simmer until thick; serve warm over gingerbread.

QUICK GINGERBREAD
Favorite of the Young Set

2 cups baking mix	½ teaspoon cloves
¼ cup sugar	1 egg, beaten
½ teaspoon cinnamon	½ cup milk
½ teaspoon ginger	½ cup molasses

Combine baking mix, sugar and spices in a medium bowl; mix in egg beaten with milk and molasses only until combined. Pour into a well greased, floured 8x8-inch pan. Bake at 350° for 40 minutes or until an inserted wooden pick is free of batter. Serve warm with ice cream. Yields 6 servings.

Variation:

GINGERBREAD WAFFLES: Add 1 tablespoon oil. Pour batter on preheated waffle iron.

ROSE'S ITALIAN BISCOTTI
Means Twice Baked

½ cup butter	2 cups all-purpose flour
1 drop anise oil, (licorice flavor)	2 teaspoons baking powder
1 cup sugar	½ cup walnuts or pecans,
2 eggs	chopped
½ cup milk	

In food processor, combine butter, anise oil and sugar until creamy; process eggs with mixture. Add milk to process. Pour processed contents over flour mixed with baking powder and nuts. Combine ingredients; spoon into a greased, 9x5x3-inch loaf pan or a 12x4x3-inch loaf pan. Bake at 375° for 30-35 minutes.

Total mixing by hand: Combine dry mixture alternately with milk to the creamed ingredients.

Slice ½-inch thick, arrange on cookie sheet, and lightly toast in the oven. *These tasty morsels keep well; look tempting displayed in a clear container. Wonderful with a morning cup of coffee.*

Rose has precious childhood memories of this bread being tea bread or a quick dessert with fruit.

Variation:

CHOCOLATE BISCOTTI: Add 2 tablespoons cocoa to the flour; ice top of sliced toasted Biscotti with Betty Sims' White Chocolate Ganache.

PASTRY

Combine pastry, just as Homemade Biscuit Mix, with a mixer, food processor, pastry blender, fork or two knives pulling against one another. When ingredients are the consistency of coarse meal, add the ice water, one tablespoon at a time, until the dough is moist enough to barely stick together. The amount of liquid varies with the humidity and the flour type. The food processor's short on-off action will, in seconds, produce a pea size mixture of flour, salt and shortening. Chill or freeze shortening when using the food processor. Add the ice water one tablespoon at a time; process with the on-off action just until the pastry begins to form a ball.

Gather pastry dough, however processed, into a ball by hand, wrap in plastic wrap and refrigerate for about one hour or freeze for 5-8 minutes.

Roll ball of dough from center to outer edges on lightly floured surface, forming a 1/8-inch thick crust. Loosen dough sticking to surface with a thin, flat spatula. Roll crust large enough to come over the pan edge.

Roll pastry onto a floured rolling pin or fold pastry in half to transfer to pie pan. Unroll or unfold pastry, loosely fitting to pan; gently press pastry to pan without stretching the dough. Trim excess dough with a knife or scissors, leaving a 1-inch margin of pastry around outside of pan. Use a fork or fingers to form a crimped or fluted design to press pastry to the pan edge. Prick the pastry shell with a fork on the sides and bottom if baked before filling.

Cuts or designs made with a knife tip in the center top of a double crust form air vents. For a lattice effect, attach crisscrossed dough strips from one side of pan to the opposite side, pressing against pan edge. Cut animal, chicken, fruit, vegetable and leaf designs from 1/8-inch thick pastry to attach to moistened rim of pastry or place on the pie surface. Roll a long strip to tie as a bow or to form an initial for personalizing a crust. Let children shape free form birds, animals or designs for the top.

Extra Secrets for a Flaky, Tender Pastry

1.   Add only a minimum of water to hold flour and shortening together.

2.   Bake a crisp, shiny, golden crust by brushing egg white (beaten with 1/2 teaspoon of water until foamy) over top crust before baking.

3.   Cover outer edge of over-browning pastry crust with foil.

ALL-PURPOSE PASTRY

1 cup all-purpose flour	¹/₃ cup shortening
½ teaspoon salt	3-4 tablespoons cold water

Cut in flour, salt and shortening; sprinkle with enough water to moisten ingredients, mixing with a fork. Shape into a ball; refrigerate about 1 hour. Roll ¹/₈-inch thick on lightly floured surface to fit the pan. Bake at 400° for 10 minutes or until light brown. Makes 1 (9-inch) pie shell. Double recipe for a 2 crust pie.

Variations:

TART PASTRY SHELLS: Cut rolled dough with 2-inch plain or scalloped cutter. Fit each pastry into small muffin pans; prick with fork.

CHEESE PASTRY: Add 1 cup shredded cheddar cheese to the dough. Reduce temperature to 375° for 15 minutes.

NUT PASTRY: Add ½ cup finely chopped pecans, walnuts or peanuts to dry ingredients before adding ice water.

GRANDMOTHER'S OATMEAL PASTRY: Substitute ¼ cup rolled oats for ¼ cup flour.

OLD-FASHIONED BAKER'S IDEA: Cover the bottom of a 9-inch square pan with pastry. Bake; spread with a thick, sweet fruit or dried fruit filling. Cut in small squares. Optional, sprinkle with powdered sugar before serving.

MEAT PASTRY: Combine ¼ teaspoon mace, ¼ teaspoon mustard and ¹/₈ teaspoon pepper with dry ingredients. When dough has chilled, roll in desired size for encasing a small, about 1 pound, cooked ham or roast. Seal seam side, placing on lightly greased pan. Use extra dough to form decorations or pastry top.

SWEET PASTRY: Add ¼ cup powdered sugar and substitute 4 tablespoons cream for water.

DAD'S SWEET PASTRY TOPPING: Omit salt and water; substitute butter or margarine for shortening. Add ½ cup sugar with flour; mix until crumbly. Sprinkle crumbs on top of pies or over fruit casseroles.

DAD'S SWEET CHEESE PASTRY TOPPING: Add 1 cup shredded American cheese to Dad's Sweet Topping.

CINNAMON-SUGAR PINWHEELS: Use leftovers to please the young or not so young. Roll pastry thin; sprinkle with cinnamon and sugar. Roll as a jelly roll; place (cut slices) on a lightly greased pan. Bake at 375° until crisp, not brown.

AUNT MARY'S APPLE-CHEESE CRISP: Prepare 1 recipe of Dad's Sweet Cheese Pastry Topping.

5 cups sliced apples (5 apples)	**1 teaspoon grated lemon rind (1 lemon)**
1 teaspoon cinnamon	**1 tablespoon lemon juice**
½ cup sugar	**¼ cup hot water**

Slice apples into a greased 9-inch square baking dish. Cover with spice, sugar, rind, juice and water. Crumble pastry evenly over the apple mixture. Bake at 350° for 55 to 60 minutes or until apples are soft and pastry is light brown. Serve hot with ice milk. Serves 6 to 8. A special request from all the men in our family!

BETTE'S OLD SOUTH BUTTER ROLL: Cut pastry (all-purpose recipe, doubled) into 12 pieces. Roll each piece on a lightly floured board to a 6-inch circle. Place approximately 1½ tablespoons cold sliced butter, in chunks, and 1½ tablespoons sugar on each circle. Sprinkle generously with nutmeg and/or cinnamon.

Pull dough sides over the butter-sugar combination; gently seal the edges. This will resemble a poorly formed egg roll. Place 8 rolls seam side down in a generously buttered 2-quart rectangular oven-proof casserole. Bette places the other 4 rolls in an 8x8-inch buttered pan to share with a friend. Don't overcrowd rolls. Use at least a 2-inch deep pan to prevent milk from boiling over.

Pour 2 to 3 cups milk to cover all the rolls, except for the top ¼-inch. Sprinkle ⅔'s cup sugar over the 12 rolls. Dot each roll with a drop of vanilla and a sprinkling of cinnamon. Shake pan gently to slightly moisten sugar. Bake at 350° for 60-80 minutes or until milk has almost cooked away. Serve warm with a scoop of ice cream. Better made within 3 hours of serving. If necessary, refrigerate formed and covered rolls; just before baking, add milk and other ingredients.

A seldom found, delicious remembrance of the deep South! This juicy treat was the cook's sweet surprise when fruit was not available. Some cooks used less butter and more cinnamon, but the results were the same...compliments and more requests.

RUTH'S EGG PASTRY

Perfect for Fruit Pies

3 cups all-purpose flour	1 tablespoon vinegar
1 teaspoon salt	1 egg
1 cup shortening	4 tablespoons ice water

Mix flour and salt; cut in shortening. Add vinegar beaten with egg; sprinkle only enough water over dough to form a ball. Chill for 1 hour. Roll dough, fit in pan and prick sides and bottom. Bake at 400° for 10 minutes or fill and bake. Makes 3 (9-inch) pie shells.

"PITTY PAT'S" FRUIT 'N' CRUST PIE

Almost "as fast as a cat can wink his eye!"

¼ cup butter	2 cans peaches, cherries or
½ cup sugar	apples (16-ounce) cans or use
1 cup baking mix	4 cups fresh, sweetened fruit
1 cup liquid from fruit or milk	

Melt butter in a 2 quart baking dish. Combine sugar, baking mix and liquid; pour on top of butter. Cover with fruit, sweetened if necessary, and any extra juice. Bake at 400° for 25-30 minutes or until brown. Break up crust with a spoon; serve hot with ice cream. Serves 6.

CORNMEAL PASTRY

Try with Fish, Beef or Mexican Fare

½ cup cornmeal	⅓ cup shortening
¾ cup all-purpose flour	3-4 tablespoons ice water
¾ teaspoon salt	

Mix cornmeal, flour and salt; cut in shortening until fine. Add water, 1 tablespoon at a time, until mixture is moist enough to form a ball. Chill, covered in plastic wrap; roll on a lightly floured board to fit a 9-inch pie pan or muffin pans. Fill with cooked meat and vegetables. Bake at 400°, 20-25 minutes or until pastry is done and filling is hot. Sprinkle top with grated sharp cheese.

CREAM CHEESE PASTRY
The Kimbrough Girls' Favorite for Savory or Sweet Fillings

1 (3-ounce) package cream cheese	½ cup butter
	1 cup all-purpose flour

Combine softened cream cheese and butter with the flour by mixing. Using the food processor, process ingredients with cold sliced butter until combined. Form into a ball; wrap in plastic to refrigerate overnight or a few hours.

INDIVIDUAL TARTS: Form 24 small balls. With fingers, press balls into small muffin cups. Prick with a fork if to be baked before the filling is added. Bake at 400° for 10 minutes. Fill baked tarts with chicken salad or ½ pound ham (chopped) mixed with 1 tablespoon toasted sesame seeds, ¼ teaspoon Worcestershire sauce, 2 teaspoons Dijon mustard and ¼ cup mayonnaise.

PASTRY TURNOVERS: Roll pastry thin, about ⅛-inch thick on a floured surface. Cut a 2-inch square or a 1x2-inch rectangle. Add 1 teaspoon filling in center. Fold pastry over, gently pressing edges with a fork to seal; prick top with fork.

ALMOND LEAVES: Add 1½ teaspoons almond extract to the Cream Cheese Pastry dough. Roll out dough ⅛-inch thick on a lightly floured surface. Cut with leaf cookie cutters or use appropriate seasonal cutters. Press toasted, finely chopped almonds into pastry. Bake only until a very pale edging of brown forms, 8-10 minutes. Easy, decorative nibbles for a pastry tray or buffet table.

PHYLLO PASTRY
Filo (fee low) or Strudel Pastry

Versatile phyllo dough can elegantly hold any thick, sweet or savory fillings used for pastry or yeast dough. Use for appetizers, main dishes and desserts. Commercial phyllo gives uniform, paper-thin leaves of pastry which keep well, airtight, in the freezer or refrigerator. Unroll as needed, covering pastry with waxed paper covered with a damp cloth to prevent drying.

Use a sharp, serrated knife for cutting; press pastry together to repair. Thicken runaway sweet fillings with bread crumbs; Parmesan cheese rescues runaway, savory fillings. Because butter is brushed on phyllo sheets, use casseroles or pans with sides, allowing hot pastry to stand a few minutes before cutting.

ELEGANT BAKLAVA
The Ultimate of Greek Delectables

1 pound phyllo dough   ½ cup sugar
1 pound walnuts and/or almonds ½ teaspoon nutmeg
1 pound butter   1½ teaspoons cinnamon

Cover phyllo dough with waxed paper and a damp cloth. Evenly layer 4 sheets of phyllo, each brushed with melted butter, on the bottom of a greased 11x16x2-inch pan. Sprinkle with thin layer of nut mixture. Cover with 3 phyllo sheets; brush each with butter. Continue this procedure with all phyllo sheets and nut mixture until all are used. Finish with 4 sheets on top, brushing each with melted butter. Cut into diamond shaped squares. Bake at 350° approximately 1 hour until lightly browned. Remove from oven and cool. Pour warm syrup over baklava. Makes 36 squares.

SYRUP: Simmer until a syrup consistency; remove lemon half.

1½ cups sugar   ¼ cup honey
¾ cup water   ½ lemon, juice plus lemon half

CHEF CARO'S APPLE STRUDEL

Starting in his native Germany, Chef Alfred Caro has served as an international chef for 54 years. Working in South America, New York City and Anniston, Alabama, he has a following of ardent admirers. One of his most popular specialties is his Apple Strudel. He shares the following easy version.

7 sheets Phyllo pastry   ¾ teaspoon cinnamon
Melted butter   1 cup lightly toasted, coarsely
1 (1 pound 5-ounce) can of apple   chopped pecans
   pie filling (drain excess sauce) 6 ounces almond paste

Place 2 sheets of Phyllo on a greased 13x9x2-inch casserole or jelly roll pan. Brush only top sheet with butter. Add 2 more sheets of phyllo on top of first set; brush butter only on top sheet. Cover with 2 more sheets, brushing top with butter; top with last sheet, brushing top surface with butter.

Place apples in a single layer 4-inches from the long side of the phyllo sheets. The apples will take up another 3¾ to 4 inches. Sprinkle with cinnamon and pecans. Crumble almond paste over apples. Fold a 4-inch margin of phyllo pastry over the apples and the almond paste.

Bring over the opposite phyllo to totally cover and tuck under apple filling. Brush entire strudel with butter. Bake at 350° for 30-35 minutes or until light brown. Serves 10.

EVELYN'S QUICK AND SPICY STRUDEL
Easy version of strudel pastry

Pastry:
1/3 cup refrigerated butter
1 1/3 cups all-purpose flour
1 tablespoon sugar
1/4 teaspoon salt
1 egg
1/2 cup sour cream
Filling:
2/3 cup thick grape, cherry, apricot, orange or peach preserves or marmalade, mixed or matched

1/4 cup brown sugar
1 teaspoon cinnamon
1/8 teaspoon allspice
1/8 teaspoon ginger
1/8 teaspoon nutmeg
1/8 teaspoon mace
3/4 cup chopped, toasted pecans
1/2 cup white raisins

Cut in butter (cut in pieces) and flour by hand or with food processor until a coarse, cornmeal consistency. Pour in medium bowl with sugar and salt; mix in egg beaten with sour cream just until moistened. Gather into a ball to refrigerate in plastic wrap for at least 1 hour. Combine preserves, sugar and spices; substitute all cinnamon as an option.

Divide pastry in half; sprinkle on more flour if necessary for a manageable dough. On a lightly floured surface, roll each dough half about 9x5-inches. Spread surface of each rectangle with preserve mixture; sprinkle with nuts and raisins. Starting with the long side, roll rectangle as a jelly roll, placing seam side down on a greased, foil lined baking sheet. Bake at 350° for 25-30 minutes or until brown. Cut into small slices. Yields about 20 slices.

Refrigerate or freeze ahead of time for a brunch or coffee.

CROISSANTS AND DANISH PASTRY

Hurried Baker's Version for Today's Fast-Paced Living

BETTY'S QUICK CROISSANTS
Use butter or solid margarine

2 cups all-purpose flour
½ cup refrigerated butter
1 package yeast
⅔ cup warm skim milk (105-115°)
¼ teaspoon salt

2 tablespoons sugar
¼ cup all-purpose flour
¼ cup melted butter
Egg glaze

Cut in flour and butter (cut in slices) in the food processor or by hand. Process until a very coarse cornmeal consistency. Remove contents to a large bowl.

Mix yeast and milk in food processor. Add salt, sugar, flour and butter, processing until smooth. Combine with flour mixture just until moistened. Cover bowl with plastic wrap; refrigerate overnight or a few days. Gather into a ball adding extra flour as necessary to be manageable.

Divide dough in half; roll each section into a 14-inch circle on a lightly floured board. Cut 10 wedge shaped pieces for smaller croissants and 8 pieces for larger rolls. Starting with wide end, roll up, placing point side down on lightly greased baking pan. Curve sides to form a crescent shape. Leave a 1-inch space around rolls for rising. Let rise, covered, until double in a warm draft-free area, for 1 to 1½ hours. Lightly brush with 1 egg beaten with 1 tablespoon water. Bake in a 400° oven for 10-15 minutes. After 10 minutes brush tops again with egg glaze. Yields 20 small rolls.

Especially delicious considering how fast! Don't tell that you didn't stay up all night baking as the Austrian and French bakers do!

CHEESE CROISSANTS: Sprinkle and press shredded cheddar cheese on dough triangle surface before rolling into its final shape. Proceed as directed.

HAM AND CHEESE CROISSANTS: Place finely chopped ham on the center wide base with a little shredded Swiss cheese. Press in place gently. Roll and bake as usual.

CHOCOLATE-ALMOND CROISSANTS: Sprinkle smallest chocolate chips or grated semi-sweet chocolate on dough triangle with finely chopped toasted almonds. Gently press into dough. Proceed as directed.

These recipes were included in an article by The Decatur Daily *about my Community Education Croissant Baking Class.*

QUICK DANISH PASTRY

For a speedy version of classic Danish pastry, use Betty's Quick Croissants, adding 1 egg to the food processor after yeast is dissolved. Dough will need about ¼ cup extra flour for rolling.

DANISH PASTRY VARIATIONS USING QUICK DANISH PASTRY

DANISH SPIRAL BUNS: Roll ⅓ of dough to a 10x10-inch rectangle. Cut into 12 strips. Press end of each strip to greased pan, circling dough around and tucking loose end under the bun. Press center of each bun to form an indentation; let rise until double. Bake at 375° only until done, pale brown in color, about 10-12 minutes. Spoon filling in the center, sprinkle with nuts and drizzle with a glaze.

BILLIE'S DANISH SQUARES: Roll ⅓ of dough to a 10x10-inch rectangle. Cut into 16 (2½-inch) squares. Place a teaspoon of filling in center of each square. Fold opposite corners of square to center. Press corners together. Let rise until double. Bake at 375° for 15 minutes or until a pale brown. Drizzle with a glaze.

ESTHER'S FRUIT-FILLED DANISH COFFEE CAKE: Roll ⅓ of dough to an 8x10-inch rectangle. Place on a greased foil-lined baking sheet. Place thick fruit filling (½ to ¾ cup) down the center of the rectangle, leaving dough on each side. Cut dough on each side in 1-inch strips. Starting at the top, fold each strip over the center of the filling at an angle, forming a braided effect. Alternate strips until complete. Let rise; bake at 375° for 15 minutes or until a pale brown. Sprinkle with spicy granulated sugar; drizzle with a glaze.

Esther and Billie use classical Danish methods for their pastries, often adding maraschino cherries, nuts, dates and raisins to the fillings.

Any favorite filling from the yeast bread section can be used for the Quick Danish Pastry or choose from the fillings on the following page.

MORE DANISH PASTRY VARIATIONS, FILLING AND GLAZE:

FRUIT FILLING: Use 1 (16-ounce) can of drained, pitted and chopped fruit such as canned purple plums. Sweeten to taste. A 16-ounce can yields about ¾ cup fruit filling. Mix in 1 teaspoon grated lemon or orange rind. Sprinkle filling with chopped toasted pecans or almonds.

Use approximately ½ cup fruit filling and ¼ cup nuts for each recipe of Danish Spiral Buns and Esther's Danish Coffee Cake (page 195). Use approximately ¼ cup filling and ¼ cup nuts for Billie's Danish Squares (page 195).

BAKER'S HINT: For time savers, use well-drained canned pie filling, adding rind and nuts.

GLAZE: Combine 1 cup powdered sugar with ½ teaspoon vanilla and ½ teaspoon orange extract or ½ teaspoon almond and ½ teaspoon lemon extract. Beat in about 1½ to 2 tablespoons milk, forming a thick pourable consistency.

ORANGE CREAM DANISH SQUARES: Roll and press ½ of Quick Danish Pastry to fit a greased, foil-lined 15x10x¾-inch jelly roll pan. Except for oranges, combine and spread dough with the following:

1 cup orange marmalade or apricot preserves	**1 egg, beaten**
1 cup sour cream, pour off any liquid on top	**½ teaspoon vanilla**
	2 (11-ounce) cans Mandarin oranges

Top with Mandarin oranges (juice removed and drained on paper towels). Form 9 rows of 8 orange segments each across the pan to form approximately 1x1¾-inch rectangles. Let rise until double in size and light to touch. Bake at 375° for 15-20 minutes or until topping is set and the bottom of the pastry is light brown. When cool, cut into 72 bite size pieces.

Variations: Sprinkle top of oranges and filling with 1 cup sweetened, flaked coconut and/or lightly toasted sliced almonds.

CHOCOLATE LOVERS: Drizzle rows with melted semi-sweet chocolate.

HURRIED BAKER: Spread ½ cup sweetened condensed milk in place of cream filling, adding oranges and coconut or replace each orange segment with a pecan half.

CHEESE CRACKERS AND SHORT BREADS

Between a pastry and a flat bread
Freeze baked crackers, layered with waxed paper,
in a heavy airtight container.

AUNT MARY'S CHEESE DELIGHTS
Cheese Straws in Slices

½ pound sharp cheddar cheese   **½ teaspoon salt**
½ cup margarine   **¼ teaspoon cayenne**
2 cups all-purpose flour

Mix shredded cheese with softened margarine; add flour, combine with salt and cayenne. Divide dough into 2 narrow rolls, 1½-inches wide. Refrigerate plastic wrapped cheese rolls for at least 1 hour. Cut into ¼-inch slices. Place slices on a greased cookie sheet; bake at 350° for 15 minutes. Ease the entire mixing process with a food processor. Refrigerate dough for a few days or freeze.

Aunt Mary's kitchen was like an adventure in good baking, with generous samples always available. Long before the days of fast foods, she could pull out — in a moment's notice — goodies hidden away in the bread box, refrigerator or freezer. Her Cheese Delights are just one of those many delicious surprises.

LAURIE'S CRISPY CHEDDAR CRACKERS
A Welcome Gift

1 pound cheddar cheese	1 teaspoon paprika
½ pound margarine	1 teaspoon salt
3 cups all-purpose flour	2 eggs beaten

Grate cheese very fine; cream cheese with margarine. Add flour, paprika and salt; mix thoroughly with eggs. If using food processor, form all ingredients into a dough. Chill dough to make it manageable. Roll dough ¼-inch thick; cut in desired shapes, dipping the cutters in flour if necessary.

Use your imagination for the occasion. Try animal shapes, alphabet letters or small cutters. Use the 1-inch heart shaped cutter or use all the card symbol shapes for your bridge club's snack crackers. Bake at 350° for 15 minutes. Yields approximately 64 slices. Watch, as small crackers bake in about 10 minutes.

These keep well only if hidden from family and friends!

FORM EACH OF THE FOLLOWING VARIATIONS into 4 narrow rolls, 1½-inches wide and 8 inches long. Chill plastic wrapped rolls; slice ¼-inch thick. Place slices on baking sheets; bake at 350° for 15 minutes. Yields 128 slices. Crackers will be crisp, not brown, on the top.

ONION-CHEDDAR CRACKERS: Omit eggs; add 1 envelope crushed onion soup mix and ¼ teaspoon cayenne. Sprinkle caraway, sesame or poppy seeds on slices before baking.

HOT PEPPER CHEESE CRACKERS: Omit eggs; substitute hot pepper Monterey Jack cheese for cheddar cheese. Sprinkle tops with poppy seeds before baking.

BENNE CHEDDAR CRACKERS: Add ¼ teaspoon cayenne for extra flavor. Roll narrow rolls of dough in lightly toasted sesame seeds before slicing.

VARIATION: Roll dough ¼-inch thick; press dough surface with a layer of lightly toasted sesame seeds. Cut out shapes with a thimble or an extract bottle top. Bake approximately 10 minutes.

BAKER'S HINT: Lightly toast sesame seeds by spreading seeds on an oven-proof plate; microwave on full power for 1 minute.

BRAN FLAKE CHEESE MACAROONS

Kids and Adults Love These; Double Recipe for a Crowd

¼ pound New York Sharp Cheddar Cheese
¹/₈ teaspoon worcestershire sauce
¼ cup margarine

¹/₈ teaspoon red pepper
¹/₈ teaspoon salt
½ cup all-purpose flour
1 cup bran flakes

Combine all ingredients in a food processor until the dough is smooth. Form into small 1-inch balls, pressing down with a fork or form dough into 2 long rolls to chill and slice. Place on a greased baking sheet; bake at 325° for 15-20 minutes. Bake only until crisp.

Without a food processor, grate cheese and crush flakes. Substituting corn flakes for bran flakes will result in a lighter product.

KITTY'S SCOTCH SHORT BREAD

A sweet pastry delicacy

1 cup butter, softened
¾ cup powdered sugar

3 cups all-purpose flour

Beat butter and sugar until creamy; mix in flour. Press dough together with hands. Pat dough evenly into a lightly buttered 14x9x2-inch pan, two 9-inch pie pans, or a short bread mold. Prick the surface with a fork; score the top with a knife about ¹/₈-inch through the dough to mark squares or rectangles for later cutting. Bake at 325° for 20-25 minutes or until light brown. While warm, finish cutting on scored marks

Delicately sweet, a crunchy addition to an assorted tray of sweet breads.

BROWN SUGAR SCOTCH SHORT BREAD: Substitute ¾ cup brown sugar for the powdered sugar; add 1 teaspoon vanilla.

FLAT BREADS

Flat breads, the very first bread, can be found in every region of the world today. This unleavened bread (ground whole grains combined with water and baked by the sunlight or an open fire) is similar to Sarah's bread in Genesis 18:6. Jewish Passover bread and communion breads made today are unleavened flat breads.

Each country has its own version of flat bread. Swedish flat bread with wheat and rye is similar to the corn tortilla. The Hunza's of Pakistan, noted for their longevity, eat freshly ground whole wheat and water flat breads called Chapatties. Bakers in India add a little butter to their flat breads calling them Parathas, while the Greeks form a hole in their flat breads to hang them in the kitchen.

Crisp flat breads are really a form of cracker—our favorite "munchies". All the flat breads freeze well. Separate bread with waxed paper, seal with plastic wrap and store in freezer bags. Thaw and heat for a few minutes, or until hot, at 350°.

COMMUNION BREAD

Communion breadbaking, a family tradition for generations in many American churches, can become a very special project for any age.

1 cup all-purpose flour   **3-4 tablespoons ice water**
¼ cup shortening

Cut in the shortening and flour in a bowl with a pastry blender until the consistency of coarse meal; slowly add just enough ice water to form into a ball. Chill dough; divide into four parts. Roll each part very thin, about ¹/₁₆-inch thick. Place on a greased cookie sheet; prick with a fork and cut in ¼x¼-inch squares with a pastry cutter or serrated knife. For larger shapes, roll dough thin, cut design and prick surface with a fork. Bake at 300° 10-15 minutes until a cracker or pastry consistency, but not brown.

While reading this recipe, Walt Sidwell recalled how his Aunt Ella had taught him as a child the reverence and ritual of communion bread baking. She baked a similar unleavened bread for the church, in large flat circles, to be passed and broken for the Lord's Supper.

MARIA'S CORN TORTILLAS

Maria Ugalde de Sandoval, an expert baker, showed me her speedy style which won acclaim at gatherings in her home, Costa Rica, Central America.

2 cups corn flour (masa harina)　　　**1 to 1¼ cups water**
(not cornmeal but a ground
hominy-type product)

Combine the corn flour with enough water in a medium bowl to hold its shape. Pinch off dough the size of a small egg. Roll ⅛-inch thick on a corn floured surface or waxed paper, forming a round tortilla. Maria, placing the dough in the center of a piece of waxed paper, moves the paper and dough as she presses the ball into a thin, round circle with the fingers of her other hand. Bake on a hot, ungreased skillet or griddle. This will not appear brown when done, but will be dry on the edges with bake spots on the surface. Turn and bake other side. Makes 12 small tortillas.

Her daughter, Olga, makes small open-face sandwiches with grilled meats, sauces and cooked vegetables. This bread is not complete without their delicious red beans and rice. If Masa Harina is not available, use equal amount of hot water and cornmeal. When cool proceed with recipe.

Variations:

DIET SWEDISH FLAT BREAD: Use Maria's Corn Tortilla recipe. Substitute all-purpose flour for corn flour. Knead the dough until smooth before dividing into 12 parts.

WHOLE-GRAIN SWEDISH FLAT BREAD: Same as Diet Swedish Flat Bread except for changing all-purpose flour to ½ rye flour and ½ whole wheat flour to measure a total of 2 cups.

INDIA'S PARATHAS: Use Swedish Flat Bread recipe using ½ whole wheat flour and ½ all-purpose flour to measure a total of 2 cups. Knead dough until smooth and elastic. After kneading dough, cut into 12 pieces. Spread butter in center of dough pieces using about 2 tablespoons in all. Stack ½ of dough with butter, rolling out each stack; cut into 12 pieces again, forming into 12 thin pancake-like circles. Bake on both sides until lightly browned. They will puff up during cooking.

INDIA'S PURI: Form as Parathas; lower in 375° cooking oil until light brown and puffed. Drain; serve warm.

BAKER'S IDEA: Great accompaniment to curry dishes. Children like the sweet whole grain flavor. Share the taste of Parathas with your children's classmates as they study geography.

LAURIE'S INDIAN FRY BREAD

The tasty Indian Fry Bread is attributed to the Pueblo, Navaho and other Southwest Indian tribes. Instant powdered milk enhances the flavor and nutrition.

2 cups all-purpose flour or 1 cup whole wheat flour and 1 cup all-purpose flour
1 tablespoon baking powder
½ teaspoon salt

3 tablespoons powdered milk, optional
1 cup water
cooking oil

Combine flour, baking powder and salt. Dissolve powdered milk in water; add to dry ingredients. Knead in the bowl until smooth, adding more flour if needed. Form dough into 2-inch balls; roll to a 4-inch circle (as thin as possible). A small hole can be made through the center. Cook in 1-inch of hot oil in skillet for 1 minute on each side. Push bread down under oil. It will puff up during frying. Drain; serve warm.

BAKER'S IDEAS: Serve hot with honey or use bread to hold hamburgers and sandwich fillings. For an Indian style pizza, add cheese and favorite pizza toppings to a circle of cooked bread; broil until cheese melts.

BAKER'S FAVORITE: Using whole wheat and all-purpose flour? Add cracked wheat and whole wheat flour while kneading if dough is sticky. Will add an extra crunchy texture.

SOUTHWEST FLOUR TORTILLAS

2 cups all-purpose flour
1 teaspoon baking powder
¾ teaspoon salt

2 tablespoons shortening
1 cup lukewarm water

Mix flour, baking powder and salt in a medium bowl; cut in shortening. Add water slowly, adding only enough to form a ball, using a fork to mix. Form dough into 6 balls. Let rest for 10 minutes. Roll each ball ⅛-inch thick on a lightly floured surface forming a round large tortilla. Bake on a hot ungreased griddle on one side and then the other. It will not appear brown as a pancake, but will be white with darker bake spots on its surface. Yields 6 tortillas.

Use the tortillas for Mexican and Spanish dishes or butter and fold as a bread. Cut in triangles to serve plain or fried with salsa or guacamole dip.

ARMENIAN LAVOSH — WHOLE-GRAIN CRACKER BREAD

1 package yeast	½ cup rye flour
½ cup warm water (105-115°)	½ cup cracked wheat
¾ teaspoon salt	⅔ cup whole wheat flour
1 teaspoon sugar	¼ cup melted margarine or butter

Dissolve yeast in water. Mix salt, sugar, rye flour, cracked wheat and whole wheat together in a bowl; add yeast and margarine. Beat until smooth and manageable. Place in greased bowl, turning to grease top. Let rise until double in size; punch down dough. Divide into 2 parts; roll as thin as possible (11x14 inches) using more whole grain flour as necessary. Place on lightly greased baking sheet. Bake at 350° for 10-12 minutes.

Bread can be crisp or chewy, depending on baking time. Serve in whole sheets or broken into pieces. For individual servings, form dough into small balls; roll into thin circles, sprinkle with salt. Baking time depends on the thickness. The crackers quickly become overly brown. Watch! Try adding 1 tablespoon honey, molasses or sugar to the dough if a sweeter taste is desired.

The delicate whole grain flavor and cracked wheat crunch adds the finishing touches to a steamy bowl of thick, homemade chili on a snowy night.

Variations:

ALL-PURPOSE LAVOSH: Substitute half or all whole grain flour for all-purpose flour. Seasoned salt, crushed dill weed, sesame seeds and crushed cumin seeds make flavorful toppings. Press toppings into uncooked cracker dough.

WHEAT GERM LAVOSH: Add ½ cup wheat germ to your choice of flour types to form a total of 1⅔ cups flour.

OATMEAL LAVOSH: Omit cracked wheat; add ½ cup oatmeal.

HONEY GRAHAM CRACKERS-IN-THE-ROUND

A Tribute to the Graham Flour Originator,
1800's Health Advocate, Sylvester Graham

²/₃ cup graham flour	¹/₈ teaspoon cinnamon, optional
¹/₃ cup all-purpose flour	¹/₈ teaspoon salt
2 tablespoons packed brown sugar	2 tablespoons butter
	2 tablespoons honey
½ teaspoon baking powder	2 tablespoons milk

Combine flours in a medium bowl with sugar, baking powder, cinnamon and salt; cut in butter. Whisk milk and honey together. Sprinkle enough milk over surface of dry ingredients to moisten for gathering in a ball. Knead dough in the bowl until smooth and manageable, if necessary add more flour. Flatten dough on a greased 12-inch pizza pan, pressing dough evenly to fit pan. Cut dough in 20 wedge shaped sections with a pastry cutter. Cut each section into 2 pieces by cutting a circle around the dough, 5 inches from the outside edge. Prick the dough surface with a fork. Bake at 350° for 15 minutes or until crisp, but not brown. Watch! Yields 40 crackers. *Vary shapes of dough with cookie cutter or cut in squares.*

WHEAT CRACKERS-IN-THE-ROUND

Circle cracker wedges around Dip or Cheese Ball

½ cup whole wheat flour	¼ teaspoon salt
½ cup all-purpose flour	2 tablespoons butter
½ teaspoon baking powder	2-3 tablespoons milk
2 tablespoons sugar	

Mix flours in a medium bowl with baking powder, sugar and salt; cut in butter. Sprinkle with enough milk to gather dough into a ball, adding more milk if necessary. Knead dough in the bowl until smooth and manageable. Flatten ball on a greased 12-inch pizza pan, pressing dough evenly over pan. Cut dough in 20 wedge shaped sections with a pastry cutter. Cut each section in 2 pieces by cutting a circle around the dough, 2 inches from the outside edge. Prick dough surface with a fork. Bake at 350° for 15 minutes or until crisp, not brown. Watch! Yields 40 crackers. *Vary cut shapes of rolled dough.*

BAKER'S SECRET: Help prevent overbrowning by lining pan with greased foil.

VERSATILE DOUGHNUTS

Bake As Well As Fry!

A recent early morning doughnut party brought remembrances to my friend, Marguerite Hamilton, of the hot, yeasty doughnuts her mother once made. The recipes were misplaced, but the memories live on with fortunate friends, family and neighbors who enjoyed them.

Doughnuts are a paradox today as we enjoy these delicacies, but wish to balance good nutrition too. Doughnuts can be a special treat with good-for-you ingredients.

If frying is not on your diet, convert your favorite quick bread doughnuts or fritters from frying to baking. Add just enough extra of the recipe's liquid (milk or plain yogurt) to form a pourable batter.

Bake the batter in small muffin pans, filled ²/₃ full, at 400° until light brown, about 10-15 minutes. Can bake the batter on a greased hot griddle until light brown on both sides. To bake yeast doughnuts, extra spice and flavorings should be added.

COOKING TIPS

Take the guess work out of doughnut cooking with a deep frying thermometer. Stanley Szczepanski, who makes thousands of doughnuts each year with the help of friends, neighbors and family using his doughnut recipe in this section, shares the following tips for yeast raised or quick mix doughnuts.

1. Organize ingredients and materials.

2. Write down the schedule for each batch of doughnuts: time for refrigerated dough to warm to room temperature, approximate rising time and actual frying time.

3. Avoid overcrowding; leave room for expansion of dough. Use shortening which can maintain 375° without disintegrating; check your favorite vegetable shortening's label. Use a cooking thermometer.

4. Using a deep heavy pan, electric skillet or deep fryer with a thermostat, arrange dough in basket to immerse in hot oil or ease a spoonful of dough, level or heaping, into oil to avoid spattering. An iced teaspoon (long handle) works well. Place shaped yeast doughnuts on a greased foil lined baking sheet to rise. Cut around doughnut and foil if shape changes when moved.

5. Maintain a 375° temperature before adding more uncooked dough. Drain doughnuts briefly over hot oil before placing on baking sheets lined with newspapers, covered with paper towels. Finish cooling on wire racks. **Supervise hot oil cooking at all times!** Do not leave this project until hot oil is in a safe place.

6. Prepare icings, toppings and doughs the night before; refrigerate.

QUICK MIX DOUGHNUTS

ROSE'S SOUR CREAM DOUGHNUTS

2 cups all-purpose flour	1 egg
½ teaspoon baking soda	½ cup sugar
½ teaspoon salt	½ cup sour cream, 4 ounces
¼ teaspoon nutmeg	1 teaspoon vanilla

Combine flour, soda, salt and nutmeg; mix in the egg beaten with sugar, sour cream and vanilla. Let batter stand while heating oil. Ease dough by heaping teaspoonfuls into 375° oil, lightly browning on both sides. Drain on paper towels; cool on metal rack. Yields about 2 dozen doughnuts. Toss in powdered sugar, or glaze warm doughnuts.

Rose divides the recipe, refrigerating unused dough to cook for breakfast or an evening snack. When cooking batter at one time, she freezes extra doughnuts on a baking sheet, storing them frozen in freezer bags.

Variations:

ORANGE AND BLACK WALNUT DOUGHNUTS: Add 1 cup chopped black walnuts and 1 teaspoon grated orange rind to the dough. After cooking and draining, roll in orange glaze, drain on wire rack and serve warm with Superb Chocolate Sauce and Black Walnut Glaze.

Pecans, almonds, peanuts or macadamia nuts can be substituted for walnuts, as well as hickory nuts.

BLUEBERRY DOUGHNUTS: Add 1 cup, fresh, canned or frozen and thawed, well drained blueberries with 1 teaspoon grated lemon rind to the dough; cook and drain; roll in powdered sugar and serve with blueberry sauce.

PINEAPPLE DOUGHNUTS: Add 1 (8-ounce) can, well drained, crushed pineapple and 1 teaspoon grated orange rind to the dough. Cook; drain. Roll first in orange glaze and next in coconut-nut coating.

DUTCH DOUGHNUTS: Add 1 teaspoon each grated lemon and orange rind and ½ cup raisins to the dough. Cook and drain. While warm roll in vanilla glaze.

Serve with Almond Glaze and Spice Glaze. Enjoy!

BAKER'S HINT: As an alternate to frying, add more sour cream or plain yogurt (about ¾ cup) to form a thinner batter. Bake on a greased medium hot griddle until light brown on both sides or bake in small greased muffin pans in a 400° oven about 12 minutes.

ROSE'S ITALIAN SFINGE

(Pronouncing Sfinge: short I as in "it" — long E as in "eel")

2 eggs
½ cup water
1½ tablespoons sugar
1 cup all-purpose flour

1¼ teaspoons baking powder
½ teaspoon salt
granulated sugar

Beat eggs, water and sugar together; mix in flour combined with baking powder and salt. Let batter stand while heating oil to 375° for deep fat frying. Add 1 tablespoon batter at a time, turning when light golden brown to cook on other side. Drain and roll in plain granulated sugar. Makes 1 dozen doughnuts.

The family's special request on a cold winter night.

Variation:

WHOLE WHEAT SFINGE: Substitute ½ whole wheat flour for ½ all-purpose flour. This batter bakes easily in small muffin pans or on a griddle. Add 1-2 more tablespoons whole wheat flour for doughnuts.

BILLIE DAVIS' DOUBLE APPLE DOUGHNUT NUGGETS

¼ cup whole wheat flour
2½ cups all-purpose flour
2 teaspoons baking powder
1 teaspoon baking soda
1 teaspoon cinnamon
½ teaspoon nutmeg
¼ teaspoon allspice
½ teaspoon salt
¼ cup brown sugar

¾ cup sugar
2 eggs
2 tablespoons melted butter or oil
2 tablespoons plain yogurt or
  sour cream
1 cup sweetened applesauce
½ teaspoon vanilla
¼ cup finely chopped, peeled
  apples

Mix the flours, baking powder, soda, spices and salt in a large bowl. Beat in a medium bowl the sugars, eggs, butter and yogurt; mix in applesauce, vanilla and apples. Combine with dry ingredients. Slide batter by heaping teaspoonfuls in 375° oil. Fry for one minute on each side or until done in center. Drain on paper towels. Yields about 3½ dozen.

Keep doughnuts warm; shake in bag of powdered sugar just before serving or coat doughnuts with a vanilla glaze. These keep well.

SWEET POTATO OR PUMPKIN DOUGHNUTS

A Traditional Fall Specialty — Halloween, Thanksgiving or After the Ball Game

½ cup mashed sweet potatoes or pumpkin
1½ tablespoons melted butter
¼ cup milk
1 egg
½ cup sugar
1 teaspoon grated orange rind

2¼ cups all-purpose flour
3 teaspoons baking powder
¼ teaspoon salt
¼ teaspoon nutmeg
¼ teaspoon ginger
½ teaspoon cinnamon

Beat potatoes, butter, milk, egg, sugar and orange rind. Mix in flour combined with baking powder, salt, and spices. Roll in small balls. Fry in 375° oil until a light golden brown, turning to brown other side. Drain. Roll in Orange or Maple Sugar Glaze. Serve warm with extra glaze. Yields about 3 dozen.

SPEEDY CALAS

Sweet Version of Rice Griddle Cakes

Years ago in New Orleans, street vendors would sing out "Belle Cala, Belle Cala", good cakes. New Orleans residents delighted in these fried, yeast rice cakes for breakfast. The following is a quick version of Belle Cala.

2/3 cup all-purpose flour
½ cup sugar
2 teaspoons baking powder
¼ teaspoon salt

¼ teaspoon nutmeg
1 egg
1 cup cooked, drained rice
¼ teaspoon vanilla

Combine flour, sugar, baking powder, salt and nutmeg; mix in egg beaten with rice and vanilla. If batter is too thin, add a small amount of flour to thicken. Ease batter, scooped by tablespoonfuls, into 375° oil. Cook until light brown; turn, cooking other side. Serve hot; roll in powdered sugar before serving. Yields 18 doughnuts.

A pancake version is on page 147.

No guarantees for speaking French after sampling these tasty morsels, but you'll agree with "tres belle calas".

SANTA FE'S SOPAIPILLAS

Fill these airy hot treats with butter and honey. Sopaipillas can be a bread or an after Mexican-Spanish dinner reward sprinkled with powdered sugar and a dash of cinnamon. Our family calls these little delicacies "sofa-pillows," because of their shape.

2 cups all-purpose flour
1 tablespoon baking powder
½ teaspoon salt

1¼ tablespoons shortening
½ to ⅔ cup lukewarm water

Mix flour, baking powder and salt together. Cut in the shortening until it resembles cornmeal. Slowly add water, using a fork to combine. Add only enough water to gather dough into a manageable ball. Roll dough about ⅛-inch thick on a floured surface. Cut into 3-inch squares; let stand for 5 minutes. Fry, a few at a time, in deep hot oil, 375°, until dough puffs and is light golden brown on both sides. Drain on absorbent paper. Olé! Serve immediately! Yields about 2½ dozen.

GRAHAM CRACKER DOUGHNUTS

Children Like These Crunchy Morsels

1 cup baking mix (page 121)
½ teaspoon nutmeg
½ teaspoon ginger
½ cup sugar

1 egg
¼ cup milk
¾ cup fine graham cracker
    crumbs

In mixing bowl, combine baking mix, spices and sugar; mix in egg beaten in milk. Stir the graham cracker crumbs into the dough. On a graham cracker crumb covered surface, roll dough ¼-inch thick; cut as desired with floured cutter. Lightly brown in 375° oil, for 2-3 minutes or until a light golden brown on both sides and done on the inside. Drain and roll in powdered sugar. Serve warm. Yields about 1 dozen.

HELEN JOHNSON'S ROSETTES

A taste of Victorian charm

Delicate Scandinavian rosettes add a note of joyful festivity to a buffet table set for any occasion. A salad plate with rosettes takes on a sense of royalty.

1 ½ cups all-purpose flour	2 eggs
1 teaspoon salt	1 cup milk
1 teaspoon sugar	2 tablespoons liquid shortening

Mix flour, salt and sugar; combine with eggs beaten with milk and shortening. Let batter stand for 1 hour. Batter should be the consistency of thick cream. Heat oil to 375°. Place iron in oil to heat; drain. Place hot iron into batter within ¼-inch of top of rosette iron. Fry until light golden brown, drain and, with a fork, slip rosette off iron. Drain and cool on wire racks. Keeps well if stored or frozen in a tightly covered container. Do not sprinkle with powdered sugar if storing. Reheat in a warm oven; sprinkle with powdered sugar before serving. Yields 5 dozen.

Variations:

TIMBLE CASES: Use a timble iron (usually comes with a rosette set); proceed as for rosettes. These can be drained, slipped off the iron, and used as pastry shells for salads, creamed foods, vegetables and fruit. Can be edible containers for a dessert; keep in the freezer to use for an emergency dessert. A plain quick pudding with a dab of chocolate, whipped cream and a cherry would now become very spectacular in this exotic case.

PAT'S FUNNEL CAKES: Add the following ingredients to Helen's Rosettes: 2 tablespoons sugar, 1 teaspoon soda and ¾ teaspoon baking powder. Heat a well-oiled griddle to medium hot; pour about ⅓ to ½ cup batter into a funnel, holding finger over tip. Release finger; move funnel in a circular motion forming a spiral. Delight adults and children by forming their initials. Turn once; cook until light brown on the edges, about 1-2 minutes. Drain; sprinkle with powdered sugar.

Pat guarantees these as an instant hit with family and guests. Only problem — they will ask for a repeat performance!

FRITTERS

Fritters cover a multitude of dishes from the simple Spanish-fried squash blossoms (try them, no one will guess) to any meat, vegetable or fruit added to a fritter batter and deep-fried. Fritters can be a side dish, appetizer, main course or dessert.

FRITTER BATTER

1 cup all-purpose flour	**1 egg**
1 tablespoon sugar	**½ cup milk**
1½ teaspoons baking powder	**1 tablespoon oil**
¼ teaspoon salt	

In a mixing bowl, combine flour, sugar, baking powder and salt; gradually add egg beaten with milk and oil. Dip drained fruits, meats or vegetables cut in small or bite-size pieces in the batter. Drain off any excess batter over the batter container. Fry fritters at 375° in deep hot oil until a light golden brown. Fry 3 or 4 at a time just until brown and done in the center. Length of time depends on the size. Drain on paper towels. Fritters should be served warm. They can be served plain, with powdered sugar or syrup.

Variations:

APPLE FRITTERS: Peel, core and slice apples, across the top or in wedge slices, ¼-inch thick. Sprinkle with cinnamon and sugar. Dip into batter; fry until light brown. Sprinkle with powdered sugar.

PINEAPPLE FRITTERS: ¼ cup drained crushed pineapple and ⅛ teaspoon nutmeg added to ¼ cup batter. Ease batter by tablespoonfuls into hot, deep oil until a golden brown. Drain on paper towels; sprinkle with powdered sugar. Chopped apples can be substituted for pineapple.

CORN FRITTERS: Mix ½ cup drained whole corn, 1½ teaspoons minced dried onion and 2 tablespoons cooked, crumbled bacon with ½ cup fritter batter. Ease batter, by tablespoons, into hot, deep oil until a light golden brown. Use a slotted spoon to lift out fritters. Lift out any excess food particles; maintain the 375° temperature.

Cooked ham or beef, diced in bite-size pieces, can be mixed with the fritter batter. A sprinkling of seasoned salt or dry herbs will add a zest to the meat.

BAKER'S IDEA: Fast - bake fritter batter in greased, small muffin pans, in a 400° oven, for about 12 minutes or on a greased, medium hot griddle.

PÂTE à CHOU or CREAM PUFF PASTE

It is baked as a cream puff, beignet or croustade holder for salads or fillings. Chou paste can be deep-fried as a French doughnut, or souffle fritter.

Leftover chou paste can be stored in the refrigerator. Mix with leftover meats, cheeses, mushrooms or vegetables to bake as an appetizer or after-school snack. If too thin to hold their shape, spread on bread or crackers and bake.

FRENCH DOUGHNUTS
Delicately Delicious

½ cup butter	1 cup all-purpose flour
1 teaspoon sugar	4 eggs
¼ teaspoon salt	1 teaspoon vanilla, orange or
1 cup water	other flavorings can be used

Heat the butter, sugar, salt and water to boiling in a heavy 2 quart sauce pan. Add flour, lowering the temperature. Stir until the mixture is smooth, leaves the sides of the pan and forms a smooth ball. Remove from heat; let cool for a few minutes. Beat each egg into the mixture until smooth and shiny. Add the vanilla. Beat a few more minutes; slip dough by teaspoonfuls into 375° hot oil. Turn, cooking both sides until a light golden brown. Roll in powdered sugar or a vanilla glaze. Yields about 30 doughnuts.

Great for any occasion. Serve these for your next bridge game with a choice of chocolate and maple glaze for dipping. Use a decorator bag with a large star tip to form small rosettes.

Variation:

CREAM PUFFS (BAKED): Using the French paste, place by tablespoonfuls on a greased baking sheet (if shape doesn't hold, beat some more). Leave about 2 inches between puffs, smooth tops of puffs. Bake at 425° for 15 minutes, lowering temperature to 375°, baking until shells are crisp and hollow. Leave puffs in oven with door ajar and heat off. Refrigerate and freeze in air tight containers. Recrisp at 375°. Cut in half for filling both sides with meat salad or a savory filling for appetizers or entrees. Puffs hold sweet custard or ice cream topped with fruit or sauce. Yields about 15 medium to 30 small puffs.

ONION CHEESE BEIGNETS (BAKED)

Serve as an Appetizer

Beignets or souffle fritters are a type of French fritter made with a chou paste or cream puff pastry. Beignets can be baked or fried. They puff or swell, as the word "beignet" denotes.

1 cup chicken broth	½ teaspoon dry mustard
½ cup butter or margarine	1 cup all-purpose flour
1 envelope dry onion soup mix	1 cup Parmesan cheese
1 teaspoon crushed caraway, dill	4 eggs
or cumin seeds	

Bring chicken broth, butter, soup mix, seeds and mustard to a boil. Over low heat, add flour all at once. Stir until mixture is smooth, leaves sides of pan and forms a ball. Remove from heat and immediately beat in cheese, then each egg, until mixture is smooth. Drop by teaspoonfuls 2 inches apart on a greased cookie sheet. Bake at 375° for 15 minutes until puffed and golden. Leave in warm oven 10 minutes with door ajar. Serve hot. Makes 60 puffs. Serve with Peggy's Cocktail Sauce.

PEGGY'S COCKTAIL SAUCE: Mix ¾ cup chili sauce, 2 teaspoons worcestershire, 2 tablespoons lemon juice, 2 tablespoons horseradish sauce, 1 teaspoon grated onion and a few drops hot sauce.

Be creative about the ingredients! Add ½ cup chopped ham or corned beef to the batter. For an extra cheese effect, substitute ½ cup grated sharp cheddar or grated Swiss cheese for ½ cup of the Parmesan cheese.

YEAST-RAISED DOUGHNUTS

KATHERINE'S FRENCH MARKET DOUGHNUTS
Beignets

1 package dry yeast
¼ cup lukewarm water
1 egg
¼ cup sugar
½ teaspoon salt
2 tablespoons cooking oil

1 cup evaporated milk or whole
    milk
3 cups all-purpose flour
½ teaspoon nutmeg
powdered sugar

Dissolve yeast in water; beat in egg, sugar, salt, oil and milk. Blend in flour mixed with nutmeg, until combined.

Refrigerate covered overnight. Roll dough ¼-inch thick on a floured surface. Cut into 2-inch to 2½-inch squares with a pastry cutter or knife. Allow dough to rise until double. With a slotted metal spatula, ease doughnuts into 375° oil. Fry until a light, puffy golden brown on both sides in 375° oil. Cook only a few at a time. Drain and thoroughly coat with powdered sugar. Yields about 3½ dozen.

Serve these hot with Café au Lait, strong coffee or Chickory Coffee with hot milk. Sit back and dream about being in New Orleans French Market. For an extra New Orleans' flair, add Speedy Calas (page 209) to the menu.

STANLEY'S MAXI-DOUGHNUTS

The 18-year Halloween doughnut-making tradition of the Stanley Szczepanski family began when their 9 children would return from trick or treating cold and hungry. The Szczepanski's would have doughnuts and hot cocoa waiting for them. As the children grew older, planning Halloween parties and giving treats to their friends, the family made more doughnuts. Last year they made 1,000 doughnuts. The "organized confusion" starts even before Halloween. For years they also made doughnuts on Shrove Tuesday, the day before Lent and six weeks before Easter.

7 packages dry yeast
1¼ cups warm water
4¼ cups milk, divided
1 cup plus 7 tablespoons
   (11½ ounces) butter-flavored
   shortening, melted

1¾ cups sugar (13½ ounces)
5¾ teaspoons salt
6 eggs, beaten
5 pounds all-purpose flour

Dissolve yeast in warm water. Heat ½ of milk with shortening, sugar and salt just until shortening melts; add rest of cold milk. When mixture is cooled to 105-115°, mix in yeast. Add 1 pound of flour at a time and stir. Cover with a damp cloth and let rise 1½ hours or until double in bulk. Punch down dough, roll out, about ¼-inch (½ the desired finished thickness) and cut doughnuts placing on waxed paper. Let rise 2 hours until light and double in size. Dip a slotted metal spatula into the hot oil to ease risen doughnuts from the pan into the 375° oil. Cook on both sides until a light golden brown. Let drain on rack over cookie sheets covered with paper towels.

ICINGS: Choose chocolate, powdered sugar glaze, chocolate with coconut, glazed with coconut, cinnamon and sugar, powdered sugar or Stanley's Mega Icings. Stanley has these ready on trays and in bowls.

STANLEY'S MAXI-GLAZED VANILLA ICING: Combine 1 box powdered sugar, 1 teaspoon vanilla and enough water to form a thin icing.

STANLEY'S MAXI-CHOCOLATE ICING GLAZE: Add 2 (1-ounce) squares of melted chocolate to the vanilla icing.

SZCZEPANSKI'S FILLED DOUGHNUTS: Cut dough in squares as French Market Doughnuts. Cook as usual, being sure the inside is done. When cooled, make a small hole in side; use a pastry tube to fill with any flavor bought or homemade pie filling, fruit jelly or preserves. Sprinkle with powdered sugar. These are always eaten first.

MEMPHIS DOUGHNUTS
Light Airy Puffs That Melt in Your Mouth

This is ½ of Aunt Mary's Potato Roll recipe.

Use any leftover sweet dough, brioche or roll dough. Cut in ¼-inch thick squares or triangles. Let rise until double in size. Fry in 375° oil until a light golden brown on both sides. Drain. Roll in powdered sugar or serve warm with a large bowl of apple butter with dinner or as a snack.

¼ cup sugar	¾ cup water, 120-130°
1 teaspoon salt	½ cup milk
⅓ cup instant potato flakes	⅓ cup shortening
1 package dry yeast	1 egg
3-4 cups all-purpose flour, divided	

In large bowl thoroughly combine, with mixer, sugar, salt, potato flakes, yeast, and 1½ cups flour; beat in liquid mixed with shortening. Beat in 1 cup flour and egg. Add enough flour to form a soft manageable dough. Refrigerate over night in a greased covered bowl or floured plastic bag. The next morning or when doughnuts are desired, knead dough on a floured board until manageable. Roll dough ¼-inch thick; cut the doughnuts with a doughnut cutter, placing doughnuts and doughnut holes on a greased foil-lined baking sheet. Let rise until light and double in size. With a slotted metal spatula, slip doughnuts into deep oil, 375°. Brown until a light golden color, turning to brown other side. Drain doughnuts before placing on paper towels. Glaze with your favorite glaze, sauce or icing. Yields about 2 dozen.

BAKER'S IDEA: Cut out miniature doughnuts, using a small glass for the outside and an extract bottle top to cut out the center. For smaller, faster doughnuts, scoop dough by teaspoonfuls; roll in balls, let rise and fry or bake.

This light doughnut brings back memories of the wonderful family dough-nut shop in Memphis, Tennessee, with its fragrant, hot doughnuts.

Variation:

BAKED MEMPHIS DOUGHNUTS: Add 1 teaspoon cinnamon, ¼ teaspoon nutmeg and ¼ teaspoon ginger to the yeast mixture. Roll dough ½-inch thick; cut with a doughnut cutter or cut 3x½-inch strips, twisted if desired. Bake at 400° for 10 to 12 minutes or until a light golden brown. Dip while hot in warm cooked glaze or glaze with your favorite icing. Serve with bowls of extra glaze, apple sauce or apple butter. Add more spice as desired.

DOUGHNUT GLAZES AND TOPPINGS

Dip or roll warm doughnuts in a thick sauce or pour on a glaze; drain on wire racks over a pan. Reuse excess sauce or glaze. Save extra glaze in a bowl; serve with glazed doughnuts.

Roll doughnuts or toss in a bag of powdered sugar or sugar coating. Powdered sugar works best on warm doughnuts, just before serving. If storing doughnuts, do not add plain powdered sugar until later. Store, labeled, in air tight containers in the refrigerator or freezer. Warm before serving.

COCONUT-NUT COATING: Combine ingredients; roll warm doughnuts in mixture.

1 cup coconut, toasted and broken up with a rolling pin

1 cup toasted, finely chopped nuts

SUGAR AND SPICE COATING: Mix well in plastic bag. Lightly shake warm doughnuts in bag or sprinkle over glazed doughnuts.

1 teaspoon cinnamon
¼ teaspoon nutmeg

1 cup granulated sugar

COLORED SUGAR TOPPING: Mix; let dry. Sprinkle over muffins or doughnuts for a festive look. Make special colors and flavorings (orange extract with orange color or lemon extract with yellow color.)

1 cup sugar
add a few drops of food coloring depending on shade desired

optional, add drop of appropriate flavoring

CITRUS SUGAR TOPPING: Combine ingredients; sprinkle over muffins or glazed doughnuts.

1 teaspoon grated orange rind
1 teaspoon grated lemon rind

1 cup granulated sugar

DARK CHOCOLATE GLAZE: Melt butter and chocolate; whisk in rest of ingredients. Pour warm glaze over doughnuts or dip tops of doughnuts.

2 tablespoons butter
1 (1-ounce) square unsweetened chocolate

1 cup powdered sugar
2 tablespoons hot water
¼ teaspoon vanilla

SUPERB CHOCOLATE SAUCE: Melt chocolate with evaporated milk on low temperature; add other ingredients, cooking and stirring until desired thickness. Serve warm.

2 squares unsweetened chocolate	1 teaspoon vanilla extract
	½ teaspoon almond extract
1 (5.6-ounce) can evaporated milk	1¼ cups powdered sugar

BLUEBERRY SAUCE: Adjust combined ingredients to form a thick, pourable consistency.

1 cup powdered sugar	½ cup mashed blueberries
3 tablespoons milk	

ORANGE GLAZE: Combine ingredients to form desired thickness.

2 cups powdered sugar	1 teaspoon grated orange rind
¼ cup orange juice	

HONEY-LEMON GLAZE: Combine ingredients; if desired, add powdered sugar to thicken.

½ cup honey	½ teaspoon grated lemon rind
1 teaspoon lemon juice	powdered sugar

ALMOND GLAZE: Combine ingredients to form desired thickness.

2 cups powdered sugar	1 teaspoon almond flavoring
¼ cup milk	

BLACK WALNUT GLAZE: Beat all ingredients well.

2 cups powdered sugar	1 teaspoon black walnut flavoring
¼ cup milk	

MAPLE SUGAR GLAZE: Beat and adjust ingredients until desired consistency.

1 cup maple sugar syrup	powdered sugar

SPICE GLAZE: Combine spices and sugar; beat in milk and vanilla.

1 teaspoon cinnamon	¼ cup milk
½ teaspoon nutmeg	1 teaspoon vanilla
1 cup powdered sugar	

VANILLA GLAZE: Beat ingredients until smooth and desired consistency.

2 cups powdered sugar	1 teaspoon vanilla
¼ cup milk	

ENTERTAINING WITH DOUGHNUTS

CHOCOLATE AND COMPANY COFFEE
Mocha Coffee - Hot Chocolate

Almond Glazed Orange and
  Almond Sour Cream Puffs
Superb Chocolate Sauce

Vanilla Glazed Miniature
  Memphis Doughnuts
Orange Glaze

Arrange warm glazed doughnuts around the sauces. Guaranteed to be warm and comforting.

DOUGHNUT PARTY

Sour Cream Blueberry
  Doughnuts
Blueberry Sauce
Double Apple Nuggets
Cinnamon-Nutmeg Glaze

French Doughnuts
Dark Chocolate Glaze

Coffee   Tea   Fruit Juice

Glaze all doughnuts the night before; allow to drain. Cool and refrigerate in labeled, sealed plastic bags. Reheat doughnuts on a foil-lined baking sheet at 250° until warm. Use a folded card to label doughnuts and sauces.

Place bowl or bowls of dip or glaze in the center of a platter with the corresponding doughnuts around them. Use your imagination. Let guests dip, spoon or pour small amount of glaze over doughnuts on their plate.

BREADCRUMBS AND COMPANY

The Case for Saving Bread — Breadcrumbs Reap Frugal Rewards!

These are the "lost in the refrigerator bread treasures," — the end of a loaf or very dry slices. Save these goodies in a designated freezer bag in the freezer. Don't waste even the crumbs of homemade bread!

Breadcrumbs: Slice leftover bread to uniform thickness; place on a baking sheet. Slowly bake in a 200° oven until the desired color and dryness. After bread is thoroughly dried, crush with a blender, food processor or rolling pin until fine crumbs are formed. *Breadcrumbs add crunch to fish, meat coatings and coffee cake fillings. They add flavor and body to soups and yeast breads. Substitute crumbs for flour in pancakes, bread puddings and pie crusts.*

Soft Bread Croutons: Croutons can be left plain, lightly toasted in the oven or stirred until light brown with olive oil or margarine. Use approximately 1 to 2 tablespoons oil to 1 cup croutons; add a finely minced garlic clove or garlic powder for added flavor. Toss croutons with dried herbs or leave plain. A sprinkling of one or more of parsley, pepper, thyme, paprika and onion powder adds zip. *Use croutons to layer between sliced vegetables before baking in the oven or as a casserole topping, on salads and in savory dressings.*

Dried Bread Croutons: Cut in desired uniform thickness; bake in 175° oven until dry and crisp. While still warm, toss with Parmesan cheese or herbs.

Cracker crumbs: Don't forget not-so-crisp, but still tasty, crackers. Recrisp at 175°; when cool, use blender to form crumbs. *Makes a delicious crunchy coating for seafood.*

Breadcrumbs are a baker's lagniappe, meaning a bonus or gift, in the finest of Louisiana tradition. The Breadcrumbs and Company chapter is my lagniappe to you! A little something extra: sweets and savories to add to your meals. Bon Appétit!

CROUSTADES

Hollow out any size muffins, loaves of bread, biscuits or brioches to hold food. If you want to use the top of the bread, cut wide enough to form a sturdy lid for replacing over filling or leaning against croustade. Use a small, sharp, serrated knife and spoon to gently remove center of bread so that firm walls remain.

If the filling is a heavy dip, the bread holder can be buttered and toasted lightly in the oven. The removed pieces of bread can be used for dipping into the filling or turned into bread crumbs or croutons.

OYSTER SANDWICH IN A CROUSTADE: This Louisiana treat was a gourmet specialty of Bay Naylor's father, a native of the Mississippi Delta. His directions were as follows: Cut approximately 1-inch below the top of an unsliced loaf of bread to form a lid; hollow out the inside of the loaf, leaving substantial walls and bottom. Layer breaded fried oysters, cocktail sauce, thinly sliced onion rings and mild cheese; replace lid. Bake at 350° until hot throughout; cover loosely with foil if top becomes too brown. Slice as a sandwich. Serve with a green salad.

DORIS' MOCK CRAB BALLS
Make Ahead Appetizers

1 pound sausage
½ onion, minced
1 (8-ounce) package cream
  cheese
1 teaspoon worcestershire sauce

1 (2 pound) can chopped kraut
¼ cup dry bread crumbs
3 eggs, beaten
bread crumbs

Cook sausage and onion; drain. In a large bowl, combine cream cheese with sauce and sausage mixture until smooth. Drain kraut, rinse in cold water and drain again, squeezing out extra liquid. Mix kraut and bread crumbs with sausage mixture. When cool, shape into bite size balls. Roll in beaten eggs; roll in fine bread crumbs. Ease into 375° oil, deep enough to cover balls. Cook only a few balls at a time. Turn to brown both sides. Drain on paper towels. Serve warm with Peggy's Cocktail Sauce (page 214) or with Honey-Mustard Sauce (page 223).

BAKER'S IDEA: Can cook the night before, refrigerating until time to reheat in the oven for serving. Don't tell your secret ingredients!

HONEY-MUSTARD SAUCE: Combine ½ cup honey, ½ cup mayonnaise, 3 tablespoons Dijon mustard and 3 tablespoons lemon juice. Keep refrigerated. Yields about 1¼ cups sauce.

BAY'S FRENCH TOAST
The Creoles Call This "Lost Bread" — "Pain Perdu"

6 slices (¼-inch thick), remove crusts, few days old loaf bread	½ teaspoon salt
	½ teaspoon vanilla
2 eggs	Cooking oil
½ cup milk	Powdered sugar

Prepare bread; cut sliced bread in half. Beat eggs, milk, salt and vanilla. Dip one piece of bread at a time into egg mixture. Using enough oil (375°) to cover bread, fry until a light golden brown. Drain; sprinkle with powdered sugar. A dash of nutmeg on the top gives a spicy zip. Makes 3 servings. *Pass a bowl of hot baked pears and Mandarin oranges, with sugar added to taste, a sprinkling of ginger and toasted sliced almonds.*

BAKER'S IDEA: Can bake in the oven at 350° or on a hot griddle until light golden brown.

ANN'S AND DOTTIE'S CRUNCHY BREAD STICKS
Vary with Sprinkling of Seasoned Salt and Parmesan Cheese

Use 3-or-4-day-old hot dog buns. Break buns open, cutting apart the top and bottom halves. Cut each half into 3 long sticks. Place bread sticks in pan; drizzle with melted butter. Bake in a 250° oven for 2 to 3 hours. When cool freeze or store in a dry, air tight container. Use the same method for leftover hamburger buns.

Use with salads, as crunchy snacks or with soup.

EDWARD'S HERB BREAD CRUMB COATING FOR WILD GAME AND TAME CHICKEN

2 cups fine bread or cracker
  crumbs
3 tablespoons cornstarch
1 tablespoon sugar
2½ tablespoons paprika
3 tablespoons parsley
1 tablespoon onion powder
1 tablespoon celery salt

1 tablespoon garlic salt
1 teaspoon rosemary
½ teaspoon cayenne pepper
1 teaspoon dill weed
¼ teaspoon garlic powder
1 teaspoon thyme
½ teaspoon black pepper
butter or margarine, (optional)

All herbs must be dried and crushed. Combine crumbs, cornstarch, sugar and next 11 spices and herbs. Dip food to be coated in melted butter, margarine or oil; can leave plain or spray with vegetable cooking spray. Shake in a bag until coated. Completely coat and press herb mixture on the surface of a roast. Bake in oven at 350° until done or pan fry.

Use for vegetables or casserole toppings. Store in a tightly sealed bag or jar on the shelf. Freeze if not used often.

ANN COCHRAN'S HOLIDAY DRESSING

7 cups mixed soft cornbread,
  loaf, rolls or frozen, thawed
  leftover bread.
1 teaspoon salt
1 teaspoon pepper

*1 teaspoon sage
2 cups chopped celery
2 cups chopped onions
2 cups chicken or turkey broth
6 large eggs

*Adjust to taste — Ann uses 1 tablespoon sage.

Crumble cornbread, break up sliced bread; blend in salt, pepper and sage with bread cubes. Simmer celery and onion in water to cover for 15-20 minutes or until tender. Add hot vegetables and broth with all ingredients. Stir lightly. If desired, add more seasoning. Cover bowl tightly; let stand for approximately 2 hours. Pour into a large, greased, 9½x14½x2-inch baking dish. Bake at 350° for 45 minutes or until golden brown. Serves 15.

Ann is famous for her holiday dinners. Her freshly ground pepper and eggs make this dressing my family's favorite! Save and freeze leftover biscuits, dry unsweetened cereals and whole grain breads for dressing.

Boiled eggs, giblets, chestnuts, sausage and oysters are many of the different additions to dressings. Any of these cooked and chopped add a change of flavor to the basic dressing.

VARIATIONS:

SAVORY DRESSING: Substitute lightly toasted whole grain breads, rolls and cornbread broken into small pieces. Add 1 teaspoon dried thyme, ½ cup chopped, canned mushrooms, ½ cup fresh chopped parsley and 1 chopped green pepper; sprinkle 2½ cups grated cheddar cheese over the top for the last few baking minutes.

MOCK POULET: Use Savory Dressing ingredients; optional to omit mushrooms. Add 1 can undiluted cream of mushroom soup to 1½ cups chicken broth and ¼ cup margarine. Pour over the bread pieces; spoon ½ of the bread into the greased baking dish. Cover with vegetables; layer with rest of bread mixture. Cover casserole with remaining broth, beaten with ½ cup milk, ½ cup mayonnaise, eggs and 1 undiluted can of cream of chicken soup. Refrigerate for 6 hours or overnight. Bake at 350° for 1 hour or until done. Add cheese. *Quickly disappears at a covered dish supper. If you wish to make a true poulet, add some chopped chicken or turkey.*

BREADCRUMB CRUST

1 cup dry breadcrumbs
⅓ cup melted butter

Combine ingredients; press into a 9-inch pie pan and bake at 350° for 12 minutes.

VARIATION:

DRIED HERB BREADCRUMB CRUST: Add 1 tablespoon margarine, 1 tablespoon dried parsley, ¼ teaspoon oregano, ¼ teaspoon thyme and ⅛ teaspoon seasoned salt. Optional: 1 teaspoon sesame seeds, ⅛ teaspoon cayenne and 1 tablespoon Parmesan cheese.

BAKER'S HINT: Layer the bottom of the crust with leftover cooked and drained vegetables and/or meats. Sprinkle top with grated Parmesan cheese or shredded cheddar cheese. Bake until completely hot. Serve, cool or wrap to refrigerate or freeze.

HURRIED BAKER: Use the food processor to combine all ingredients; not necessary to melt butter or margarine.

BASIC GRAHAM CRACKER CRUST

1¼ cups graham cracker crumbs   ¼ teaspoon cinnamon, optional
2 tablespoons sugar   ⅓ cup melted butter or margarine

Combine all ingredients; press all combined ingredients into bottom and sides of a 9-inch pie pan. Bake at 350° for 12 minutes. Cool before filling. *Good for ice cream, whipped topping delicacies or fruit desserts.*

HURRIED BAKER: Microwave on full power for 1½ minutes or until firm, using a microwavable container. Rotate dish halfway through baking.

ANN'S ALMOND GRAHAM CRACKER CRUST

2 cups graham cracker crumbs   ½ cup toasted finely chopped
½ cup melted butter   almonds

Combine all ingredients. Use a food processor to save time. Press on the bottom and sides of a 10-inch spring form pan for a cheese cake or for 2 (9-inch) pie crusts. Bake at 350° for 10-12 minutes.

VARIATIONS:

COCONUT GRAHAM CRACKER CRUST: Add ½ cup shredded coconut to the ingredients.

CHOCOLATE-PEANUT GRAHAM CRACKER CRUST: Substitute ¾ cup finely chopped peanuts for the almonds. Add ¼ cup brown sugar and ⅓ cup semi-sweet chocolate chips to the ingredients.

NUT-CRACKER CRUMB CRUST: Substitute wheat or other cracker crumbs for graham crackers. Mix or match up to ¾ cup chopped, toasted almonds, English walnuts, pecans or black walnuts with butter.

MERINGUE CRUMB CRUST
Glamorized Crust or Dessert

Use grease free bowl and beaters to beat egg whites that contain no yolks. For chocolate lovers, fold in ½ cup semi-sweet chocolate chips with the nuts.

3 egg whites, room temperature
½ teaspoon cream of tartar
1 cup sugar
1 teaspoon vanilla or almond
extract
¼ cup powdered sugar

½ cup dry cracker and/or bread
crumbs
½ cup finely chopped nuts
(pecans, walnuts or lightly
toasted almonds)

Beat egg whites until frothy; add cream of tartar and beat until soft peaks form. Gradually sprinkle sugar, by tablespoons, beating until stiff peaks form when beaters are raised. Fold in flavoring, powdered sugar, crumbs and nuts by hand. Mound meringue on a greased, foil-lined baking sheet, 10-inch round pie container or skillet. Form an indentation for the filling with the back of a spoon. Bake crust at 325° for 35 minutes. With oven turned off, allow crust to stay in oven until cool, or about 1 hour. Remove crust from pan to peel off foil. Cracks or breaks in the crust will be covered with topping or filling. Fill cooled meringue with pudding, yogurt ice cream or 8 ounces of whipped topping. Garnish with sliced strawberries and grated semi-sweet chocolate. Serves 8 to 10.

SWEET CRUMB CRUST

1¼ cups crumbs (dry bread, dry
cereal, cookie wafers, ginger
snaps or vanilla wafers dried
and blended into crumbs)
½ cup powdered sugar or
granulated sugar

¼ teaspoon cinnamon
⅛ teaspoon nutmeg or mace
½ cup melted butter

Combine ingredients; press into a 9-inch greased pie pan. Bake at 350° for 10-12 minutes.

BREAD PUDDINGS

Saving bread is worth the nostalgia of this comfort food. A universally beloved dish, bread pudding can be everyday or company fare. Refrigerate or freeze leftovers.

PAT TAYLOR'S EASY BREAD PUDDING

4 slices white bread, cubed
1 cup raisins
1 (14-ounce) can sweetened
  condensed milk
3 cups boiling water

2 tablespoons butter
2 eggs
1 teaspoon vanilla
dash salt

Place bread in buttered 9-inch square pan; sprinkle raisins over top. Wisk condensed milk with boiling water and butter; mix with beaten eggs and vanilla. Pour over bread; bake at 375° for 20 minutes. Lower temperature to 350° and bake for an additional 25 minutes. Cover top with foil if pudding is becoming too brown. Pudding should be soft and moist, but hold its shape. Serve warm with ice cream or "The Dip." Serves 6.

Pat and John Taylor always please their guests with creative gourmet delights, as well as nostalgic delicacies in their Sarasota, Florida home.

Variation:

"THE DIP:" Combine 1 cup cream, half and half or whole milk, ½ teaspoon vanilla and a sprinkling of freshly grated nutmeg or ground nutmeg. Ladle over hot individual servings of pudding.

This was my Grandmother's staple dish. Each warm spoonful is dipped into the pool of vanilla cream floating around the individual servings.

ANN WORD'S MERINGUE BREAD PUDDING
Reminiscent of traditional Virginia baking.

3 tablespoons butter
2 egg yolks
½ cup sugar
½ teaspoon vanilla
¼ teaspoon cinnamon
2 cups milk
1½ cups sweet or non-sweet dry
 bread pieces

1½ teaspoons grated lemon rind
Soft Meringue:
2 egg whites
¼ teaspoon cream of tartar
4 tablespoons sugar

Beat melted butter, eggs, sugar, vanilla, cinnamon and milk. Mix in bread and lemon rind. Let soak for 20 minutes. Pour into well-buttered 1½ quart baking dish. Bake at 350° for 40-50 minutes or until custard is set. Use 2 whole eggs in the pudding when not making meringue. Serves 6.

Beat 2 egg whites to the foamy stage. Add cream of tartar, beating until soft peaks form. Slowly add sugar, 1 tablespoon at a time, until egg whites are stiff and smooth. Spoon on meringue to completely cover top of pudding. Bake at 325° for 15 minutes or until edges are beginning to turn a pale brown.

Variations:

COCONUT-NUT BREAD PUDDING: Sprinkle coconut and chopped nuts over the pudding top before baking. Meringue could be added, but is not necessary.

JEWELL'S FRUIT MERINGUE BREAD PUDDING: Spread a layer of favorite fruit preserves, marmalade or thinly sliced bananas or strawberries over hot baked pudding. Spoon on meringue to cover top of pudding. Bake as directed.

This recipe is a gracious reminder of Jewell and John Norton's hospitality through the years to church and business leaders.

BETTE'S PRIZE BREAD PUDDING

A winner on her T.V. cooking show and on your table for guests!

6 cups leftover coffee cake or
   sweet rolls
4 eggs
1½ cups milk
1 cup granulated sugar
1½ cups whipping cream
few grains salt

⅓ cup melted butter
1 teaspoon vanilla extract
¼ teaspoon almond extract
½ teaspoon cinnamon
½ cup chopped candied cherries
   or candied pineapple, optional
   (can use raisins)

Break up the coffee cake or sweet rolls by hand into fairly large pieces. Toast in a 350° oven for 20-25 minutes or until slightly dried out. Set aside.

Combine eggs and milk; blend well with sugar. Mix in the whipping cream; stir in salt, butter, vanilla and almond extract. Pour into a well-buttered 3 quart baking dish or a 9½x13½x2½-inch baking casserole. Evenly add the toasted coffee cake; press down with a spoon to moisten the cake. Sprinkle with cinnamon and candied fruit; press again with a spoon. Bake on the center rack of the oven at 400°; immediately after placing pudding in oven, change heat to 350°. Bake for 30-35 minutes or until set.

WHISKEY SAUCE:

1 cup whipping cream
1 cup powdered sugar
2 tablespoons butter

2 tablespoons bourbon or
1 teaspoon bourbon flavoring

Whisk the whipping cream and powdered sugar together in a deep, heavy pan. Add butter; cook over medium heat, bringing mixture to a boil. Continue to simmer for 4 minutes; stir constantly with a wooden spoon, lowering temperature if necessary to prevent scorching. Texture should be similar to a heavy cream. Add the bourbon and pour into a serving container.

Bette serves the pudding and the sauce warm. Reheat in the microwave. Vary sauce by substituting rum, brandy or vanilla flavoring to taste instead of bourbon.

JANET'S COMPANY BREAD PUDDING

Expect... recipe requests

¼ cup soft butter
½ to ¾ loaf stale French or Italian
   bread
¾ cup raisins
4 eggs
2½ cups sugar
1 quart milk

1 tablespoon vanilla
¼ teaspoon mace
Topping:
¼ cup butter
½ cup whipping cream
⅓ cup sugar

Spread soft butter over a 9 ½x13 ½x2 ½-inch baking casserole or pan. Use enough bread, cut in 1-inch slices, to evenly cover bottom of pan; sprinkle with raisins. Cover with eggs beaten with sugar, milk, vanilla and mace. Let soak for 10 minutes. Bake at 350° until pudding is almost firm, about 45 minutes.

Remove from oven. Increase oven temperature to 375°. Place butter, cut in pieces, evenly over hot pudding; pour liquid whipping cream over top sprinkling with sugar.

Return to oven; bake 10-15 minutes to allow cream to set. Yields 10-12 servings. Best served warm.

BAKER'S HINT: Freeze leftover bread pudding for a scrumpteous "instant" dessert. Serve warm.

HURRIED BAKER: Heat bread pudding in the microwave oven. Spoon warm pudding over ice cream, frozen yogurt or ice milk for a perfect gourmet ending to a not-so-fancy supper.

Entertaining can be as simple as, come by for lemonade with tea breads or muffins fresh from the oven or freezer.

HIGH TEA

Small servings are given in separate courses, while guests are seated. Also, foods can be grouped together on a buffet table for guests to serve themselves. Make the plates or buffet very attractive with garnishes, doilies, or elegant service plates.

Yorkshire Scones (page 119)

Lemon Curd (page 120)

Rosettes (page 211)

Poppyseed Coffe Cake Squares (page 181)

Carrot Applesauce Squares (page 177)

Strawberry and Cheese Amish Muffins (page 97)

Chicken Salad in Small Cream Puffs (page 213)

Orange Cream Danish Squares (page 196)

Bishop's Short Bread Coffee Cake (page 180)

Tea   Lemon   Cream

CHOCOLATE TABLE
FOR
WEDDING OR ANNIVERSARY RECEPTION

Form small muffins and rolls; cut squares in small bite-sized servings.

Chocolate Marzipan Squares (page 63)

Chocolate Amish Muffins (page 97)

Double Chocolate Cinnamon Rolls (page 79)

Toffee Coffee Cake Squares (page 183)

Chocolate Coconut Rolls (page 61)

Strawberries with Superb Chocolate Sauce (page 219)

CHILDREN'S CORNER

NON-EDIBLE ART DOUGHS
Keep this on hand when the real dough isn't available.

ANNETTE'S FREE FORM PLAY DOUGH

Just as home baked bread means using the best ingredients, homemade non-edible play dough assures non-toxic ingredients. Clay's usefulness goes beyond creativity.

1 cup all-purpose flour   **½ cup water**
½ cup salt

Children can mix the ingredients. Dough does not hold its shape unless more flour is added.With additional flour, children's object of art, can be dried or baked at 325°. Store unused dough in air tight container. Adults enjoy too! Can dry and paint with acrylics.

ATHENS' FUNDOUGH
Makes for Happy Hands

This is my favorite homemade children's dough. It can be stored in an airtight container indefinitely. Save plastic scoops, lids, containers, cookie cutters and popsicle sticks as accessories.

2 cups all-purpose flour   **2 tablespoons oil**
1 cup salt   **2 ~~tablespoons~~ cups water**
1 tablespoon cream of tartar   **food coloring, optional**

Mix dry ingredients in a heavy pan. Stir in water and oil slowly over medium heat. Stir dough away from sides of pan until thick. Cool before gathering into a ball. Try leaving clay white as recipe contains natural ingredients found in "real" baking. This will enhance children's "baking interests". If desired, add color later.

CHARLIE'S CREATIVE ART DOUGH
(NON-EDIBLE)
Form into ornaments or decorative objects

3 slices white bread, use day old
  or let stand for 2 hours
3 tablespoons white glue

1 teaspoon glycerine
1 tablespoon white acrylic paint
3 drops lemon juice

Remove crust from bread; break into small pieces. Mix bread with glue, glycerine, paint and lemon juice. Stir until dough pulls away from sides of bowl; knead on waxed paper until dough is no longer sticky. Sprinkle with cornstarch if necessary.

Keep air tight in a plastic bag, inside a sealed plastic container. Can add color (tempera, water color or acrylic) to dough.

Add small amount of water if dough seems dry. Allow article to dry for 12 hours; paint if desired. Spray dried art object with a clear acrylic spray.

Older children and adults can form baskets, napkin rings, decorative braided wreaths and Christmas ornaments.

BAKER'S IDEA: Can use a kneaded white bread recipe, baking as directed, in various bread shapes or in creative shapes for art objects. After baking, these can be sprayed with a plastic fixative to make them more durable (although non-edible!). Paint if desired.

Can be used for wall decorations or centerpieces. Great gift ideas!

Don't leave out man's best friend.

These edible, nutritious dog treats will make Fido happy.

FIDO'S BREAD STICK BISCUITS

When Fido's not looking, humans can enjoy

1½ cups whole wheat flour
½ cup oatmeal
¼ cup Brewers yeast
1½ teaspoons garlic powder

⅔ cup beef broth, use 2 beef
   bouillon cubes
1 egg

Mix flour, oatmeal, brewers yeast and garlic powder; beat in broth and egg to form a soft manageable dough. Add more flour if necessary; knead lightly in the bowl until manageable. Form dough into 6x2-inch bread sticks or roll out and cut into bone shapes or rectangles. Gauge size of bread stick by dog's size. Bake at 350° for 30-35 minutes until hard. Try baking in the microwave for 2 minutes; turn dough over and microwave for 2 to 3 more minutes. The microwave time schedule varies with the different ovens. The garlic is said to help cut down on fleas, but if the family starts nibbling on these hard biscuits, the garlic may need to be changed to taste.

Just as for humans, if Fido can't have salt, make your own chicken or beef broth.

These were unanimously endorsed by the neighborhood dogs; orders have been received for Christmas!

FIDO'S CORNBREAD CAKE

For doggie's birthday, let the children help make a quick cornbread with meat broth or a bouillon cube in the liquid. Everyone can have a piece of that dog cake!

FLOUR AND ASSOCIATES, LTD.
Contains B Vitamins, Protein and Iron

BASIC INGREDIENTS BAKER KNEADS

FLOURS

ALL-PURPOSE FLOURS: A blend of hard and soft wheat flours with a long shelf life due to low-fat content. A balanced flour will have enough gluten, the protein which gives flour its strong elastic qualities, to make yeast breads, but not too much for quick breads. The balanced all-purpose flour usually contains about 11 grams of protein in a 5 pound bag, while the softer wheat flour has a protein content of 9. Biscuit and pastry bakers often use only soft Southern wheat flours.

UNBLEACHED ALL-PURPOSE FLOUR: A creamy colored, not oxidized flour, which is used the same as all-purpose flour. White all-purpose or bread flours have a long shelf life because of the low fat content.

SELF-RISING FLOUR: Salt and baking powder added (each cup of flour contains 1½ teaspoons baking powder and ½ teaspoon salt). Self-rising flour cannot be stored as long as other white flour due to the baking powder.

BREAD FLOUR: From high protein (higher gluten content) wheat to give better volume and texture to bread. It is adapted especially for breadmaking with long risings and kneading. Some yeast bread makers prefer using half bread flour and half all-purpose flour or use all-purpose flour entirely. Yeast breads made with bread flour must be kneaded or beaten to totally develop the gluten.

HOMEMADE OR COMMERCIAL BAKING OR BISCUIT MIXES: Contain the correct ratio of flour, shortening, baking powder, salt and sugar for a basic quick bread. Be in control of the ingredients and save money by making your own baking mix.

WHOLE-GRAINS

Contain the whole-grain; bran layer, endosperm and wheat germ. High in proteins, B vitamins and iron, but low in gluten. Whole wheat and rye have the best gluten as other whole-grains have very little or none. Refrigerate or freeze freshly ground whole-grain flour.

WHOLE WHEAT: Cracked wheat is coarsely cut pieces of whole grain. Use small amounts of cracked wheat and bran to prevent cutting strands of gluten. Graham flour is whole wheat flour coarsely ground and unsifted.

BUCKWHEAT: A malty flavored flour used mostly in pancakes.

BARLEY FLOUR: A heavy flour often used as a stabilizer in bread flours.

CORNMEAL: Use the whole grain, not degerminated, if nutrition conscious. See cornbread section.

OATS: Contains good quality protein, but no gluten. Excellent nutritional boost for breads.

RYE: Types of flours are dark (hard to find, except in Europe), medium and light flour.

SOY FLOUR: Ground from the soybean, soy has more nutrients, except for gluten, but fewer calories than whole wheat. Soy and wheat compliment each other forming a complete protein.

LEGUMES: Soy beans, lentils, split peas and most beans can be blended into flour, forming a complete protein when combined with wheat flour.

LEAVENINGS AND FLAVORINGS

YEAST: When activated yeast plant grows, carbon dioxide gas forms, which makes the dough rise and the bread light.

SODA AND SOUR MILK: Soda, first sold commercially in 1846, was combined with an acid liquid such as buttermilk to form carbon dioxide gas for leavening.

BAKING POWDER: Before the first commercial baking powder was made in 1870, cream of tartar was added as an acid with baking soda to leaven quick breads. Double acting baking powder reacts with liquid and heat giving the cook more time and flexibility.

AIR AND STEAM: Many breads use air enclosed as the leavening agent. Air is added by beating eggs, creaming sugar and shortening, beating and folding batter and by folding and rolling dough. Steam is formed as the liquid in the batter or dough is heated.

SALT: Salt adds flavor and controls the rate of rising. When salt is lowered in the ingredients (due to dietary needs) do not allow dough to over rise.

SUGAR: Sugar, molasses, honey and other syrups add flavor to bread and helps it brown readily. Sugar speeds yeast activity as it acts as a food for the yeast.

EGGS: Eggs add a rich flavor, nutritional value and extra lightness when beaten. Eggs give bread a delicate texture and an extended freshness.

LIQUID: Liquid helps combine ingredients and is necessary to develop the gluten in yeast breads. Use milk, water, potato water (from cooking potatoes) or fruit juice. Milk makes the crust brown and increases the nutritional value.

FAT: Fat increases the tenderness of flour mixtures by shortening the long gluten strands, adding flavor, developing the crisp crust and adds better keeping qualities.

BATTER BREADS vs DOUGHS:
Now you can judge the ingredients in a recipe!

Thin Batter is approximately 1 cup liquid to 1 cup flour. Rosettes, timbale cases, popovers and fritters are some examples.

Medium Batter is about 1 cup liquid to 1 ½ cups flour. Waffles, griddle cakes and thick cover batters come under this heading.

Thick Batter is about 1 cup liquid to 2 cups flour. Muffins, sweet breads, batter yeast breads and quick pan breads are included in this list.

Soft Dough is approximately 1 cup liquid to 3 cups flour. This portion could include soft roll dough, sweet yeast dough, heavier batter breads, doughnuts and yeast breads.

Stiff Dough is approximately 1 cup liquid to 4 cups flour. This would include flat breads, pastry, some yeast doughs and crackers.

BAKING EQUIPMENT

Besides the essentials, the following make baking easier and faster: bread thermometers registering 40-130° Fahrenheit, deep fat thermometers registering 375° Fahrenheit, wooden spoons, rolling pins, cake testers, spatulas, spreaders, dough scrapers, whisks, graters, serrated knives, electric knives, measuring spoons and cups, large and small oven proof glass measuring cups, heavy sauce pans, deep fryers, mixers, blenders, food processors, microwave ovens and convection ovens.

The food processor is valuable for chopping and combining ingredients. The lower power on some microwave ovens can be used to warm refrigerator dough for a few seconds, thaw frozen dough, speed rising for yeast breads, warm baked products and bake totally or partially some quick breads. Carefully check the time and doneness. Toppings to cover quick breads or dark colored quick breads will eliminate browning in an oven. Manufacturers directions and settings must be followed for the food processor, microwave ovens, breadmakers and convection ovens for bread products.

TYPES OF BAKING CONTAINERS: The array of containers suitable for bread baking is endless. Iron skillets, dull metal pans, shiny pans, baking sheets, ovenproof glass, clay containers, dutch ovens and disposable aluminum pans are all acceptable bread baking pans. Each has advantages.

Be creative by saving vegetable, soup, coffee and ham cans. Wash and smooth down sharp edges to use for sweet breads, batter breads or yeast breads.

Collect unusual pans from yard sales, antique dealers, kitchen shops and department stores. Small individual loaf pans joined together are a baker's dream. With these pans, cooking time is shortened and the size is perfect for gift giving. Unusual molds yield breads perfect as an edible festive centerpiece or an attractive addition to a buffet. Long narrow pans or circular molds yield breads easily sliced. Cylinders for French bread and baking stones for pizzas or free form loaves are available in kitchen stores. Iron skillets or shallow iron pans are great for the oven as well as the campfire. Unique bread pans can double as a wall decoration, a big help with storage.

The heaviness of pans is important for quick breads and yeast breads. For more thickness, stack 2 cookie sheets and line with aluminum foil for free form breads. They burn easily on thin pans. A heavy metal baking sheet is perfect for a biscuit pan. Breads baked in dark pans have a darker, thick crust. If this is not desirable, line pan with foil. Non-stick pans, a real time saver, demand care with the surface.

A favorite all-purpose bread pan is a heavy, natural finish, aluminum or steel. It gives even baking and the lighter sides help batter and dough reach maximum height before hardening into a crust. Rounded corners brown more evenly than the sharp corners. Line pans with foil to form rounded corners.

SIZE OF BAKING CONTAINERS: Size of the pan is not a problem with yeast doughs or quick breads as extras can always fit in another small container — it seems that with home baking there are often extras. Make allowance for rising as most doughs and batters will double in size. Most pans are filled ½ to ⅔ full except for some sourdoughs which rise triple their size. Adjust cooking time to the pan size. Set the timer and watch!

Dough risen in a greatly misjudged pan, the size too large or too small, can be salvaged. For yeast dough, punch dough down, reform, adjust pan size and allow to rise again. For quick breads, quickly spoon part of batter into another container.

A large standard bread pan 9x5x3-inch holds, approximately, 3-3½ cups flour in a dough recipe or 3½-4 cups batter. A medium pan is an 8½x4½x3-inch loaf pan, which holds about 2¼ to 3 cups flour in a recipe or 2½-3 cups batter for each loaf. A small, individual 5⅞x3⅜x2-inch loaf pan will yield 4 loaves in a recipe designated for 1 standard loaf pan. A mini-pan is 5¼x2¾x1½-inch size, which will make 8 loaves from a recipe using a standard loaf pan. These are just a few of the pan sizes; adjust your dough or batter to fit your particular pan.

The entire set of rolls can be lifted out of the pan for freezing with a round or square cake pan. The oven safe glass rectangular casseroles are my favorite for rolls, large coffee cakes and juicy sweet rolls. I can watch the rate of browning during baking; freeze or store and serve from the same container. Glass and ceramic absorb and hold heat making breads cook quicker, but rather than lowering oven temperatures, I prefer to check the bread as it bakes. Don't forget oven-proof mixing bowls which are perfect for baking round, crusty loaves of bread. Experiment with containers to find the ones best suited to your needs.

PREPARATION OF BAKING CONTAINERS: Pans greased with butter, margarine, shortening or the new baking sprays help keep breads from sticking; grease and flour special problem pans. Wax paper liners are especially helpful for very large loaves, sweet breads or breads with fillings. If the entire pan cannot be lined, place waxed paper in the center of the pan, the most usual place for breads to stick; grease as usual. Do not take off immediately; allow quick breads and fruit filled yeast breads to stand a few minutes before removing from pan.

KNEADS OF YEAST BREADS

Overheard comments from some of the best cooks..."never had any luck with yeast breads" or ..."always wanted to learn how to make rolls".

Grab your spoon and bowl, electric mixer or food processor....

LET'S GET IN THE DOUGH

YEAST: Give the microscopic yeast plant the correct temperature, liquid and flour to make the dough rise. The temperature of the mixture is essential for success with yeast breads. Too cold retards the yeast growth and too hot kills the yeast. Sprinkle yeast over warm water (105-115°); stir until dissolved. Test water inside wrist, should feel slightly warmer than body temperature.

Use higher liquid temperatures (120-130°) only when dried yeast is thoroughly mixed with other dry ingredients before adding the liquid. A thermometer should be used for the higher temperatures used in rapid mixing and with rapid yeast.

MIXING OR BEATING: When not mixing sourdough or yeast dough by hand, use a heavy duty electric mixer with beaters or dough hooks. Dough hooks for mixing and kneading cut the work time in half. Dough is quickly formed by a food processor designed for mixing and kneading doughs. Manufacturers directions must be followed. When beating dough add only enough flour to form a soft manageable dough. Flour amounts are only approximate due to the humidity and type of flour - avoid adding too much flour. Beating will activate the protein gluten in the flour faster.

BATTER BREADS: They are beaten (not kneaded) until the batter comes away from the sides of the bowl and the dough appears stringy.

KNEADING: Gather dough into a ball placing on a lightly floured, flat surface. Sprinkle on more flour if dough becomes too sticky for handling. Roll up your sleeves and flour your hands as you start the following steps.

1. Flatten ball and pick up farthest edge of dough, folding over to closest edge.

2. Curve the fingers of both hands over the folded edge of the dough. Push down with the heel of the hand, pushing dough away from you. Give the dough a quarter turn clockwise.

3. Repeat folding, pushing and turning the dough in a rhythm until the dough is smooth, elastic and springy. Actual time for kneading depends on the previous beating or mixing, type of ingredients (whole-grain flours require more kneading) and your speed in kneading.

DOUGH RISING: Allow kneaded dough, not required to rise before shaping, a 10 minute, covered rest for easier handling. Dough can be placed, covered, in the refrigerator to slow the rising or placed uncovered in a warm oven (85°) with a bowl of hot water to speed rising (the steam acts as a commercial proofer). The bowl of dough, covered with a damp cloth, can be placed in a larger bowl, partially filled with warm water, placed on a rack above a pan of hot water or placed in a warm, draft-free area until doubled in size. **Check the temperature.**

BAKER'S RESCUE: Dough not rising because of problem with yeast; knead or mix in fresh yeast dissolved in 2 tablespoons water. Add more flour as necessary.

PUNCHING DOWN: When dough is double in size, flatten dough center with fist. Form dough into a ball. Let covered dough rest for 10 minutes to make shaping easier.

STIRRING DOWN: After rising until double, batter doughs are stirred to original volume. Pour into greased containers for second rising.

SHAPING ROLLS OR LOAVES: Form rolls into desired shapes; place in greased containers. For even textured loaves, flatten dough into an oblong shape, roll dough into a rectangle or gently knead out gas bubbles. If forming into rectangles, roll dough into a roll (as a jelly roll), starting with the short side. Seal edges and ends by pressing dough; turn ends under. Place seam side down in well greased loaf pan.

RISING AND BAKING FOR LOAVES AND ROLLS: Allow formed rolls and loaves to rise, covered, in a warm, draft-free area or use ideas under Dough Rising. Bake in a preheated oven after the dough doubles in size, feels light to touch and does not move back when dented with tip of finger. The bread will continue to rise for a few minutes in the hot oven, called oven spring.

TESTING FOR DONENESS: Tops are usually brown when done and loaves sound hollow when tapped. If not done, continue baking, turning loaf upside down in the pan to speed browning.

COOLING AND CUTTING: Remove bread from the pan when done, placing on a wire rack to cool. Slice when cool unless hungry folks are on hand. A serrated or electric knife yields uniform slices.

STORING AND FREEZING: Wrap thoroughly cooled bread in plastic bag or foil to store in the refrigerator for a few days or the freezer for several months. Wrap slices individually for easy removal. Unbaked yeast dough or shaped rolls or loaves can be frozen before rising for 4 weeks. Thaw at room temperature before continuing recipe directions. Let baked bread thaw in freezer wrapper for a couple of hours. Microwave oven can speed the process. When dough begins to warm, stop the microwave. Check dough's outside surface temperature.

BAKER'S SECRETS

What If...?   **Could be...**

Uneven Shape ....Wrong proportions of salt or yeast; out of date yeast or temperatures too hot for yeast; improper shaping; wrong size pan; insufficient rising time; insufficient heat circulation around pans; oven temperature too low or too high.

Irregular Crumbly Texture........Temperature too high during mixing and rising for yeast; dough too stiff; allowed to rise too long; over baked.

Tough, Heavy Texture........Out of date yeast; insufficient or too much rising time before baking; overbaking.

Displeasing flavor........Old ingredients; too much salt.

Remember, don't throw these away — they make good "kitchen bread," toast or crumbs.

DEAR BAKER AWARD

KISSES TO THE BAKER

IS HEREBY CERTIFIED,
In Gourmet Bread Baking,
Qualified to Unequivocally Deem
all Baked Products "Excellent"
no Matter How Unique,
Unusual, or Unforgettable.

Index

When the Knead Rises

Please send me _____ **Copies**

When the Knead Rises @ $14.95 each .... $ _____

add postage and handling @ $2.25 each .... $ _____

Alabama residents add sales tax @ $0.60 each ..... $ _____

Total $ _____

Name _____

Address _____

City _____ **State** _____ **Zip** _____

Charge to ❏Visa or ❏Master Card # _____ Exp. Date _____

Or make check or money order payable to:

Gingerbread Press, Inc., P.O. Box 2332 Decatur, AL 35602

When the Knead Rises

Please send me _____ **Copies**

When the Knead Rises @ $14.95 each .... $ _____

add postage and handling @ $2.25 each .... $ _____

Alabama residents add sales tax @ $0.60 each ..... $ _____

Total $ _____

Name _____

Address _____

City _____ **State** _____ **Zip** _____

Charge to ❏Visa or ❏Master Card # _____ Exp. Date _____

Or make check or money order payable to:

Gingerbread Press, Inc., P.O. Box 2332 Decatur, AL 35602

When the Knead Rises

Please send me _____ **Copies**

When the Knead Rises @ $14.95 each .... $ _____

add postage and handling @ $2.25 each .... $ _____

Alabama residents add sales tax @ $0.60 each ..... $ _____

Total $ _____

Name _____

Address _____

City _____ **State** _____ **Zip** _____

Charge to ❏Visa or ❏Master Card # _____ Exp. Date _____

Or make check or money order payable to:

Gingerbread Press, Inc., P.O. Box 2332 Decatur, AL 35602

Please list any book stores or gift shops in your area that you would like to handle this book.

_____

_____

_____

_____

_____

- -

Please list any book stores or gift shops in your area that you would like to handle this book.

_____

_____

_____

_____

_____

- -

Please list any book stores or gift shops in your area that you would like to handle this book.

_____

_____

_____

_____

_____